COLD WAR FUGITIVE

Other books by Gil Green

CUBA at 25, The Continuing Revolution (1984)
What's Happening to Labor (1976)
Portugal's Revolution (1976)
The New Radicalism (1971)
Revolution Cuban Style (1970)
The Enemy Forgotten (1956)

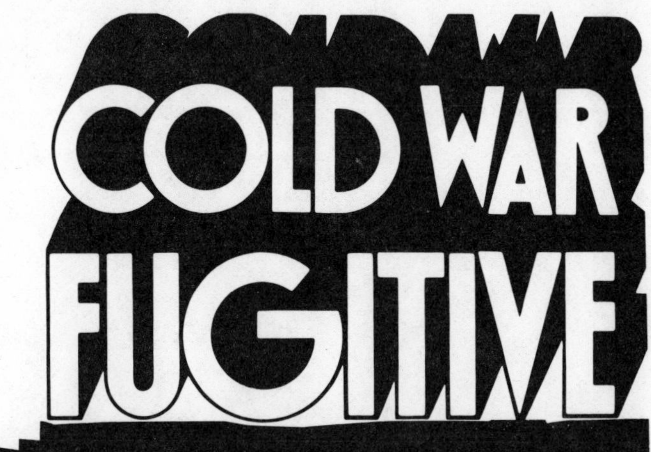

A PERSONAL STORY OF THE McCARTHY YEARS BY GIL GREEN

INTERNATIONAL PUBLISHERS, New York

First edition 1984
Printed in the United States of America

Library of Congress Cataloging in Publication Data

Green, Gil, 1906-
Cold war fugitive.

Includes index.
1. Green, Gil, 1906- . 2. Communists--United States--Biography. I. Title.
HX84.G74A34 1984 324.273'75'0924 [B] 84-22433
ISBN 0-7178-0615-4
ISBN 0-7178-0616-2 (pbk.)

CONTENTS

I—–GATHERING STORM

II—–FUGITIVE!

III——LEAVENWORTH

Photographs and Reproductions follow I, II, III.

PREFACE

This book is a personal account of an extremely difficult period in my life, my family's, and of countless thousands of other Americans. It was the time of McCarthyism. For nearly five years I was a fugitive from the FBI. After I voluntarily surrendered, I served 5½ years of an eight-year sentence in Leavenworth Penitentiary.

Why I and others went "underground," where and how I lived and worked, the people who befriended and worked closely with me, and how we avoided FBI detection are described for the first time. (I use fictitious names for those who could still be victimized, even three decades after the events.)

Revealed herein are the methods the FBI used in its search for me. Some of these I knew from personal observations and from facts later gleaned from my family and friends. But not for 27 years, until in December 1978 I began to receive my FBI files under the provisions of the Freedom of Information Act, did I fully appreciate the scope and vindictive nature of this effort. Even now, as these words are written, I do not possess all the facts.

First, the heavily censored FBI files deal nearly exclusively with the hunt for *me,* touching only incidentally and inferentially on the search for the other fugitives. Second, the FBI has not given me *all* the files pertaining to me, only a select portion amounting to over 20,000 pages, out of what was—as they informed my attorney Edward Greer—somewhere in the neighborhood of a *million pages.* Furthermore, those given me are full of blacked-out excisions—from a word to most of a page. What I was permitted to see, therefore, is a highly sanitized version of my FBI files. Whatever the FBI was determined to keep from me—and from the public—was ruthlessly suppressed. It is logical to assume, therefore, that what it sought to hide are precisely those of its practices most blatantly indefensible.

In 1979, when the FBI would permit me to see only 4,800 pages, and these with huge blacked-out deletions, I wrote a letter appealing this withholding of my files to the then Deputy Attorney General:

> Now that many of the past policies and practices of the Justice Department and the FBI are under public scrutiny—[it was the post-Watergate period]—and serious violations of the law by these agencies have been uncovered, I seek a full disclosure of *all* the facts pertaining to the conviction of myself and my colleagues. I am convinced that these will show the same kind of malfeasance and hence lead to a public reexamination of the circumstances and evidence surrounding our convictions. . . . Now that nearly a quarter-of-a-century separates my trial and prison term from the present day, all documentation pertaining to both should be completely declassified and released. Time itself has made absurd the claim of national security. . . . It represents, instead, a deliberate attempt to hide from public scrutiny the many FBI violations of civil rights.

Yet what I did get from the FBI—up to the summer of 1981 and expurgated though it was—is highly revealing. These files show how ludicrously far afield the search for me went, at what cost to the public, and to what extent cruel and vindictive methods were used to harass and persecute the members of my family.

The files also disclose differences within the Harry Truman Administration—particularly with J. Edgar Hoover and the FBI—over how far and fast to go in the roundup and prosecution of Communists. In addition, the files give evidence of FBI frame-up techniques including forgery of handwriting and forgery by typewriter.

I had been urged over the years to write a personal account of the McCarthy witch hunt. I hesitated to do so because it required re-living a chapter of my life painful to recall. I also disliked writing in the first-person singular; it would tend to make the story too subjective. I had been but one participant in the mass passion play of those years.

There was, however, one real hero in our family. It was my wife Lil. For more than a decade she had carried the full burden of the family, being both mother and father to the children and earning a living at the same time. But she could no longer tell her story; she had died of cancer barely three years after my return home.

Another hesitation came from the fear of throwing a spotlight on my children. They had suffered enough. But when they urged me to write the story, not only for them but for their children—my grandchildren—I began to relent. What finally convinced me was the insistence of my wife, Helen, whom I married some years after Lil's death. Another lovely and brave woman, Helen's urgings were decisive. I had been reluctant to undertake a task that would engross me in lengthy meditation over a past period of my life she had not shared, although she, too, had stood up to the horror and terror of that time. But not only did she bear with me, she scrutinized every page I wrote to make suggestions.

My personal account starts on July 18, 1948, the day I and eleven other Communist leaders were indicted by a federal grand jury. The story ends thirteen years later, on July 29, 1961, when I was released from prison. Part I covers the period from the indictments through our nine-month long trial to June, 1951—in the midst of the Korean War—when the Supreme Court upheld our convictions and ordered us to begin serving our sentences. Part II tells of my years as a fugitive. Part III narrates my life in Leavenworth.

ACKNOWLEDGMENTS

I am greatly indebted to a large number of people for helping me in various ways to write this book. Each of the people that I could reach, who had worked closely with me in the underground, readily cooperated in providing me with their own recollections. The same was true of a few men in Leavenworth. I am grateful to all of them for their cooperation and help.

I am likewise indebted to those who read the entire manuscript. These include, in addition to family members, John Abt, Lloyd and Lily Brown, Louis Diskin, Sender Garlin, Simon Gerson, Gus Hall, Martha Millet, Michael Myerson, Nathan Solomon, William Weinstone, Carl Winter and Henry Winston. Each made contributions.

I owe special thanks to Sender Garlin. He prompted me to write the book and then made thoughtful suggestions, often together with his wife Martha, to each chapter of the book.

I am extremely grateful for Henry Winston's cooperation. He, who lost his eyesight in prison, had been my very closest comrade and friend during the years of our common existence as fugitives.

Thanks also go to Prof. Edward Greer of Northeastern Law School. He generously donated his services as attorney to help me get my FBI files. I am likewise greatly indebted to Rev. Victor Obenhaus and Prof. Robert J. Havighurst, both of Chicago, for their fund appeal to help defray costs of travel and research, and of legal expenses other than those of attorney fees. With the generous help of William Sennett and the cooperation of the Capp Foundation of San Francisco, their appeal netted $3,142. To each and every person who contributed, my grateful thanks.

While many valuable suggestions were made by others, I alone bear full responsibility for what appears in this book, including inadvertent errors of judgment or fact.

"It is time to cease muting the fact that Dr. [W.E.B.] Du Bois was a genius and chose to be a Communist. Our irrational obsessive anti-Communism has led us into too many quagmires to be retained as if it were a mode of scientific thinking."

Dr. Martin Luther King, Jr.
February 23, 1968

At the Du Bois Centennial Celebration,
Carnegie Hall,
New York City

I——GATHERING STORM

1

Grim News

The knock on the door came in bright daylight. But I wasn't home to answer it, nor was anyone else. Neither was I to be found at the Communist Party's Illinois office at 208 N. Wells Street, in Chicago's Loop.

All this was purely coincidental. I had no way of knowing that on this particular day—July 20, 1948—the FBI would be looking for me with a warrant for my arrest.

I had other plans. My youngest brother, Ben, and I had agreed to take off from work to drive our families to a small lakeside cottage about sixty miles northwest of Chicago. We had rented the place from a friend of a friend for ten dollars a week. My wife, Lil, my sister-in-law Florence and the children would be able to spend some time away from the sultry heat and the noise and grime of the city, to glory in sun, water, grass and trees.

The children were up earlier than usual. We too were ready, bent on dodging the traffic in the midday heat. Ben and I had planned to get to the cottage early. We wanted this day to frolic with the kids, for we were to return to the city next morning and would not see our families until the following week.

It was a clear summer day and the trip was uneventful. To keep the children occupied and happy, we sang, played games and counted cows and "marble orchards" (cemeteries) along the way. We were in a gay, carefree mood, intoxicated by fresh air, the fragrance of new-mown hay and the sight of row upon row of growing corn, crowned here and there with golden tassels. At last we arrived.

Exhausted by too much sun and trying to keep up with the kids, we greeted the dusk and gladly put them to bed, washed the dishes and sat back to relax. We would turn in early, after listening to the radio for the ten o'clock news from Chicago. It was then that we learned that a Federal grand jury in New York had indicted twelve members of the

Communist Party's National Board for violating the Smith Act. They were charged with "conspiracy to teach and advocate the duty and necessity to overthrow the U.S. Government by force and violence."

There were two indictments: the first for being leaders of the organization; the second for membership. Each called for a maximum prison sentence of ten years, plus a $10,000 fine. Nine of the accused lived in New York; the other three in Cleveland, Detroit and Chicago. I was the one in Chicago.

The newscast went on to report that the FBI had hunted me at our apartment on the old West Side of Chicago and at the Party's headquarters. Zealous newsmen, spurred to the chase, had interviewed neighbors. They were told that we were a quiet, friendly family, the children well-behaved and courteous. Sometimes, they reported, I was seen playing catch with my oldest, Danny, or riding the two younger ones, Josie and Ralph, on the handlebars of my bike. None of our neighbors knew where we had gone.

We listened to the news in grim silence, each of us groping with this sudden new reality. It was not about something happening to others, or to everyone in general. This time it was happening to *us,* in a most direct and personal way. It was as if a sudden violent storm had burst into our lives. None of us could foresee its consequences.

The thought of sleep having vanished, we began to talk. The news of the indictments had come as a surprise, even as a shock, yet not entirely so. There had been ample evidence that a repressive wind was blowing, and we had good reason to expect increased anti-Communist attacks. But we just hadn't known what form they would take and how soon—or even if—they would actually occur.

In hushed, strained voices we discussed the disturbing news. We noted how far the professedly liberal Truman Administration was prepared to go to placate the extreme Right and to further whip up the mounting anti-Communist and anti-Soviet hysteria. Particularly ominous was the second indictment, which by making membership a criminal offense, seemed to foreshadow a move to outlaw the entire Party.

Our immediate concern was whether the FBI's search for me would lead to the cottage we had rented. We concluded that this was unlikely. Had we been followed that morning, we surely would have heard of it by now. We therefore agreed that Ben and I would stay overnight as originally planned and return to Chicago next morning.

With the lights out and unable to sleep, Lil whispered to me, "I'm frightened. Not for myself alone, but for the children. How will they take all this? And what if you have to go to prison?"

"I know, honey, I know," I replied, "but what can we do? We'll have to face things as they come."

In some ways the children had been prepared for this moment. Our political views were no secret to them. They were constantly exposed to radical political talk. Our home was something of a Movement center and a stopover for out-of-town speakers and organizers. We took the children to demonstrations and Party events. They were personally acquainted with Party leaders. Benjamin J. Davis, Jr., a New York City Councilman and a Communist, had once given Josie a birthday gift she would never forget—nothing less than Central Park itself, as long as she would let others use it, too. The children had also heard of police brutality, lynchings, political arrests and frame-ups, and of the Cold War engulfing our country. Yet how much of all this could they really grasp, viewing the absurd adult world through the kaleidoscopic fantasy lens of a child's imagination?

Danny was not yet eleven, intelligent, dependable and self-reliant for his age. He traveled on his own via public transportation and sometimes acted as sitter for the younger ones. He knew about my political activities and even helped distribute leaflets and gather signatures on petitions. Yet at times he openly resented the demands upon my time that he felt were incursions on his time. On one such occasion, when a new emergency kept me from spending a promised Sunday with the family, he burst out: "You're concerned with the rights of the whole world, but what about my rights?" It was a rebuke I would not quickly forget.

Now his rights were to be violated wholesale. For many years he would have to be the man of the family, shedding his childhood long before its time. Would he know whom to blame for this?

Josie, lovely, sensitive Josie, with her dark flashing eyes and black curly hair, was going on seven and the most vivacious of the clan. One day in the midst of all our troubles, bored with nothing exciting to do and apparently still immune to the surrounding tension, she complained to her mother, "Nothing ever happens in our family!" The time would soon come when she could no longer make this complaint, though the family often reminded her of it.

Ralphy, the baby of the family, was three, a lovable child. The adult goings-on were certainly outside his ken, and that was indeed a blessing, for as long as it would last.

So Lil had good reason to worry. But even she could not foresee the long years during which she would have to carry the full load of providing for and raising the family. Nor could she anticipate to what lengths the FBI would go to hobble her every move.

As we lay in the dark, waiting for sleep to come, my mind raced back to a time when we both were young: I was twenty, she only sixteen. She had told me she was eighteen and I had no reason to doubt her. For she had been earning her living as an office worker for some time. A bit later she admitted to me that she was only seventeen, and some years after that, when she wrote to Cleveland for her birth certificate, she learned, to her surprise and chagrin, that she was a year younger than she had been led to believe. Her folks had added a year to her age to get her into school earlier.

Hand in hand, absorbed in one another, we had slowly strolled south on Chicago's Kedzie Avenue toward its intersection with Roosevelt Road. She lived with her parents three blocks west on Roosevelt, near Homan, in a three-story walk-up with a store on the ground floor.

As we approached her home, I realized there was still one subject I had not broached. "Honey," I said, "there is still something we need talk about. I'm committed to the Movement, to the struggle for socialism. This will determine how I live and what I do. This commitment may lead to hardships, even to prison. Look at the repression that followed the war and the thousands who were arrested in the Palmer Raids of 1920. Can we be sure that it won't occur again? This means we'll have to forego the luxury of children. It isn't right to bring kids into the world without being sure we can care for them properly."

"By this time you ought to know," she replied, "that I share the same beliefs and commitments. I have no desire to be a lady of leisure. I intend to keep earning my own way. As for children, I agree, they're not for us."

As the years passed we kept our commitments. I gained experience and increased responsibility in the ranks of the Young Communist League; first while working at various manual jobs; later, as a full-time organizer. Lil, too, worked, most often in an office, but for short periods in factories to help in union organizing efforts.

But with the passing years our views about having children changed. What seemed logical and right at twenty and sixteen seemed so no longer as we began to approach thirty. "At least one," we finally agreed, and Danny was the first. When I told William Z. Foster, the Party's National Chairman, that Lil was expecting, he said, "You're making a mistake. A revolutionist should never be burdened with children. And you can't stop with one. The first is for the parents' sake, the second for the first one's, and so on."

When I related this to Lil, she laughed. "Bill may be right, but I notice that when he married, Esther already had two young children by a previous marriage, and that didn't seem to cramp his style."

Josie arrived four years later and Ralph four years after that. On each occasion Lil reminded me, "In case of trouble I'll manage alone, somehow."

Now suddenly this prospect was upon us, although I was sure she would not be completely alone. Ben and Florence could always be counted on. And Lil would have scores of friends and comrades to help her when she needed them. I knew Lil was worried, but I also knew she would be true to her word. "I can handle the big crises of life," she would say, "but it's the daily little ones that get me down." She was to have more than her share of both.

Sleep that night, facing the unknown future, came in fitful spurts. City folks like to think that the countryside is blissfully quiet at night. But the hoot of an owl, the wind rattling a windowpane, the rustle of a bush, or a squirrel on the roof can be startling and ominous sounds. Only the dawn brought respite.

2

A Flight Backward in Time

Since we did not know how the Government would attempt to prove the charge against us, or who its witnesses would be, we could not determine in advance of the trial how many or which defendants would take the stand. Yet each of us had to be prepared. From the outset, however, it seemed quite certain that I would be one of them.

Sometime later, when I met Abraham J. Isserman, my attorney in the case, he urged, in addition to other preparations, that I try and recall something of my early life and experiences, particularly those that had led to my socialist views and my becoming a Communist. He thought it important to be able to question me on my past, so that the jury could get an idea how my political outlook had evolved.

I had never met Isserman before but knew of his record as a labor and civil liberties lawyer. A member of the New Jersey Bar, he was on the national board of the American Civil Liberties Union, and was the counsel for the American Newspaper Guild and the Consumers Union, among other groups. Abe, low-keyed and not given to courtroom pyrotechnics, understood the significance of our trial, not only for the defendants and their party but for civil liberties in general. He was painstaking in his preparations. From the start, he and I hit it off well. I respected his skill and tried to follow his legal advice.

What influences had led me to the prisoner's dock? What had made me what I am?

So many things occur in one's lifetime, especially in childhood and youth, that it is nearly impossible to say that this or that incident, or incidents, was decisive in determining later development. Yet certain events and people did stand out in my memory.

There was, of course, my father. He was not a radical, quite the contrary. But why had he died at 33, when I was only nine? It made me, the oldest, grow up too fast. Even before the diabetes had done its fatal work (insulin had not yet been produced synthetically in 1915), I became my mother's confidant.

We lived behind a wooden partition in a cleaning and tailoring shop, for my father could no longer seek work as a custom tailor of men's suits. It was here that my parents eked out a living, working as a team. During the last months of his life, when he was in a coma much of the time, I traveled regularly by streetcar (the half-fare ride cost three cents then) from Archer Avenue on Chicago's South Side to the Owl Drug Store in the Loop. It was the only pharmacy in the city that carried the medicine prescribed for my father.

After his death we moved to the Jewish ghetto on Chicago's West Side. My mother tried to support the family. A small sign, *Dressmaker,* hung out of the window of our first-floor flat. Since she did not earn enough for us to live on, she had to apply for public assistance, then called "Home Relief." Ma was an intensely proud woman, ashamed of receiving charity, and she tried her best to keep this a secret. The monthly check went for rent, but she would never dream of giving it directly to the landlord; she would first get it cashed at the bank.

Ma even tried to keep the disgrace from my two younger brothers. But this failed. Mrs. Law, the caseworker who visited us regularly, and unexpectedly, would look everything over to see what had been bought—a chair, a pot, shoes—even if secondhand. Having learned that my mother sometimes gave us a penny after lunch for candy, she periodically stationed herself where she could observe the candy store to make sure we were not being extravagant at public expense.

How we hated Mrs. Law! Any little thing that was not on her list of permissible Spartan necessities put us in a sweat. When my brother Harry and I wanted to go to the movies on Saturday afternoon to see another thrilling episode of the latest cliff-hanger serial, we first scouted the block to make sure she was not watching us. I am sure she had other things to do besides observing our family. But to us she was the devil incarnate, with horns inside the hat she always wore.

I guess she, too, unwittingly influenced my early perception of things.

To get a bit more income for the house, Harry and I (Ben was still too young) tried to earn a few cents here and there. But Ma did not like the thought of our hawking newspapers or selling chewing gum. Too demeaning for *her* sons. So she set out to find me an after-school and Saturday job that would be "respectable" and have a future. She succeeded with a pharmacist on Roosevelt and Turner. When I was about 13, I became his bottle washer, bottle filler, errand boy, soda jerker and general helper. To Ma, this was a perfect job. I would earn money, meet nice people, learn about pharmacy and, who knows?—maybe someday become a pharmacist or even a doctor.

My boss was a plump, easygoing, good-natured man. "Son," he said, "you can eat all the candy and ice cream you want, but if I ever find you taking any out with you, you're through." I consumed so much the first day that I wouldn't touch a thing after that. Wise man. My mother was right; I was earning two dollars a week and meeting the right kind of people.

It was 1919, the beginning of the Prohibition Era. To buy a pint of good whisky legally required a doctor's prescription. The purchase of the coveted bottle took place in a drugstore, which received its regular supply directly from the government. Stock was replenished monthly, a new bottle for every prescription turned in.

This arrangement would have worked perfectly, but for the druggist's kindheartedness. He hated to see people downing poisonous bathtub gin and wood alcohol-spiked moonshine while his pharmacy basement was filled with good stuff. So he asked several doctor friends to sell him their excess government allotment of whiskey permits. After himself filling in the doctor-signed prescription blanks with fictitious names, he was able to sell many pints "under the counter" and for a raised price.

This worked fine until the beginning of the holiday season. Then, as the rush for bottled cheer got under way, the doctors caught the spirit too. They forgot their pledge to provide prescription blanks to the druggist. After all, there were many sick folk they could make well and happy at the same time.

My boss was also outdoing himself making the season a joyous one, confident that his doctor friends would provide him with the necessary prescription blanks.

Then came the hangover. He had sold hundreds of extra pints and had no December blanks to show for them—and there were none to be gotten. He was frantic. His good humor was gone. The doctors were in a panic too. What if this led to an investigation that disclosed their own shenanigans? What to do?

I knew about the situation, and wondered how they were going to escape from their dilemma.

On Monday afternoon when I came to work, I found the pharmacist his cheerful, happy self again. With a straight face, he told me that the store had been burglarized over the weekend and the basement emptied of its liquor stock. This was a crime, a disgrace, he made clear to me, but what could he do about it? It wasn't his fault. The government would understand—of course.

What could I say? I knew there'd been no bottles left to be stolen. I said nothing, for I still needed the job. But it was never the same again. My youthful, wide-eyed illusions had been shattered. If this was how nice people acted, did I want to be like them?

Sometimes a seemingly minor childhood incident leaves a deep scar, always painful to recollect. This had happened to me in a classroom at the John Lawson Public School when I was ten or eleven.

To reward the class for good behavior during the week, the teacher permitted us ten minutes of play before dismissal on Fridays. Tag was our favorite game. We sat with head and arms resting on our desks, our eyes closed, while one of us who was It would circle the room and then tag someone on the shoulder. The tagged one would then rise and try to beat the tagger to his seat, and failing, would become the new It. The game was usually ended by the dismissal bell.

There was one Black child in the class. She had entered in midterm, when her family moved into a basement flat. Her father was the janitor of that apartment house. Mary had no friends, came and went by herself, and sat alone on a stoop during recess, an untouchable in a class of some forty white children.

The same ostracism occurred in our weekly game of tag. All of us had been tagged a number of times, but she, never. I watched this with a growing sense of shame, and finally decided to correct the injustice next time I was It. The day came. I gently nudged her on the shoulder, but she did not rise and chase me. Believing she had not felt my tap, I went back and poked her again. This time she began to cry. Embarrassed, the teacher abruptly ended the game and dismissed the class.

I saw Mary many times after that, and sometimes our eyes would meet for an uneasy moment. She said nothing to me and I said nothing to her. But each time I felt a personal sense of shame and guilt.

What had made me more sensitive to racism then the others in my class? I am not sure. My own family was not free of racial prejudice, yet we had all felt the lash of anti-Semitism many times. When we lived behind the store partition on Archer Avenue, during the last months of my father's life, we felt our Jewishness keenly. It was a Polish-Irish community, the nearest Jewish family blocks away. Harry and I knew of no other Jewish children at public school. When we first enrolled there and children learned our family name was Greenberg, the cruel taunts began. More than once we had to run all the way home, pursued by what seemed to us a murderous wolfpack yelling at the top of their lungs, "Christ killers! Christ killers!"

We learned how to sprint; we also learned something about bigotry and prejudice that we could never have learned from books alone.

3

Soapbox Thespians

Socialism was not a strange and foreign "ism" when I was growing up. Eugene V. Debs was a name widely known and respected, and not only in Chicago's working-class communities. In 1920, while serving a ten-year prison sentence in Atlanta Penitentiary for opposing U.S. entry into World War I, Debs polled over 900,000 votes as the Socialist Party candidate for President. S. P. halls dotted the city. There was one in my neighborhood, on the corner of Roosevelt and Sawyer, above the O'Conner and Goldberg shoe store. It was a gathering place for lectures, social affairs, meetings of workers' sick-and-death-benefit societies, and a Socialist Sunday school for children. A mile east on Roosevelt near Western, a German *Turnverein* occupied a three-story building. And an uncle of mine (on my mother's side) was a Socialist Party member.

This was an age before radio and automobiles, and long before television had radically altered cultural patterns. Our first radio was a simple crystal set, which my brother Harry and I secretly built. Ma wouldn't contribute a penny for the venture, saying that only damn fools thought sound could come "from thin air." One night we surprised her. She came home to find our homemade contraption, which used a bedspring as an antenna, with ragtime music flowing through the earphones. From the way she boasted of this "miracle" to friends, it was her sons who had invented radio!

Life was centered in the community. The common meeting ground was its main stem, Roosevelt Road. Weather permitting, or sultry heat having made it imperative, neighbors would leave their overcrowded flats after the evening meal to promenade up and down the avenue. Here one joined friends, scanned store-window displays, marveled at the glittering marquee above the new movie house and reveled in the oratory of soapboxers.

Loudspeakers were still in the future; the orators needed lusty voices to be heard above the din of passing streetcars, honking horns and heckling wiseguys. What a variety show of strange personalities and causes it was, with Saturday night reserved for the best!

It was the last of the golden age of in-person oratory, when public speakers had to be thespians as much as logicians. A bit of knowledge went a long way when properly mixed with passion, humor and wit, and some improvised statistics. For me, Roosevelt Road was a university.

One evening I stopped to listen, attracted by the antics of a speaker on vegetarianism. "I know why you eat meat," he told us. "It's because you want to be as strong as a horse. But stop and think: What does a horse eat?" This was logic so overwhelming that while I didn't go over to eating raw oats and grass, I did, there and then, become a vegetarian. A week later I still wanted to be as strong as a horse, but in a carnivorous way.

Once a week, on the corner of Roosevelt and Spalding, a blind orator held forth on history and socialism. One lecture might be about primitive communal society, another about ancient slavery or feudalism; but these were always related to modern capitalism and socialism. He constantly repeated a central theme: It is morally wrong for a man who does no useful labor to amass hundreds of millions of dollars, while millions who toil all their lives barely make enough to live on. I was amazed at his erudition and fascinated by his ability to marshal facts in so orderly a fashion. It seemed especially wonderful to me because the man was totally blind. After questions were answered, the hat would be passed, and literature (largely his own printed lectures) sold.

I went to hear this man regularly, and much of what he said took root, for he dealt with problems that increasingly troubled me. Why such appalling poverty in a land so abundantly rich—the richest on earth? Why do those who work the least, or not at all, get the most? What about the Russian Revolution of 1917? Could it, would it succeed? Could society get along without capitalists? Why was Debs in prison for opposing war?

These questions nagged at me, alongside those of my own work experiences, even while I was still attending school. I wrapped packages after school at a mail-order house, washed dishes weekends in an ice cream parlor, worked one summer as a millwright's helper in a bedspring factory. Another summer I stamped holes in leather belts in a factory, and during a third, filed mountains of papers in an insurance house. Wages were miserably low. There were no unions, no right to bargain for conditions. Entering the workplace, one shed all sense of personal dignity, as well as elementary rights.

My uncle Isidore, the Socialist, worked as a luggage maker. During World War I, when additional workers were needed, the trade union movement seized the opportunity to augment its ranks. From less than three million organized workers prior to the war, unions grew to some five million. But once the conflict ended and the need for labor declined, the employers set out to drive the unions out, and with them the wartime wages and improved conditions. Their "open shop" drive provoked a period of intense class conflict, of brutal assaults on unionism and workers' conditions.

My uncle was one of the victims of this drive. The workers in the luggage shop refused to accept nonunion status and a wage cut, and went out on strike, picketing for many weeks. Then hunger forced one worker after another to accept defeat.

But not my uncle. He vowed that he would never go back; he would not be a scab. Meanwhile, the union had disintegrated, and there was no one to call the strike off. But my uncle stuck to his guns. He was a union man and a Socialist, and would not break a strike. Of course, by this time he would not have been rehired by the company, and his militancy and intransigence resulted in his being blacklisted throughout the industry.

This episode produced a crisis in our family. My uncle was married and had several children to feed. There were no family savings, no strike benefits, and unemployment compensation was something still far off in the future. I recall lugging pots of food from our flat to theirs, a few blocks away. My uncle's wife Ida, my mother, my other aunt, Clara, were all hostile to Iz. They too, they said, favored unions, but feeding the family must come first. He had no business staying on strike so long! They accused him of not loving his family enough.

In my youthful eyes, however, Iz was a brave and noble knight. His principled stand appealed to my idealism. My anger was directed at the company, not at my uncle for courageously defying it.

Uncle Iz didn't get to go back to work at his trade until the great CIO organizing drive of the mid 1930s. In the interim he worked on many jobs; for a long spell he was a milk deliveryman.

As I became aware of the grim side of life, I became immune to the rags-to-riches fiction still current among teenagers at the time. I turned to the social realism of Jack London, Upton Sinclair, Emile Zola, Mark Twain, Theodore Dreiser and Sinclair Lewis. I was deeply moved by Jack London's novel *Martin Eden,* and by E. L. Voynich's *The Gadfly.* These books stirred my imagination and appealed to my youthful romanticism. (Many years later I learned that the *E.* in Voynich's name stood for Ethel. I had never suspected that the author was a woman.) Gradually I began to think of myself as a Socialist.

In bull sessions with my boyhood pals on the corner of Turner and 13th Place, invariably I took the side of the underdog. I defended Gene Debs against those who considered him a traitor. I argued the case of striking workers. (When Chicago's streetcarmen walked out on strike, paralyzing the city's public transit system, I wished them well, and gladly walked more than two miles each way to my summer job at the bedspring factory on Halsted Street.) When our street corner discussions touched on the famine-ridden, infant "Soviet Russia," I not only argued that it would survive but unabashedly prophesied, "Within ten years it will have a higher standard of living than we have here." How simple it all seemed to me then.

After one of our impromptu exchanges, my friend Nate said to me, "My piano teacher thinks much the same as you, Gil. Why don't you come with me and meet him sometime? He's a swell guy and has a big library with many books on socialism. You can look them over while I take my lesson."

A week later I accepted Nate's invitation. I was curious to meet Mr. Leibich and, above all, there was the lure of his library.

Rudolph Leibich, I was to learn, was an extraordinarily fine musician, a pianist who sometimes performed at radical affairs, and an arranger and harmonizer of music for workers' orchestras and choruses. His living-room shelves were lined with books, many on socialism. Week after week I would return, often becoming so absorbed in what I was reading that I had to be reminded Nate's lesson was over.

Leibich appeared to me an old man, with a head of unruly gray hair that fell to his shoulders, in looks a blend of ancient prophet and future hippie. Despite the age gap, we became fast friends. He was soft-spoken, kind, anxious to help, and natural and unassuming in his manner, with not a touch of condescension. After my first few visits, he permitted me to borrow books, skillfully guiding me from one enlightening volume to another.

It was from his library that I read Edward Bellamy's novel *Looking Backward* and Jack London's *The Iron Heel.* Both books contained highly romanticized versions of how socialism would come to the United States. Yet how different the vision of each! Bellamy's view was idyllic, London's apocalyptic. It was as though they were describing two different worlds. Only many years later did I realize that each was reacting to a different side of American life—the one to democratic, constitutional rule; and the other to wholesale violence and often the fiercest of class warfare.

At Leibich's suggestion I read Charles A. Beard's *Economic Interpretation of the Constitution* and Augustus Myers' *History of the Great American Fortunes.* Most important for my grasp of socialism as a theory rooted in history was my first contact with the writings of classical Marxism. *The Communist Manifesto,* written by Karl Marx and Frederick Engels (1847-48), and Engels' *Socialism, Utopian and Scientific,* opened my eyes to a panoramic view of history, a synthesis of the past, present and future.

While engaged in this private educational venture, I was taking a two-year commercial course at Chicago's Marshall High School. The only thing I learned there that has stayed with me over the years, and for which I am grateful, was touch-typing. For the rest, I spent time in class burrowing into books not included in the curriculum, concealing them within the covers of prescribed textbooks. When I graduated, some of what I had learned from these other books found its way into my valedictory address.

My presentation, as planned, was mildly radical, expressing some of the post World War I disillusionment current among thoughtful people at the time. But it was far too extreme for the faculty member assigned as my adviser. He told me that my speech would have to be changed. I responded heatedly that the content of my address was not his affair; that it was I, not he, who had been chosen by the graduating class. He then warned me that unless I changed the text I would not be permitted to deliver it, and it would not appear in the school yearbook.

Incensed, I took things into my own hands. Assured of classmate support, I gave my copy to the school printshop without telling them anything of the dispute. When the faculty adviser, acting as censor, learned of this, it was too late—the yearbook had already gone to press. He was indignant and threatened to have me flunked. But the speech appeared as written, was delivered in its original form, and the walls of Marshall High did not come tumbling down. And when I reread that speech years later, I did not find it all that radical.

One day Leibich invited me to accompany him to an affair at which he was to perform. It was a gathering of young Communists, the West Side branch of what was then called the Young Workers League. I eagerly agreed. I wanted to see what an organized group of radical young people was like, and also why some Socialists were now calling themselves Communists.

The event took place in an old, two-story former private dwelling (now divided into public meeting rooms), located in the neighborhood where I grew up. As I entered the hall I was struck by the ages of the young people assembled. They were all—about thirty-five of them—in their middle or late twenties, which for me at seventeen, was a generation apart.

The evening was pleasant, and they all tried—in their words—to make me "feel at home." Iz Gabin, whom I got to know well in later years, sat next to me. At every break in the program he would ask, "How do you like it, kid? How do you like it?" I liked it—but not the "kid" part.

Before leaving I was urged to attend their next meeting, which would feature a lecture. I did come back, and once again Gabin sat next to me, playing the role of mentor. He was so concerned with getting me to feel at home that, this time, he nearly drove me away for all time.

The speaker of the evening reported on some world congress that he had recently attended. But what it was all about went completely over my head; I could make no sense of it. But Gabin was sure that anyone with an ounce of intelligence could understand it all. Assuming that I possessed that ounce—otherwise, what was I doing there?—he doggedly concentrated on getting me to participate.

When the speaker ended his talk and the questions began, Gabin continued to prod me. "Ask a question, kid, ask a question. Say something, don't be bashful, you're among friends." All I could mutter was, "Not tonight, next time."

When that next time arrived, I made sure to get there after the speaker had finished. Gabin seemed delighted to see me, and when the meeting was over asked me to join the group. The invitation took me by surprise. Influenced by stories I had read in the press, I imagined a Communist organization to be a semi-secret society, difficult to join, for which applicants first had to prove their worthiness. Yet here, in spite of knowing so little, I was being *invited* to join. I felt flattered and agreed immediately. I was already committed to socialism as a goal, and I wanted to work with others toward its realization. Even my failure to understand some of what was being said, and the rather esoteric language employed, whetted my appetite to learn more. Before many weeks had passed I was actively helping to form another branch with young people nearer my own age.

One thing did stay with me. Every time I saw new faces at a meeting I wondered whether what was being said—sometimes even when *I* was the speaker—was comprehensible to them.

Of course, I had many romantic and unrealistic notions of how soon the Revolution would come to the United States. But the illusions were not mine alone. Shortly after I joined up in January 1924, I organized a meeting of my young friends to "hear a Communist speaker." He was Harry Gannes, a gifted young Marxist. (A few years later he became my brother-in-law, and in the 1930s he was the foreign editor of the *Daily Worker.*) Gannes spoke briefly and convincingly. After presenting the case for socialism, he cited the successful Russian Revolution as evidence that world capitalism was now on its last legs. "If it could happen in semi-feudal, backward Russia," he said, "it can't be long before the Revolution comes to the developed capitalist countries, including the United States."

The very first question asked, one in which we all were intensely interested, was: "How long will it be before the socialist revolution comes to this country?"

Gannes smilingly shook his head and replied, "I can't answer that question; no one can." He explained that Marxism was a social science, not an exact science like mathematics. "It is about people, society, social classes and class conflicts. No one can say precisely when the American workers will set socialism as their goal. Nor is it possible to say how deep the crisis of capitalism will become, or how soon, or whether a revolutionary leadership will arise capable of taking the country out of the crisis."

Then, looking at our eager, expectant faces, he added, "But don't worry; your generation is lucky. Before any of you reach the age of twenty-five you will have lived through the American socialist revolution."

That didn't seem too long to wait—even for impetuous teenagers. Gannes's forecast expressed the euphoria engendered by the Russian Revolution and the wave of revolutionary events that had swept central and eastern Europe at the end of the war. Monarchies were toppled, the Austro-Hungarian Empire split apart, a number of ancient nations won independence, and in the short-lived German Revolution of November 1918, Workers', Soldiers' and Sailors' Soviets (Councils) sprang up. In the words of Eugene Debs, uttered from behind prison bars, "The day of the people has come." Harry Gannes spoke to us toward the end of that period, but its glow lingered on.

If anyone had told me then that a decade later fascism would hold power in Germany, and a quarter of a century later I would be facing criminal prosecution and prison for my Communist beliefs and affiliation, I would have found the thought incomprehensible, perhaps even laughable.

4
Hired and Fired

I soon learned the art of job-hunting. First I would scan the Help Wanted columns of the early edition of the Chicago *Tribune*, which came out the night before. If there was a lead, I was up early in an effort to be among the first to apply. If there were no leads, I was still up early to canvass the many private employment agencies strung along Wells Street, on the west side of the Loop. If these turned up nothing, I joined with a crowd of other job seekers in front of the printing plant of the Chicago *Daily News*, the afternoon paper that carried the largest Help Wanted section, in order to grab a copy hot off the press. If an ad offered some hope, I dashed to the nearest streetcar or El station.

Most often it turned out to be a wild-goose chase. Anyone with access to a car (few had them then) could beat me there with ease. Frequently the jobs had been filled even before the paper went to press. And not infrequently the ad was nothing more than a decoy. Corporations used this device to intimidate their workers by luring to their factory doors a long line of jobless men and women seeking work, any kind of work.

As the weeks passed, I became adept at pounding sidewalks. Ma had been looking forward to my leaving school and increasing the family income. But I was beginning to wonder whether I would ever find a job. One day, however, with an assist from a snowstorm, luck came my way.

I went to the Board of Education's employment office, as I had a number of times before. This time I was told that there was a job opening for a young man out of high school prepared to do physical labor, but who could also type. They were sure the job would be mine if I got to the Sinclair Refining Company that day.

But getting there was no simple matter. A storm had blown into a typical late-winter Chicago blizzard. Traffic was snarled; some streets were impassable. Yet I had long way to go, to Western Avenue at 44th Street. I caught a Western Avenue streetcar, which laboriously inched its way southward. But at 39th Street it gave up, unable to push through the mounting drifts piled up by the high winds racing across the prairies. I trudged through the snow the rest of the way, my feet soaking wet and freezing cold. When I got to Sinclair, they were so surprised that I promptly got the job.

The shipping department needed an additional worker because winter was drawing to a close and the spring rush for gasoline and motor oil was about to begin. In those days most autos were open, with only flaps on the side, and the street and road conditions in winter were miserable. Many owners preferred to put their cars away and take them out only with the arrival of warmer weather.

There were about sixty workers at Sinclair. Their distribution reminded me of the social pyramid I had seen depicted on an old radical poster, with the largest mass, the most exploited at the bottom. The bottom or basement floor resembled the boiler room of a coal-burning steamer. Immense cauldrons, in which crude oil was refined to various grades of lubricating oil, filled the air with hot oil and chemical fumes. Most of the men who worked there were Polish immigrants or sons of immigrants.

On the floor above, where I worked, there was a loading dock for trucks on one side and another for railroad boxcars and tankers. Between the two platforms were gigantic kettles of oil, protruding from the floor below. The man in charge of the shipping department was Hugh Glasgow; I was his helper. Working out of the same cubbyhole office was Tom Miller, the plant foreman. Bill Moore was the only Black worker. He was the cleanup and handyman.

On the third floor were the quarters of the managerial, technical and clerical personnel. These were divided into a large general office, a smaller laboratory, and a more luxurious private office for the plant superintendent, Mr. Barlow.

My job was to help in shipping and to take responsibility for the routing of boxcars and tankers to their destinations. I weighed drums after they were filled, stenciled their tops, tilted them from an upright position and roll-maneuvered them to one or the other loading dock. When a boxcar had been loaded, we nailed two-by-fours around the lot of upright drums to make sure they would remain stationary when the freight train's motion caused a side-to-side listing or a forward lurching.

I also checked the railroad tankers when they brought in oil or took it out. This required climbing to the top, breaking the seal, taking the oil's temperature, and recording the height the oil reached on the tanker's ruler-gauge. Since oil is poured when hot and condenses as it cools, and each type of oil has its own specific density and viscosity, it required some figuring to know the exact quantity of oil each tank car contained.

In addition to these duties, I had to type the bills of lading and the information placards attached to the side of the boxcar or tanker, noting the trunkline to which the car was to be switched. I brought this information to the brakemen when the freight train pulled in, sometimes climbing into a cozy caboose to warm up and chat, while the air filled with the pungent fragrance of bacon or porkchops frying on the little potbellied stove.

It was hard work, but I enjoyed it. The job gave me a chance to get around and to become acquainted with the men. When there was no shipping to be done, I was available to help out where needed. For many of the men I must have been a bit strange, the first Jew who ever worked there and the first one most of them ever had close contact with. When they were drinking, their prejudice showed. Yet, as we got to know one another, they engaged in good-natured banter, which I gave as often as I took.

I was aware when I started the job that the plant was nonunion. I knew this because unions were few, particularly for production workers, and because working conditions were so poor. We put in 50 to 54 hours a week, depending on how many hours we worked on Saturday. The work was greasy; oil covered and penetrated everything. We changed clothes at the beginning and end of the day—shoes, socks, cap, everything. Oil spills were frequent; the floor often dangerously slippery. When the filling of a large order was an emergency, we worked Sundays as well, without bonus for the extra hours. Time-and-a-half for overtime was a concept still a long way off, at least for the Sinclair Refining Company. We did not get extra pay for holidays, nor did we rate a week's vacation.

My weekly pay was $18 the first year and $21 the next. The average wage was not much higher. Yet my job was far better than most, for I could get around instead of being riveted to a single spot. My tasks varied, and I escaped monotony. I could also breathe fresh air when loading drums on boxcars or trucks, or doing chores on the railroad siding. Compared with the jobs on the floor below, mine was certainly better.

An important objective of the Communist Party and the Young Workers League at the time was to help in the unionization of production workers. That became my objective. Of course, I had no desire to lose my job, and I had next to no experience in union organizing. I began slowly, feeling my way. I soon learned that the men who needed a union most, those working on the floor below, were the most resistant to the mere mention of the word "union." They feared for their jobs and had their doubts about me. They were older, with families to feed; there was also a cultural gap. Moreover, my job was different from theirs and brought me in frequent contact with Tom, the foreman. From their point of view, therefore, they had good reason to be wary.

Hugh Glasgow, with whom I worked closely, was hostile to the idea of a union. He regarded himself superior to the "ignorant foreigners" on the floor below. He was Irish-American and had attended high school; what did he have in common with the others? he thought. Bill Moore, like the men at the vats, kept his thoughts to himself. He felt deeply his ostracism and his assignment to menial labor, nor was he permitted to forget he was Black. The only worker with any union experience was Old Jack, the cooperage man. He worked in a nook by himself, repairing and replacing slats and hoops on wooden barrels, bemoaning the slow death of his craft. He spoke favorably of unions but disparagingly of the unskilled. I was not getting very far, but I was not discouraged. At least a few of the men were being made to think about unionism.

In my second year, something occurred that brought the workers' discontent to the surface. The season was busier than usual, and keeping up with demand was extremely difficult. Several times we were asked to work beyond the usual hours, and increasing exhaustion stirred rising bitterness. Then, one Friday, a rumor swept the plant: Superintendent Barlow was going to work the plant on Sunday. He was cursed with vehemence and a variety of oaths, in a number of tongues. If the order to work came, the men vowed, they would all say no.

Saturday work proceeded as usual, but with greater tension. As quitting time neared, the men began visibly to relax. It had been only a rumor after all. We were joking and laughing as we changed clothes, when suddenly Barlow entered our filthy, foul-smelling dressing room. He was greeted with silence.

"Men," he said, "I have bad news for you, but there's nothing I can do about it. We're working tomorrow. That means every one of you."

There was a low muttering in the room, but no one said anything audible. Even John, one of the younger men, who had said he would speak up if this moment ever came, sat with eyes cast down, saying nothing.

I waited, hoping the silence would be broken. Barlow was about to leave, and I felt that if no one else would speak, I must. I knew I was not the best representative, but better I than no one. "Mr. Barlow," I began, "I have something to say. It's unfair to make us work tomorrow. Sunday is only one day of the week, but for us it's the sum of the entire week. It's the only day that's ours. Most of the men have families; Sunday is their only day together."

As I spoke, Barlow's face flushed with anger. At the same time the men around me were raising their heads, nodding assent. From the corner of my eye I could see even John looked as though he wanted to speak.

But the next and last word was Barlow's. "You," he said, pointing at me, "are too young to know what you're talking about. You'd be a lot smarter if you kept your mouth shut. I don't intend to argue. The man who doesn't show up tomorrow needn't show up on Monday." With that he swung around and left.

All was silence as we finished dressing. No one asked who was coming in the next day. We knew that we all were. But one thing had changed. In their eyes I saw a confidence and respect for me that had not been there before.

On Monday morning I was called to Barlow's office. I expected the summons and even that I might be fired. Instead, he gave me a dressing-down; he said I was a good worker but young, hot-headed and stupid. I was warned against "doing something like that again."

Two weeks later, I was again called to Barlow's office. He told me he knew I'd been attending Communist meetings on Friday nights and discussing unionism. "I should fire you now, but I won't. I'm giving you another chance because when I was young, in England, I too had some radical, socialistic ideas. Only in later years did I realize how foolish I had been. You can't change human nature, boy, you just can't. I'm giving you another chance because I like you, but if you go to another meeting I'll have to let you go."

I was shocked that he knew about my weekly meetings. *How* did he know? Who was the informer? And what was I to do about it? One thing I knew: Although I wanted the job and needed it, I was not going to quit the Movement. But I had to have time to think.

I sent word to the chairperson of my branch that I would not attend meetings for the next few weeks and would explain when I saw him. For days, I tried to recall the conduct of individual members. I was unable to pin suspicion on anyone. Maybe there was no one to suspect? Perhaps it was a company spy who had followed me to the hall. I decided to check that out.

I let a few weeks pass. Then, one Friday, I asked Ma for an extra sandwich since I was not coming home directly from work. I went to the hall, on Roosevelt just east of Kedzie, immediately after work, making sure that I was not being followed. I slipped into the hall between six and seven o'clock and waited for over an hour for the meeting to begin. I was sure no one was watching on the outside. But on Monday morning, at about 9:30, Tom Miller was called on the phone from Barlow's office and told that I was fired. I never did learn the identity of the stoolpigeon.

So came and went my first steady job. I needed nothing more to reinforce my political convictions. What I had heard of Pinkerton agents and company spies was not fiction, but fact. I had been a conscientious, reliable worker. Even Barlow admitted that. But I had dared to speak up for the men, and that was apparently an unforgivable offense. It triggered the investigation that led to my dismissal. No wonder unions in industry were so hard to come by.

At home, I said nothing about having been fired. Why worry Ma? Why get her agitated, when she was already upset about my Communist activities? Surely I would find another job soon. But jobs were not to be found; when I failed to bring home a paycheck, the truth was out.

Once or twice it looked as if I had gotten a job, only to have it evaporate after my application had been scrutinized. Was my name now on a Chicago industrial blacklist? I wasn't sure, but it seemed so. Or was it because I was Jewish? Plants in many areas of work discriminated. Gradually I found I had better use an assumed name when applying for work.

It was as George Gilberts that I finally found work at the McCormick Works of the International Harvester Company. I started as a punch-press operator and moved up to a milling machine. The building I worked in was the one—wooden floor, wooden stairway and all—that had witnessed the great strike demonstration for an eight-hour day on May 1, 1886. Here May Day was born. Yet when I worked there forty years later, the only union was a company union.

To help bring bona-fide unionism to the plant, I joined a local of the International Association of Machinists. I was its only member working in a large industrial plant; the others were employed in small machine shops. Nor were they interested in trying to organize the McCormick Works. They simply didn't believe it possible.

There was in the plant a Communist Party group, which met regularly. We discussed working conditions, the problem of unity among the many different races and nationalities employed there, and how to build the first nucleus of a future industrial union. We issued a regular monthly, four-page, half-tabloid-size paper, which exposed the company union, preached unity and struggle, and kept alive the tradition of 1886 and the goal of socialism. I helped to edit that little sheet and to distribute it surreptitiously inside the plant—mainly by leaving copies in washrooms and other spots where workers would find them.

It would take another decade, however, before a multitude of such efforts, and changed conditions, culminated in a new wave of militancy among the workers, finally bringing industrial unionism to the farm equipment industry.

So my personal work experiences, as I told Abe Isserman, had a great deal to do with my being a Communist.

5

What J. Edgar Hoover Wanted

When the twelve members of the National Board of the Communist Party first learned of their indictment under the Smith Act, in July 1948, they had no way of knowing how far the Truman Administration intended to go. However, it was clear that the timing of the indictments was part of a campaign maneuver. Running for reelection, Truman sought to steal the anti-Communist thunder from the Republicans while at the same time embarrassing the Henry Wallace third-party bid for accepting left-wing support. Wallace was nominated the Progressive Party's candidate for President at its convention on the same weekend as the indictments.

But what were the Administration's intentions beyond this? Were the grand jury's indictments the signal for a wholesale assault on the Party and the roundup of active Communists? Or would the Administration wait until our case was first tested in the courts?

We had no definitive answer to these questions, only speculation. Some in the Party's leadership took a dire view; others, less so. My own opinion was that the Administration would hesitate before spreading a wider net so long as the Cold War did not turn into a hot one. It would wait until after successfully prosecuting the twelve before moving toward wholesale indictments.

As it turned out, this guess proved largely correct. But it would not have been had J. Edgar Hoover fully had his way. This I learned only in the summer of 1981 from portions of my FBI files, obtained under the Freedom of Information Act (FOIA).

On February 5, 1948, a half year *prior* to the date of our indictments, Hoover had submitted a rather unusual document to Attorney General Tom Clark. Titled "Brief to Establish the Illegal Status of the Communist Party of the United States of America," it was marked Strictly Confidential.

An unusual feature of this brief was its length. It was all of 1,795 pages, typed single-space, divided into ten "books." These cover the origin, history and ideology of the Communist Party—as interpreted, of course, by the FBI. Like the man whose sole interest in literature was to search for erotic passages, the FBI "historians" had combed through the many works of Marx, Engels and Lenin, and the often turgid writings of lesser Marxists or self-styled Marxists for every mention of violence or forceful overthrow. Yet, significantly, they could not cite a single case of the advocacy or use of violence on the part of Communists in the United States.

One "book" of this bloated FBI brief (from which 47 pages had been deleted in my copy), listed three groups of possible witnesses to be used in court proceedings against the Party: former members, confidential informants and special agents. Three volumes consisted of possible exhibits that could be introduced as evidence—from books, pamphlets and articles or extracts from them.

The unusual length of the brief and its enormous detail suggest that it may have taken years to produce. What the FBI had in mind was further revealed in a special memorandum dated January 22, 1948, two weeks before the brief was delivered to the Attorney General. The author of this FBI inner-departmental memo was D. M. Ladd, assistant to Hoover and director of the FBI's domestic intelligence division.

Ladd strongly urged the prosecution of "Important officials and functionaries of the Communist Party" as an "immediate objective." Such action is urgent, he wrote, because it would "result in a judicial precedent being set that the Communist Party as an organization is illegal."

The Ladd memo went even further. Once this judicial precedent is established, it went on to say, *"then individual members and close adherents and sympathizers can be readily dealt with as substantive violators."* (Emphasis added.)

Thus the dragnet was to reach out and envelop those whom the FBI listed in the somewhat amorphous categories of adherents and sympathizers.

Ladd argued that "setting this precedent has an important bearing on the Bureau's position *should there be no legislative or administrative authority at the time of the outbreak of hostilities* which would permit the immediate apprehension of both aliens and citizens of the dangerous category" (Emphasis added.)

Note that Ladd's strategy, and Hoover's, was predicated on the inevitability of war, for he did not say "Should" hostilities break out, but *"at the time"* they do.

Another FBI memo, dated July 23, 1948, three days *after* the indictment of the twelve members of the Party's National Board, bore no signature and was stamped *SECRET* in large, block letters at the top and bottom of its two typed, single-spaced pages. The author of the memo was indignant that only twelve Communist Party leaders were indicated. This was proof, he believed, that the Administration was "insincere" in its anti-Communist drive. He accused it of playing politics, of engaging in "a political move . . . timed to break just before the convening of the Wallace-for-President convention in Philadelphia today." He stated that the same evidence used to indict the twelve could have been used to indict all fifty-five members of the Party's National Committee and many more. The failure to do this, he complained, gave the Party's organizations time to "protect members" and to make it "practically impossible for the Government to locate vital [membership] records." Here a full paragraph is blacked out.

The memo gives an example of what a "sincere" effort on the part of the Truman Administration would have been:

> It had been hoped that the Grand Jury investigation would be carried out in much the same way as the investigation of the Industrial Workers of the World (IWW) in 1917 during World War I. The IWW case was inaugurated by a simultaneous national move against every IWW headquarters throughout the United States. All national and local leaders of the IWW were indicted for conspiracy by the Federal Grand Jury in Chicago, were convicted and over one hundred sentenced to long prison terms. As a result of this joint national action the IWW was crushed and has never revived. *Similar action at this time would have been as effective against the Communist Party and its subsidiary organizations.* (Emphasis added.)

A clue to the authorship of this revealing document is offered in the last sentence:

> The writer was in an executive position in the federal service at that time and had an important part in the IWW prosecution and thus knows from experience that a local prosecution is not effective against a national organization if those in charge of the prosecution sincerely desire to suppress conspiratorial activities of the sort engaged in by the Communist Party.

The person who wrote the above words could have been none other than J. Edgar Hoover. It was he who entered the Justice Department in the spring of 1917 and had a hand in the raids and prosecution of the IWW that fall. As assistant to Attorney General A. Mitchell Palmer, Hoover played an equally ignoble role during the Palmer Raids. On a single night—January 2, 1920—simultaneous raids took place on workers' halls and homes in 70 separate cities and towns, with thousands, beaten and arrested, and many forcibly deported, all without "due process."

This is apparently what Hoover and Ladd sought to duplicate in 1948. Because President Truman and Attorney General Clark were not prepared to go that far, at least not at the outset, they evoked Hoover's bitter denunciation. That he dared put in writing his charge of "insincerity"—an act of gross insubordination from someone within the Administration—only shows how certain Hoover felt that the President would not fire or even reprimand him.

It would seem that the purpose of the Hoover memo was to get word around within the Bureau, and to Hoover's friends in Congress and the Administration, that Truman was not to be taken off the "soft on Communism" hook.

That was only 1948. Joseph McCarthy was still unknown nationally, and the term "McCarthyism" had not yet been coined. Before the witch hunt was over, 146 Communists would be indicted and thousands more persecuted, many losing their jobs. But they were not the only victims. Hundreds, even thousands, of liberal and progressive-minded people were harassed and victimized. Dissent and protest were stifled within the labor movement and the liberal community.

6

Our Day in Court

"They shall have an American trial," promised Federal Judge Hubert Leibell shortly after our indictments. Later, Harold R. Medina, who presided over our trial, echoed, "They will have an American trial." Neither troubled to indicate just what kind of a trial that would be.

Even a cursory reading of U.S. history, or a day's stay behind prison bars, would swiftly disabuse anyone of the notion that all persons are equal in the eyes of the law. Justice for the poor is all too often cruel injustice. And every generation has witnessed the frameup of those who challenged the established social order.

We were lucky. We had comrades and friends, thousands of ordinary—or rather extraordinary—people who selflessly helped raise the huge sums needed for bail and court costs, so that we could get our proverbial day in court. Our "day" lasted nine months, the longest federal trial in U.S. history. Yet the only fair trial would have been no trial, as is now widely acknowledged.

The trial opened on January 17, 1949. We were convicted on October 14. A year and a half later, in the midst of the Korean War (June 1951), the Supreme Court upheld our convictions without even reviewing the sufficiency of evidence. Six years later, with the Korean conflict over and the Cold War waning (and Frederick Vinson replaced by Earl Warren as Chief Justice of the Court), it did review the evidence against Communist defendants in the *Yates* (California Smith Act) case and, in effect, reversed itself. Fourteen trials and 140 convictions later! Court decisions are not retroactive, so this reversal did not apply to those of us still in prison.

As the charge and evidence were essentially the same in all these trials, it is clear that the "crime" for which we were convicted never took place. This obviates the need for a lengthy recapitulation of our Foley Square trial. Yet some aspects of the case call for comment.

The New York *Times* report the morning after our indictments said we were charged with "conspiring to overthrow the United States Government." This was *not* the charge, as the *Times* should have known. But it was what the public was led to believe.

We were *not* charged with conspiring to overthrow anything. We were charged with "conspiring *to teach and advocate*" a social doctrine. We were not even charged with actual teaching and advocacy, only with *conspiring*—that is, agreeing—to do so. And the conspiracy consisted (according to the government) of our being members and leaders of the Communist Party and believing and teaching the social theory of Marxism-Leninism.

To inflame public opinion against us, however, it was necessary to create the appearance of an actual plot to overthrow the government. A remark made by Judge Medina before the trial even began reveals this purpose. Abraham Unger, the Party's general counsel at the time, appeared before Medina with a request for a 90-day delay. John F. X. McGohey, the U.S. Attorney and later chief prosecuting attorney in our trial, vigorously objected. It would allow the defendants, he argued, 90 more days to continue their "alleged unlawful activities." Medina agreed: "If we let them do that sort of thing they'll destroy the government."

At the time this flagrantly prejudicial remark was made, Medina had not yet been chosen as our trial judge. His subsequent selection, despite his demonstrated bias, sheds light on the fairness of the judicial system under which we were tried.

Even more revealing of the same attempt to frighten the nation with the specter of a dangerous revolutionary plot was what occurred on the opening day of the trial. The New York Police Department let it be known that it had assigned 400 men and women to protect the court—"no fewer than 45 detectives, 40 traffic policemen, 38 superior officers, eleven mounted patrolmen, three policewomen, and 260 foot patrolmen." The *Times* reported that this armed contingent was "the largest detail for a court case in police history."

Commenting editorially, the *Times* noted that the defendants "are not charged with any overt act to overthrow the government." Why then, it asked rhetorically, did the Police Department muster so large an armed force, and why did it make this fact publicly known? It was "certain to make headlines as the trial began"

It did make headlines—that was its real purpose. Nor is it likely that the police had acted without prior consultation with the judge and prosecutor.

On the morning of January 17, 1949, in Room 110 (the largest courtroom at the Foley Square courthouse), the trial opened. Eleven of the defendants were present. (William Z. Foster, the Party's chairman, had been severed from the case because of a heart ailment.) We sat in a long row facing Judge Harold Medina. Immediately in front of us sat our defense lawyers; directly behind us was the rail separating the trial participants from the spectators.

We had a highly skilled group of lawyers as our defense team, but we had also decided that one of us—specifically Eugene Dennis, the Party's general secretary—would act as his own defense counsel. This enabled a defendant to make opening and closing remarks directly to the jury, to participate in the questioning or cross-examination of witnesses, and to attempt to assure that the political nature of the trial did not become obscured in a maze of legal technicalities.

At the outset, before the work of selecting the jury began, we challenged the undemocratic manner in which the members of federal grand juries were chosen in the Southern district of New York. We put forth evidence showing systematic discrimination against Blacks, Puerto Ricans, workers, poor people and women. Most members of federal jury panels, we demonstrated, came from white, upper-middle-class communities, and from special lists drawn up, many from employees of utility and insurance companies. During the previous year, no jurors had been called from either Harlem or the Lower East Side.

Our challenge to this blue-ribbon jury system took up the first month of the trial, with Judge Medina accusing us of delaying tactics to prevent the *real* trial from beginning. Delay was not our intent, nor did we have illusions as to how Medina would finally rule on the issue. But we did feel that we had to try to expose the class, race and sex bias in the federal court system. Although we were overruled, we won one important admission from Medina. He conceded that the jury panels were not truly representative of the people in the district, but insisted that we had failed to prove that this was *by design.* A few years later—I must believe we helped prepare the way—the federal jury selection system was reformed. Jurors are now drawn from voter registration lists.

No overt act of violence or advocacy of such had been charged or could be proved against us. So the Government's conspiracy theory boiled down to interpreting our *beliefs;* that is, the twisted version of them as constructed by the FBI and its trained witnesses. Our use of the term "Marxism-Leninism," and the reading, study and sale of the voluminous literature of historical Marxism were made to seem horrible "proof" of the existence of a plot.

Thus was enacted a melodrama of the grotesque. Copious selections from the writings of Marx, Engels, Lenin, Stalin and others—often entire books—were introduced as evidence. The defense countered with other selections, usually from the same works. It was a grand battle of quotations. But where was the plot? And where were the plotters?

Supreme Court Justices Hugo Black and William Douglas, in their opinions on the Yates case (July 1957), commented on this bizarre aspect of the Smith Act trials:

> The kind of trials conducted here are wholly dissimilar to normal criminal trials. Ordinarily, these "Smith Act" trials are prolonged affairs lasting for months. In part this is attributable to the routine introduction in evidence of massive collections of books, tracts, pamphlets, newspapers and manifestoes discussing communism, socialism, capitalism, feudalism and governmental institutions in general, which, it is not too much to say, are turgid, diffuse, abstruse and just plain dull. Of course, no juror can or is expected to plow his way through this jungle of

> verbiage. The testimony of witnesses is comparatively insignificant. Guilt or innocence may turn on what Marx or Engels or someone else wrote or advocated as much as 100 or more years ago.

How true of our trial! There were moments of real excitement and drama, but these were lost in a mountain of minutiae. For the defendants and their lawyers, forced to watch this charade day after day, it was an exercise in frustration, a burlesque form of cruel and unusual punishment.

The defense tried to break out of the Government-imposed strait-jacket, but without success. Early in the trial, our attorneys vigorously objected to the introduction of books into the record. "I submit," argued Richard Gladstein, a well-known California labor lawyer who was a member of our defense team, "that it is not proper in a court of law to try men upon the fact that they recommended for study a book." My own attorney, Isserman, told the court that putting books into the record in this manner was like putting books on trial. Was the jury to acquit or convict books—or us with them?

Medina overruled these objections. "This book is, as I understand it," intoned the judge, "one of the implements that are alleged to have been used by the defendants in forming the conspiracy that is alleged in the complaint or in the indictment."

Thus, according to Medina, books were to be likened to a burglar's tools.

To maneuver in this scenario of the absurd, the defense sought to introduce evidence of what we actually advocated; even more important, what we did to further that advocacy. But the prosecution and the judge strongly objected to evidence of that kind.

When Gene Dennis's opening remarks to the jury outlined the evidence he would present, Medina broke in: "I don't know how, Mr. Dennis, to disprove a charge of conspiring to teach and advocate the overthrow of the United States Government by force and violence, it is going to be relevant for the defendants to show what very good boys they were in some other respects."

This sort of thing led to frequent heated exchanges. When the defense tried to introduce evidence of the Communist Party's actual program and activities, these were generally ruled out by Medina as "irrelevant." Suppose, he asked rhetorically at one point, a plan to blow up the White House were put on paper and surrounded with

750 pages of extraneous matter showing "how good all these people were. What would be the use of admitting the 750 irrelevant pages?"

But the Party's program *was* the "plan," indicating what we were actually doing, and planning to do. The comparison of the defendants to terrorists plotting to blow up the White House was not a chance remark. It was part of the effort to plant in the public's mind, and in the jury's, a conviction that we were violent criminals.

In this respect, the Government sought to damn us on two opposite grounds. First, we were depicted as people without moral scruples, for whom the end—an evil end, of course—justified the means, *any* means. Then, we were portrayed as so diabolical that we did "good" things, were "very good boys," but for evil ends.

Thus the trial took on a Kafkaesque surrealism. The things we did may have been good—for Black freedom, for organizing the unorganized, for winning progressive social legislation. All these were good, but we were totally bad. All others were to be judged by what they *did*, but we alone by what the fantasies of some and the interests of others presented as our real motives.

As we saw it, socialism would come to this country as the end result of a long, difficult and many-sided struggle to extend democratic rights—economic, political and social. We believed that in the course of these struggles the present two-party system would break up, leading to the successful formation of a strong, popular coalition party of labor and its allies. And finally, we held that the victory of such a new political force could bring about major social and economic reforms aimed at so curbing the excessive power of the corporate ultra-rich that, in time, a relatively peaceful transition to a socialist society could be made. Violence had no place in our projection, although we warned of the danger that violence would be used by entrenched power to thwart the will of the majority. We believed this could be prevented to the extent that the overwhelming majority of people were united.

Our socialist goal was not at odds with what we were doing, but was its logical extension.

From the very outset we recognized that the cards were stacked against us. The judge was prejudiced and the jury was not of our peers. The most we could hope for was a hung jury; that one or more persons with enough independence, integrity and courage would say no to the witch-hunt. But such persons would not be easy to find under conditions where the mere charge of being "soft on Communism" could lead to the loss of employment and public ostracism.*

One question puzzled me. How would the prosecution get around the Party's explicit condemnation of violence and its espousal of revolutionary change by the most peaceable means possible? The rise of fascism in Europe had made us more conscious than previously that the democratic gains won by the people over generations of struggle could not be taken for granted. They had to be defended.

Revolution could come only through the conscious action of the great majority, never through plots and conspiracies. These views were embodied in the Party's constitution and in its basic programmatic documents.

The prosection got around this by an alchemist's trick turning the meaning of words into their opposites. This feat was performed by the Government's first witness, Louis F. Budenz, who had been a member of the Party and for a period the managing editor of the *Daily Worker*. At the very onset of the Cold War, Budenz had left the movement, to be taken to the bosom of the Inquisition. He became its professional "expert" on Communism, and on the witness stand he showed that he had what the syndicated columnist Joseph Alsop characterized a few years later as "belated recollection."

During his testimony, Budenz was asked whether the phrase "basing itself upon the principles of scientific socialism, Marxism-Leninism" bore any relation to "other language which may appear and does appear throughout the [Party's] Constitution?"

He had a ready answer: "It implies that those portions of the Constitution which are in conflict with Marxism-Leninism are null in effect. They are merely window-dressing asserted for protective purposes, the Aesopian language of V. I. Lenin. Marxism-Leninism," he testified, is the code word for violent overthrow of the Government.

Budenz was like the man who came to a psychiatrist complaining that everything he saw reminded him of a nude woman. Everything

*"We will probably never have a complete record of the number and variety of people who lost their jobs, their careers, or even their lives because of repressive policies of the Truman years. But it would be accurate to say that nearly everyone who lived through those years was diminished by the attacks against freedom of thought in the United States. Nearly everyone learned to be careful, to be anxious, to fear; not to sign a petition, not to join an organization, not to give money, not to be seen with certain books, not to speak your opinion lest someone misinterpret, accuse, inform." (Robert Sklar, Introduction to *The Truman Era,* by I. F. Stone, Random House, N.Y., 1953.)

the Party said or did, no matter what, reminded Budenz—and the prosecution—of violent overthrow, their own pet phobia. All else to them was mere camouflage.

I was staggered by the sheer brazenness of this assertion. The fact that we had *not* advocated violent overthrow was being used to prove that we had! Bundenz referred to Lenin. To get around the Czar's censors, Lenin had used what *he* called "Aesopian language," in writing his book *Imperialism.* For example, he later explained, he had spoken of Japan, not czarist Russia, when discussing the tendency of imperialist states to annex foreign territories. In the same way Aesop, the legendary slave in ancient Greece, had felt compelled to make his criticisms of the slave system in the short moral allegories he wrote with animals as the characters. But neither Aesop or Lenin said the opposite of what they believed. Their meaning was abundantly clear. That is why Aesop's fables have lived on to the present day, why Lenin's incisive critique of modern imperialism has stood the test of time.

The absurdity of the charge that we were conspiring to advocate a violent overthrow of the Government is only comprehensible in the context of that period. No one seriously believed that the country was threatened by revolution. But many people had been infected with fear that war with the Soviet Union was inevitable, even imminent. To heighten this fear became a major Government objective.

A dubious character, arrested in Pittsburgh a year earlier for illegal possession of firearms, was the Government's star witness that the Russians were coming. Charles Nicodemus testified that he had attended a Communist Party school at which he had heard it said (*not* by any of the defendants) that a "revolution wouldn't be successful in this country without the help of the [Soviet] Red Army." Nicodemus testified that he had asked "how the Soviet Union could possibly ever invade the United States without a navy," and been told, "the Russians could invade Alaska down through Canada and they could even destroy Detroit."

Defendants and spectators in the courtroom joined in the laughter. No one with even the slightest notion of the logistics involved, not to speak of the politics, could believe anything so wild. Medina, however, did. "It may seem funny to the defendants, but I don't think it is."

Turning to the witness, he asked, "They could even destroy Detroit, as I understand it. Did you say that?"

"That is what I said," replied Nicodemus evenly.

It was a time of hysteria, of spy scares, of the Alger Hiss and Judith Coplon trials. It was a time when the United States had a monopoly on the atom bomb and when frenetic voices, many in high places, were urging its use in a "preventive war" against the Soviet Union. But that monopoly ended before our trial was over, when the Soviet Union successfully tested its own bomb in September 1949. Hysteria then rose to new heights, and the stage was set for the judicial murder of Julius and Ethel Rosenberg.

In this setting it became possible to confuse people by tearing Marxist quotations out of context and reading into them the desired fantasies. Listening to the Government's mockery of the Marxist classics droned into the court record, and to selections of our own writings—some, unfortunately, jargonized—it became painfully evident that the average person would have a difficult time understanding any of it.

It is true that Marxism-Leninism as a philosophy and social science has a technical language of its own. But it is also a movement of working people, and as such needs to use a language understandable to them. "Marxism is not a dogma but a guide to action," is an oft-repeated phrase in Communist circles, and to us its meaning is clear: Marxism is a method by which to analyze reality, not a catechism of do's and don'ts to be memorized and ritualistically applied. It should be understood as only a *guide* to action, with emphasis on the word "guide." By switching the stress to *action,* the prosecution gave the phrase another and, to many, a sinister meaning: that Marxism is a social doctrine that requires action. Then they made the word "action" synonymous with violence.

7

Family Reverberations

Since neither Lil nor I had any idea how long the trial would last, and we did not want to uproot the children, the family remained in Chicago. Early in the trial, I visited home for a weekend about once a month, usually coupled with a speaking engagement. But there were so many comrades and friends to see that the brief intervals snatched for family intimacy made even more painful the long weeks of separation.

For Lil and the children it was even more difficult than for me. With the Foley Square trial in the daily news, and our home address public knowledge, Lil was constantly concerned about harassment of the children. The witch hunt had its share of mentally twisted people, and crank phone calls were frequent. At the same time Lil was increasingly often asked to speak publicly, which was total agony for her.

When she addressed an audience, whether in the living room of a worker's home or from a more formal platform, she appeared calm, spoke in measured, convincing words, completely in command of herself. Few knew what this effort took. Days before, she would begin to worry and fret, and would have restless, sleepless nights and stomach upsets. Yet how could she refuse to speak under the circumstances?

Actually, hostile incidents in the neighborhood were rare. Persons who were politically prejudiced tended to keep their views to themselves. Those who were sympathetic were in no rush to make themselves known, fearing reprisals. But some brave souls went out of their way to show sympathy. Others made theirs known by a meaningful glance, a hurried clasp of the hand, or some act of kindness to the children. Generally, there appeared to be a sense of guilt, even of shame, that something like this could be happening.

Of the three chidren, Danny had to face the problem openly. He knew what it was all about. One traumatic experience must have seared him deeply, although he has never referred to it. Some weeks after our indictments I traveled to New York as a delegate to the Party's national convention. I arrived the day before it was to start and met Danny, who had spent a few weeks at Camp Wo-Chi-Ca, a left-wing children's camp then located near Fort Murray, New Jersey. That night I attended the convention's opening rally at Madison Square Garden. The hall was full, an estimated 18,000 people attending. Then Danny and I retired to a room at the Riverside Plaza Hotel, where the convention's sessions were to take place. The room had been reserved for me, since I had been named to the resolutions committee with its expected far-into-the-night meetings.

Danny was scheduled to return to Chicago the next morning. But I was informed by Abe Unger and David Freedman, the Party's lawyers, that the U.S. Attorney's office had called with the request that I appear at ten o'clock the following morning to clear up a technical matter. I agreed to do so.

I awoke early, shaved, and went into the shower. Suddenly I heard Danny's voice. "Dad, there's someone at the door. What should I do?"

"Open it," I shouted back, "and find out what it's all about. I'll be out in a minute." I hurriedly grabbed a towel and began drying myself, coming out just in time to see two men roughly shove Danny aside as they strode into the room.

Startled, and suspecting violence, I demanded to know who they were and what they meant by this roughhouse entrance. They answered by flashing FBI badges. Then I was asked who Danny was, told I was under arrest and that their orders were to bring me in.

"Under arrest? For what?"

"For violating the Smith Act."

"Are you crazy? I've already been arraigned under that charge in Chicago and released on $5,000 bail. What is this, an arrest on top of an arrest on the same charge?"

"We have nothing to do with that. You're now under the jurisdiction of the New York court. Get dressed and let's get going."

"What am I to do with my son?"

"Leave him or take him with you, but let's go."

"I'll not take him to be locked up in a pen for whatever time it takes to straighten out this idiocy. And I won't leave him here until I find someone I can trust to take care of him."

"That's no affair of ours. Get dressed and get going."

"Hell no! I'll not leave until my son is taken care of. Until that's done, I'm staying right here. If you want to take me, you'll have to drag me out by force."

This was something they had not expected. They hurriedly conferred. Then one of them picked up the phone and called headquarters. I was told I could make the necessary phone calls, but to hurry. It was obvious that this early-morning arrest had been arranged to avoid a scene when convention delegates began to gather. Least of all, therefore, did they want a situation in which delegates might see me taken by force.

After a number of phone calls, I finally reached a friend. When he arrived and was introduced to Danny, I got dressed and left with the two agents. Later that afternoon I was released. My lawyer had to post another $5,000 bond, with the understanding that the bond placed in Chicago would be returned.

At the time this incident occurred, I was furious—not for the inconvenience caused me, and not even for the indignity, but because ten-year-old Danny had been subjected to so shocking and frightening an experience.

Recently, from portions of my FBI files obtained under the FOIA, I learned something more about this shameful episode. Documents dated August 3, 4, and 5, 1948, disclose that the U.S. Attorney's office in the Southern District of New York was fully aware that I was preparing to appear in person to straighten out whatever technicalities had arisen from my surrender in Chicago. But they also show that Irving H. Saypol, the Assistant U.S. Attorney, had other ideas:

> Mr. Saypol advised that it would appear to reflect on the Government and particularly on the FBI if the subject were given the opportunity to surrender as it might appear to indicate that the FBI could not pick him up; that insofar as Mr. McGohey and he were concerned, it was no longer necessary to adopt the kid glove policy relative to these subjects.

But on this matter, D. M. Ladd, Assistant Director of the FBI, disagreed. Ladd

> questioned the desirability of the Bureau picking up Green inasmuch as the warrant was served on him in Chicago and he is presently under bond. He advised that such procedure would furnish the CP grounds for criticism [and] they might even try to claim we were trying to break up their convention.

Ladd therefore proposed that the matter be referred to the Attorney General for resolution.

I do not know on what level a decision was finally made, but it is clear that Saypol's hard line carried the day.*

Josie, too, was learning that something was seriously wrong—that I was in trouble, that this was why I was away from home and why children whispered to one another while looking in her direction. The political implications of what was happening were still, of course, beyond her.

Ralphy, only three, was more insulated from the events, but undoubtedly also suffered. At the same time he was the recipient of a great deal of affection from family and friends and even from strangers, as the youngest innocent victim of the political malaise at large.

In some ways my mother suffered most of all. Widowed at thirty, when I was only nine, she had transferred all her affection to her three boys. As each of us grew to manhood we had to gently tear away from her embrace. Ma was a handsome, strong-willed woman, extremely self-reliant and stubbornly independent. In her mid-sixties, she was still working in a garment shop. An immigrant who had come to the United States at the age of twenty, she never learned to write beyond her own signature. She followed events by word of mouth and by assiduously listening to the radio. She was passionately devoted to her sons, believed they could do no wrong, and respected their political beliefs to the extent that she understood them. My predicament and the threat of a long prison sentence were a terrible burden and caused her great grief.

As winter slowly gave way to spring and the trial dragged on, we began to look eagerly toward the approaching school vacation when we would at last be together again. Lil and the children would come to New York; we would rent a room from an old friend in Far Rockaway and I would commute to and from court as long as the trial lasted. Certainly this grim charade at Foley Square would be over before school reopened in the fall.

That was the long view. The short one had to do with the even closer Memorial Day weekend. I promised that I would spend the

*Saypol played a part in our trial and in the second Hiss trial, and was the government prosecutor in the Rosenberg-Sobell trial. *Time* magazine referred to him as "the nation's number one legal hunter of top Communists."

days in Chicago, and the five of us began to plan for at least ten days of activities to be crowded into three.

It was to be otherwise. The prosecution now rested its case, and it was our turn. I was to be the second defense witness. It became clear that I would not be in Chicago for the extended weekend. I had to spend every spare minute preparing my testimony with my attorney. How could I assuage the deep disappointment—even anger—of the children? How could I convey to Lil how much I missed her and how terrible I felt about this latest development?

I held off informing them until the last minute, hoping against hope that I could still get away for at least part of the time. But this only made their sense of letdown more acute. I wrote Lil: "I know how the kids must feel about my failure to come home after such fulsome promises. But I hope you understand."

8

To Tell the Truth

If ever there was a political trial, it was ours. Yet the judge and prosecution blandly insisted that it was just an ordinary, if somewhat more important, criminal case. Time and again, when my co-defendants or I tried to explain a political concept as we understood it, or as it had evolved in our thinking over the years, we were stopped. The Government objected, and the judge upheld it.

"Where was this said?" "Who said it?" "At what meeting?" "Who was there?" became their refrain. It was as if a murder had been committed and all they needed to know was the participants and witnesses to the crime. As I told the court, I had participated in meetings far too numerous to recount. How could I recall specific dates and places, and who said what, when the span of the government's inquiry covered more than a decade?

It soon became clear, even before I took the stand, that the prosecution had a motive in demanding to know who was present at meetings and functions. Its aim was to enlarge the already swollen lists of the damned and to compel defense witnesses under oath to give testimony against them. For those unable to see this, the refusal of the defendants to name names seemed proof of something conspiratorial and sinister. "Hadn't they sworn to tell the *whole* truth? What are they afraid of? What are they hiding? They must be guilty—of something!"

This issue came to a dramatic climax shortly after our first witness, John Gates, a defendant, took the stand. Gates had fought in the Spanish Civil War and was also a veteran of World War II. Asked to name the members of the Party's committee on veterans affairs, he declined. Medina insisted. Gates again declined. The judge then found him guilty of contempt and sentenced him to 30 days in jail, beginning at once.

An uproar followed. Enraged at this act, Gus Hall and Henry Winston leaped to their feet in protest. Winston compared the action to a legal lynching, Hall to a kangaroo court. Medina promptly revoked their bail and remanded them to jail for the duration of the trial. For a short while after that the pressure upon us to name names subsided, but only for a time. Later, Carl Winter, another defendant, was also cited for contempt and sent to jail for 30 days. And a few days after I took the stand, I too found myself remanded "to the custody of the court." That is, to the West Street Federal Detention jail.

In preparing for my testimony, I had referred Isserman to an article I had written many years before we were indicted, jointly with Gene Dennis. "Notes on the Defense of American Democracy," dealt with the issues posed by the trial, though it was written in 1938. It had appeared in the Party's theoretical publication, *The Communist*. Isserman agreed that the article was an important piece of evidence. We were confident it would be accepted as such without question.

Once again we were in for a surprise. The prosecution objected; the judge sustained the objection. During the colloquy that followed, I turned to Medina and said, "Your honor, I thought we were going to be given a chance to prove our case. This article is germane to the very heart of the issue." That did it. For the remaining months of the trial, Winston, Hall and I were taken, handcuffed, to court by prison van, locked in a bullpen during the lunch hour break, then handcuffed and taken back to prison when court adjourned. Leaving and returning included the humilitation of being ordered by prison guards, "Lift your balls, men, then bend over and spread your cheeks." I never learned what they were looking for.

My previous arrests had been for picketing during the New Bedford, Massachusetts, textile strike in 1928; in the Sopkins dress strike on Chicago's South Side in the early '30s; for soapbox speaking on a street corner in Gary, Indiana, then a company town totally controlled by U.S. Steel; and I had been picked up once for distributing leaflets. Each time I was released without penalty. This time, however, in the midst of the trial and while on the witness stand, I was to experience jail. Since this indignity was forced upon me during the first days of my testimony, I had to prepare for the rest of the trial, with my lawyer, in the "privacy" of a prison anteroom.

I dreaded jail. My only consolation was the knowledge that Hall and Winston would be there with me, and that five days a week we would leave for the "free world" of the courtroom.

By far the worst part of this episode was that, once again, it made a reunion with Lil and the children impossible. They had just come to New York after school closed. At last we were going to be together again, we thought. Whatever the outcome of the trial, whatever fate held in store for us aferward, at least now for the summer, we would make up for the long months of separation.

Instead, we could now see each other only in the courtroom, in the bullpen behind it, or through the glass of the barrier in the visiting room at West Street. Lil was a bundle of nerves. After an emotional outburst at the courthouse, I wrote her: "What occurred at recess time has disturbed me. Please relax and take things in stride, the trial won't go on forever." As she had developed a gloomy outlook, I tried to reassure her that even if we were convicted, we would still be free for a time. "After all, there are far too many constitutional issues involved for them to deny us bail during the period of appeal. Of course, if the war danger becomes acute, things could change for the worse, but I don't believe that development likely."

Then, to change the mood, I wrote about my jail experience in a jocular vein and ended up, "From all of the above, you can see that instead of feeling sorry for me you should feel jealous. No worries. All problems settled for you—what you eat, when you get up, when you go to sleep, where you stay. It's really a great life—I wonder why I want to get out of here at all!"

Much of my time on the witness stand was spent in interrogation about my trips abroad. I told the court that during the 1930s, when I played a leading role in the Young Communist League, I traveled abroad regularly, attending conferences of Communist, Socialist and progressive youth organizations. In the summer of 1935 I was a delegate to the Seventh World Congress of the Communist International (Comintern) and was elected to its Executive Committee as one of three young people representing the world Communist youth movement. Some weeks later I also attended the Sixth World Congress of the Young Communist International, was elected to its Executive Committee, and later to its smaller Secretariat.

The most important gatherings of progressive and anti-fascist youth that I had attended were the first and second World Youth Congresses. The first was held in Geneva, Switzerland, in 1936; the second, at Vassar College in Poughkeepsie, New York, in 1938.

The Geneva Congress took place a few weeks after the armed fascist rebellion against the legally elected Popular Front government of Spain. To show our solidarity with the embattled Spanish Republic, and to get a first-hand view of what was happening, a delegation of North Americans headed by Joe Cadden traveled from Geneva to Spain. Among the delegates from the United States, in addition to Cadden, were James Lerner, Waldo McNutt, Elizabeth Scott, Edward Strong and myself. From Canada came Margaret Crang, Roy Davies and William Kashtan, and from Cuba, Carlos March.

When we reached the Spanish border in France, we found that train connections with Spain had already been severed. We therefore made our way on foot through the dark half-mile railroad tunnel that pierced the Pyrenees and linked Cerbere, France, with Port Bou, Spain. From Port Bou we took a local train to Barcelona. As our locomotive pulled into the station there, we saw a huge crowd gathered on the platform, smiling and waving banners. We were sure it was for some important person aboard, but it was for us. Evidently word of our expected arrival had preceded us. We were swept up in a tumultuous, emotional welcome that became a parade up the concourse of the beautiful tree-lined boulevard, Las Ramblas.

Although only a month had passed since the Civil War had begun, already anti-facists from nearby European countries—in particular refugees from Mussolini's Italy and Hitler's Germany—were crossing the border to help the democratic republic in whatever way possible, preferably with arms in hand. When we visited the military command post at the Guadalajara front in the mountains north of Madrid, the young man who acted as interpreter when we interviewed the front's *comandante*, Francisco Galan, was a young Italian Communist, Guiliano Pajetta, whom I got to know quite well many years later when he became a member of the Central Committee of the Italian Communist Party and was elected to Italy's Chamber of Deputies.

We visited Valencia, Madrid and Toledo, and stopped at a few smaller places along the way. Then we returned to Barcelona for a last stop before leaving Spain. An unexpected visitor came to see us at our hotel—Dolores Ibarruri, the Spanish Communist leader affectionately known as La Pasionaria. Ibarruri was above average in height, with pitch-black hair, dark eyes and an extremely expressive face. Her eyes lit up in a beautiful warm smile as she greeted us. But when she began to speak her face clouded and her eyes became deep pools in which one saw mirrored the anguish she shared with all of democratic Spain.

La Pasionaria had just returned from Paris. She had heard of our delegation and desired to say something to us before we left for home. She had gone to Paris, she told us, to meet with Leon Blum, the French Socialist leader and Prime Minister in the Popular Front Government. She had appealed to Blum to lift the arms embargo that he and his government had imposed on the Spanish Republic jointly with Great Britain and the United States. With bitterness she described to us how Blum had wept, protesting his sympathy for Spain, but had refused to do anything to lift the embargo. She charged the Western democracies with hypocrisy for imposing an arms embargo in the name of neutrality, when they well knew that Hitler and Mussolini were shipping huge quantities of arms, planes and men to help crush the Spanish Republic. She asked us to tell the story of Spain when we got home, and to do what we could to influence the Roosevelt Administration and Congress to lift the embargo.

This we tried to do. A pamphlet, *Spain 1936*, describing our visit was written on behalf of the delegation by Joe Cadden and widely circulated.

One year later I visited Spain again, this time to attend a meeting of representatives of the Communist and Socialist Youth Internationals. The meeting's specific purpose was to draw up a unity pact on behalf of the Spanish democractic struggle. There were three delegates from each International. Representing the Communist youth were Raymond Guyot of France, Michel Woolf of Czechoslovakia, and myself from the United States. The conference was successful and I was happy to be part of the group that helped make this beginning in Socialist-Communist unity possible. The chief credit, however, was due the Spanish youth, who some time before the civil war had merged the Socialist and Communist youth organizations into a single United Socialist Youth League of some 200,000 members.

During this second visit to Spain I visited Madrid again. This time it was under siege by fascist armies. I also spent time with Americans in the Abraham Lincoln Brigade, who were already in Spain fighting on the side of the republic. After watching the Americans drill at the training base in Albacete, I said a few words of greeting. Then a young man of about twenty introduced himself as a member of the Young Communist League in the States. After noting that he and I were about the same height and weight, he said he had a new suit he would like me to have. "I appreciate your offer," I replied, "but keep it, you'll need it when you get back."

"But what if I don't get back?"

Unsettled by his remark, I tried to reassure him. I never learned whether he did get back. About 1,500 young Americans did not. I'm ashamed to admit that in this fleeting encounter I didn't catch his name.

Many of my close friends lie buried in Spanish soil. Among them Dave Doran, who had been a member of the National Board of the Young Communist League before enlisting in the Abraham Lincoln Brigade.

I had traveled to Spain despite a State Department ban on such travel. To the Federal prosecutor at the Foley Square trial, this was still further proof of how dangerous a person I was. But my visits to Spain, as well as to the other countries, were in what I believed to be the very best interests of the United States and the American people. It is now clear to millions that the Spanish Civil War was the rehearsal for World War II. Hitler and Mussolini well knew it, and acted accordingly. The Western democracies, however, imposed a cruel arms embargo against the legal government of Republican Spain, under the hypocritical guise of "neutrality" and "nonintervention." The Soviet Union, to its great credit, came to Spain's assistance to the extent that it could, across the wide expanse of a hostile continent. Mexico also stood by the Spanish Republic. Had fascism been turned back in Spain, there is more than a likelihood that World War II, with all its horrors, might have been averted.

After the Spanish Republic had been crushed, President Roosevelt indirectly admitted culpability in its defeat. In a message to Congress he stated: " . . . our neutrality laws may operate unevenly and unfairly—may actually give aid to an aggressor and deny it to the victim." (Sept. 21, 1939).

Those Americans who stood on the side of democratic Spain, especially those who fought and died there, did indeed serve the best interests of the American people, and of the world.

But in praising the Communist role in the Spanish struggle, I do not wish to imply that our judgments were always sound. Costly errors were made, even in respect to the fight against fascism. It took the world Communist movement two whole years to draw the lessons of the Hitler victory in Germany and to reverse a narrow "class against class" policy into one that sought the unity of Communists, Socialists, and all democratic forces into an all-inclusive people's struggle against fascism and war.

9

Visiting the USSR

In its cross-examination of me, the prosecution showed an excessive interest in my visits to the Soviet Union. U.S. Attorney McGohey tried to make it appear that there was something sinister and conspiratorial about these visits. When I could not recall the name of the boat on which I had crossed the ocean on one of my trips (there was no trans-Atlantic air travel then) or the exact time of departure and return, he insisted that I did know but was trying to conceal something. At one point, after being badgered about a certain trip, I responded, "I do not recall the *exact* time I made it, but all the facts are at the disposal of the Government. I traveled legally. I left the Port of New York and came back to the Port of New York each time."

This reply was not to the liking of Judge Medina. "Mr. Green, he admonished, "you simply have got to avoid these unresponsive answers." Then with a majesterial sweep of the hand, he ordered, "Strike out the latter part of the answer."

But my answer *was* both responsive and pertinent. The Government may not have known what cities I visited, or whom I saw, but it knew the exact time of each departure and return. It was all in the public record. Furthermore, when I returned home from a trip I made no secret of it, including when I visited Spain without the approval of the State Department.

My first trip abroad, to Germany and the Soviet Union, had been in 1932. I remained in Berlin for about a week. Part of that time I awaited a Soviet visa, for none could be obtained then in the States. Although the Soviet Government had been in existence for fifteen years, Washington had not yet recongized it. (Diplomatic relations were finally established in November 1933.)

I didn't mind waiting; Germany held a special fascination for me. It was the native land of Marx and Engels. It was where, as I understood it, the workers were socialist-minded and highly organized, and where the Communist Party was the strongest in the West. Germany was where I and others expected the next socialist revolution to take place.

However, what I saw was not encouraging. I had read about Nazi storm troopers, but to see them was a shocking experience. They strutted the avenues arrogantly in their brown shirts and swastika armbands, rudely accosting passersby with "Heil Hitler" shouts and clicked-heels, stiff-arm salutes. They acted as though Germany were already theirs, yet at the time two-thirds of the electorate was still voting against them. But the anti-Hitler opposition was sharply divided, and the Socialists and Communists were warring against each other. It was a disturbing spectacle.

Ever since I had read John Reed's *Ten Days That Shook the World* I had dreamed of the day I could set eyes on the land of the first successful socialist revolution. Although the chief reason for my trip to the Soviet Union was to become acquainted with the leaders of the Young Communist International (with which the YCL in the States was then affiliated), it was the thought of realizing some of my dream that stirred me emotionally and intellectually.

I did not expect utopia. I knew of the indescribable hardships through which the country had passed: the blood-letting and destruction of World War I, the economic collapse and mass hunger that followed four years of civil war and foreign armed intervention. But now things were looking up and production was rising.

My first sight of the Soviet Union came from a train window. I saw endless miles of snow-covered rolling plain, which reminded me very much of the topography of my native Illinois. Missing, however, were the large cities, the industrial smokestacks, and the paved highways with their endless stream of swift-moving cars.

At station stops along the way, peasants huddled in small groups, their belongings tied in bundles. Men wore fur or leather hats with earmuffs reaching to their chins, while women wore heavy knit shawls that covered their heads and were wrapped around their necks. At one stop a young peasant entered our car, taking a seat in our compartment. One of the two friends who traveled with me knew some Russian and asked the peasant how things were going. "Better than last year," was the laconic reply. Then, putting a hand into the pocket of his sheepskin coat, he drew up something. "Last year we didn't even have this," he said as he opened his hand. It was filled with sunflower seeds. He didn't have to say any more.

On our first night in Moscow,* we went for a walk to get the feel of this very different city, a closer look at the many nearby Byzantine-style churches with spiraled and onion-shaped domes. But soon the bitter cold began nipping at our noses and ears and we turned back to the hotel. It was then we noticed people buying something from an elderly woman partially sheltered in a doorway. It seemed to me she was selling—of all things—*halvah.* Surprised that this delicacy should be sold on the street and in such bitter cold, but remembering my mother's ecstatic praise for the halvah she had eaten as a child in Odessa ("you've never tasted anything so good"), I decided to buy a chunk, letting the woman take the right amount of money from the rubles I held out in my hand. But no sooner did my lips touch the stuff than I spat it out. It tasted of lye. It was a coarse laundry-type soap.

*I was accompanied on this trip to the Soviet Union by two other YCL leaders, Jack Kling and John Marks.

There was an acute shortage of soap in the city, as we learned, and peasants were selling their homemade products on the streets.

I was appalled at the harsh conditions of life in 1932, yet moved and inspired by the spirit of the people I met. Things were bad, they admitted, but better than yesterday. Now hard times were partially self-imposed, a temporary belt-tightening that the country had to undergo to obtain the wherewithal to carry through the ambitious program for rapid industrialization. And this, it was pointed out, would make possible much higher living standards and the transition to a society based on abundance.

But the feverish drive to industrialize rapidly was impelled by something more—the omnipresent fear of another war. By January 1933, when Hitler gained power in Germany, this danger became even more apparent. On subsequent visits to the Soviet Union during the 1930's I noted evidence of vastly improved conditions, but also of rising apprehension and tension. The dread of war was pervasive. Greatest of all was the fear of a two-front war with Nazi Germany and militarist Japan.

10

Comintern

In Moscow in 1932, I met with the leaders of the Young Communist International, the representatives of the most important Communist youth organizations, hoping to learn from their greater experience. And I did learn, although much of their experience was not applicable to the States.

Even when conditions appeared the same, they were only superficially so. The setting was different. The labor movement in the United States was weaker, and the working-class awareness much lower, than in most other capitalist countries. Nor did we have an independent electoral party of labor such as existed elsewhere. In our country at that time, not even the principle of progressive social legislation embodied in unemployment compensation and social security had yet been won.

Two contrary views of the United States were expressed in our discussions. The dramatic, militant demonstrations of the jobless that were taking place in the States had been reported in the European press, and there were some who read into this activity a level of radicalism that was not there. Thus they found it difficult to understand why the Communist movement in the States was still so small. Either we in the States were underestimating our own potential, or the Depression conditions were not really that bad, This latter conclusion was reached by many, for it corresponded with a long-held view abroad that everyone in the United States was prosperous.

Even though the Communist leaders I met in Moscow in 1932 found it difficult to understand the political complexities of our country, I regard the personal friendship I established with them then and in subsequent years as an experience for which I shall always be grateful. They may not have learned much about the United States from me, but I learned much about the world from them. For the first time in my life I was meeting with people from other, far distant—and for me, strange—lands, with histories, cultures and traditions far different from my own.

In the Comintern building near the ancient Kremlin wall, in the corridors of the Lux Hotel or in its restaurant on the ground floor, I would meet foreign visitors and anti-fascist refugees who had heard I was from the States; some of them told me of their conditions and struggles, requesting that I bring their stories back to the American people. I met Communists who had spent long years in prison dungeons; they told me of colonial oppression and of fascism, not as abstractions but as first-hand experiences. A number of the people I first met in this way would later become heads of government, members of parliament, mayors of cities, and leaders of important parties and national independence and labor movements. As we talked, often in their hotel rooms or mine, and sometimes with wine, vodka or tea to toast our friendship, I felt a deep kinship with them, which has remained with me over the years.

My generation of Communists had profound admiration for Soviet achievement and tremendous respect for the opinions and experiences of its leaders. The Russian Revolution had shown the way. This, the poorest, most underdeveloped land in Europe had taken a great leap forward and had held its ground despite military intervention and the inevitable trials and errors that accompany any great venture into the unknown.

World War I had exposed the bankruptcy of the Second (Socialist) International. Most of its parties had rushed to support their own capitalist governments in a war for imperial gain. When revolution came to Germany in 1918, the Social Democrats led it not to socialism but to the restoration of capitalism. Thus, engraved in our minds were the lessons of these two opposite paths.

As is true after every great revolution, there was a tendency to read mechanically into the *specific* features of the Russian Revolution a universal application, and that was harmful. But despite such doctrinaire and sectarian interpretations of Lenin's contributions to Marxism, it was from him that we learned the deeper meaning of monopoly capitalism and its integral relationship to modern-day imperialism. He helped us recognize the immense significance of the struggle of the oppressed colonial and semi-colonial peoples for complete independence. He amplified Marx's famous slogan "Workers of all countries unite!" to read, "Workers and oppressed peoples of all countries unite!" This was a seminal concept, unknown in socialist ranks before that time. The vast revolutionary changes in the world since then have borne out the immense significance of Lenin's international foresight.

Similarly, with respect to the status of Black people in the United States, the impact of Lenin's insight was profound. The Socialist Party, in the days when Eugene V. Debs was its acknowledged spokesman, still regarded Blacks as just poorer working people, not as a racially oppressed people. Hence the Socialist Party did little to fight for full racial equality or to combat racist prejudices even within socialist ranks. But the Communists understood that Black-white unity was of decisive importance for all social advance in this country. They drew close to and were inspired by the insight and courage of Black leaders such as W.E.B. Du Bois and Paul Robeson, following in the historic tradition of Frederick Douglass.

We also learned from Lenin that a working-class political party is more than an electoral vehicle. It must prove its right to leadership as a daily combatant for the needs of the people and in the best interests of the nation.

11

Guilty!

Our trial ended with no last-minute surprises. All eleven defendants were found guilty. Ten were given five-year sentences and a $10,000 fine each. (The former maximum term of ten years for violating the Smith Act had been reduced by the U.S. Congress to five years, so we were receiving the maximum sentence under the law.) Robert Thompson, who had won the Distinguished Service Cross for exceptional bravery in the Pacific theater in World War II, received a reduced sentence—three years.

True to form, Judge Medina refused us bail pending appeal, despite the clear constitutional issues involved. The eleven of us were handcuffed, hustled into a prison van and driven to the Federal House of Detention on West Street in New York City. There we remained from October 14 to November 5, 1949, when the U.S. Court of Appeals granted us bail.

During the weeks awaiting the bail decision, Hall, Winston and I, who had by this time become old residents at this exclusive men's club, were able to initiate the others into the intricacies of prison life. We knew the ropes—what to expect, how to get around the rules, what was being cooked in the kitchen, whom to avoid, which guards were downright mean and which halfway decent, who was who among the inmates, and how to get a hard-boiled egg slipped under your pillow at bedtime. We also found more time to talk with one another, in a leisurely sort of way, than had ever been the case when we were on the go outside.

Prison life was not without its humorous moments. One day a number of us were discussing the outcome of our trial with other prisoners, when one of them burst out, "There's no fuggin' justice in this country. Look at me, I'll be getting from 15 to 25 years behind the high wall for knocking over one lousy bank, but you guys got only five years for trying to knock over the whole goddam government. I don't call that justice."

He was in deadly earnest, but we thought it funny. How many other people believed that we had actually tried to "knock over" the government?

While we had expected Medina to throw the book at us, we hardly anticipated the sentences imposed on our five courageous lawyers, ranging from 30 days to six months. Isserman was given a four-month sentence, and later was disbarred from practicing law in his home state, New Jersey.* All of them had been charged with "contemptuous behavior." In addition to my attorney, the lawyers were: George Crockett, Jr.,** Richard Gladstein, Louis F. McCabe and Harry Sacher. Their sentences were a warning to the legal profession that a zealous defense of the constitutional rights of Communists was a dangerous pursuit.

Other trial personalities fared considerably better. No sooner was the news of our conviction made public than President Truman rushed to appoint prosecutor McGohey to a Federal judgeship. The New York *Sunday News* (Oct. 16, 1949) carried a headline, *"McGohey, Red Nemesis, to be Federal Judge."* Reported the *News:*

> The nomination of U.S. Attorney John F.X. McGohey to be a federal judge was sent to the Senate by President Truman yesterday in the wake of McGohey's successful prosecution of the eleven members of the Politburo of the Communist Party as criminal plotters.

Medina's reward was also not long in coming. He was moved up to the U.S. Court of Appeals. And in 1952, Irving Saypol, the prosecutor in the Rosenberg case, would be named as a member of the New York State Supreme Court.

Our release on bail was a cause for celebration, especially for the three of us who had spent some five months behind bars. Even the sentences hanging over our heads, and the awareness of their deeper implication, did not dampen the feeling

*Eleven long years later he was reinstated by the unanimous decision of the New Jersey Supreme Court.

**Many years later, George Crockett was elected as a criminal court judge in the city of Detroit and served a number of terms. He is, at this writing, an elected Black member of the U.S. House of Representatives from Michigan's 13th District, and a member of the Congressional Black Caucus.

of total release. At last we could walk the streets again. At last we were free of the cant and hypocrisy of the trial. And at last I was to be reunited with my family.

Lil and the children were there to meet me. It was wonderful to see their beaming faces and the look of relief in their eyes. It was heaven to feel the warmth of their embraces.

As our return to Chicago would mean an immediate plunge into the daily maelstrom, we decided to take a few days off. Gus Hall and his family also sought to get away from things before returning home to Cleveland, so we made our plans together. We chose the farm of a good friend, Fred Briehl, about 90 miles north of New York City. There the crisp, fresh air, the bright sunlight, the mountains, a falling star at night, the plain but wholesome country food, the last of autumn's display of plumage, the joy of being together again, raised our spirits high. It was a brief lighthearted interlude between the grim episodes that had been and those still to come.

I had hoped that the political climate would be perceptibly improved by the time our appeal reached the U.S. Supreme Court. I reasoned that it would be only a matter of time before the anti-Communist hysteria ran its course, since it was being sustained by an irrational fear of the Soviet Union, cynically fed and manipulated by powerful interests.

This was unabashedly admitted in *U.S. News & World Report:* "War scares are easy to create," an editor wrote in its issue of Feb. 17, 1950, "and nearly surefire producers of money for arms." And, in a later issue:

> Government planners figure that they have found the magic formula for almost endless good times . . . Cold War is the catalyst. Cold War is an automatic pump-primer. Turn the spigot, and the public clamors for more spending . . . Cold War demands, if fully exploited, are almost limitless.

I was justified in believing the cold-war psychosis could not be maintained indefinitely, but I was wrong to think it would end abruptly. We were deep in the muck of a twentieth century Inquisition, but the worst had not yet come.

Our trial was a product of the current madness, and its outcome merely gave the wheel another whirl. Eleven of the most democratic and militant unions of the CIO were expelled from its ranks as t dominated." Alger Hiss was sent to prison for five and Julius Rosenberg and Morton Sobell were awaiting m spies." A new word appeared in the American vernacular and soon became known all over the world—McCarthyism.

The victory of the Chinese Revolution in 1949 had added more fuel to the anti-Communist hysteria. Within a few months a new "probe" began to find scapegoats for *our* "losing China." The mounting hysteria peaked when war broke out between South and North Korea in June, 1950. Few Americans knew anything about this strange and far-off land or could even locate it on a map. But they were told that this was all the doing of the Russians, and many believed it. They soon learned more about Korea, unfortunately, when their sons were drafted to fight and die in a war that speedily escalated.

An ill omen for the eleven of us was that the Korean conflict broke at the very time our appeal was being argued, exactly eight months after our trial. When one considers the time required to prepare the appeal briefs and to get the verbatim transcript of the trial's proceedings printed (in our case it consisted of twenty volumes of some 800 pages each) this was indeed a rapid progression up the appellate ladder. Before breaking for the summer recess, the court upheld the verdict of the lower court.

Less than a year later, on June 4, 1951, with U.S. casualties in Korea steadily mounting, the Supreme Court also rushed to wind up the case. We were ordered to begin serving our sentences on Monday, July 2.

We would be celebrating the 175th anniversary of the American Revolution behind bars.

The Supreme Court's decision was definitive. By a vote of six to two, the Court decided against us. Only Justices William O. Douglas and Hugo Black dissented. Our attorneys filed a motion for a rehearing, but we knew it would be denied.

With only a few weeks left before July 2, our need to arrive at a common estimate of the situation became urgent. From the outset of the trial, there had been differences in outlook among us. A few thought the country was sliding inexorably into an American form of fascism. Others felt this danger was exaggerated. The Supreme Court's stand seemed to lend credence to the more doleful view.

In Korea, the war continued to rage. Gen. Douglas MacArthur had demanded approval to "pursue the enemy" across the Yalu River into China. This would have led to a widening of the war and the danger of global confrontation. President Truman had rejected MacArthur's strategy and removed him from command, but his action had stirred up a national debate over which course to take. At the same time, the battlefield stalemate encouraged irresponsible demands for the use of the atom bomb to end the war "once and for all." There was no guarantee, therefore, that the situation would not get out of hand.

The action of the Supreme Court, coming when it did, had removed an important legal barrier to the further extension of the Inquisition. Before the Court's verdict, the extreme Right could still be held in check, because the legality of the Smith Act had yet to be resolved in the higher courts. Now the stage had been set for further acts to outlaw the Party and to make even membership in it a crime. More arrests, greater harassment, and a wider spread of the inquisitional net was bound to result. (The headline in the New York *Journal American,* of June 5, 1951, read: *FBI TO STRIKE AT 20,000 REDS.* The body of the story opened: "The FBI today plans a swift crackdown on the more than 20,000 Red Fascists in this area.")

In the midst of our deliberations—on June 20, twelve days before the date set for our surrender—twenty-one more Party leaders were indicted for "violating the Smith Act." They were dubbed "second stringers." And press leaks from Washington indicated that many more arrests were being prepared for Communist leaders across the country. Among the newly indicted was the legendary labor organizer Elizabeth Gurley Flynn, who up to that moment had been the only member of the National Board not indicted.

But our discussions also took note of signs of increasing public unease. The Korean War had clearly become unpopular. Pressures to extend its scope and dimensions were frightening people into a realization that the consequences could be most dangerous. Ever more individuals, many of them prominent and esteemed in their fields, were being dragged before the inquisitional committees, in an air of growing unreality. The fog of confusion and intimidation was dense; it would take time to disperse. We had confidence that it would, but for the time being we had to face the realities of intensified repression.

These two aspects of the problem had to be taken into account. It was evident that the Party would be compelled by circumstances, for how long no one could say, to work in a twilight zone of semi-legality—at best. It would have to battle tenaciously for its constitutional right to function openly, defending every inch of legal ground it still possessed. At the same time, it would have to learn to survive in semi-darkness, doing its best to protect workers and professionals from wholesale firings, and Party leaders from all being put behind prison bars.

It was therefore decided that a majority of the defendants would begin doing their time, while a smaller number remained outside of prison to work in an underground capacity. This was not a unanimous decision. Two members of the National Board argued that all should surrender. There were also varying opinions as to exactly how many should stay out. It was finally agreed that a smaller committee should fix the number and decide who they should be. All defendants were urged to prepare for either eventuality.

The days passed all too swiftly. Many comrades and friends had to be seen before taking leave. Then came the parting with Ben and Florence. Saying goodbye to my 67-year-old mother was particularly painful, for I knew the anguish she was suffering. My attempt to jolly her into believing I would be home soon was not very convincing.

To have the last days to ourselves, Lil, the children and I left for New York a week earlier. It was the time of the summer solstice, with sunlight supreme. The air had the soft warm fragrance of early summer; only the late afternoons bore evidence of hot, sultry days ahead. We drove slowly and leisurely, stopping often, whenever there was a desire to do so.

We picnicked on the grass alongside the road, climbed tree ladders to pick cherries, stopped at an inviting lake for a dip, and in Ohio ran into a huge swarm of June bugs that completely matted the windshield. On the way, the children decided they wanted to see Niagara Falls, and from both sides of the border. I begged off, fearing that, if recognized, I could be accused of trying to flee the country. Lil took them across to get sprayed by the grand splash, while I relaxed about fifteen miles away. One evening we went to a drive-in movie, splurging on popcorn and ice cream. Ralph tried valiantly, but in vain, to stay awake.

From all outward appearances, we were just another family on a carefree vacation trip. Yet the shadow accompanied us all the way, although little mention was made of it.

In New York City, four of us holed up in the apartment of two close friends on the upper West Side, while Danny stayed with David, a cousin his age. The following morning I went to the Party's national office on East 12th Street. I was told there would be a farewell party for the eleven at 4 p.m. the next day at the editorial office of the *Daily Worker*, after the weekend edition had gone to press.

I had heard nothing, either in Chicago or New York, about who had been selected to "stay out." I assumed, therefore, that I was not among them. However, during the farewell party I was called aside by a member of the Secretariat and told I was one of those chosen not to surrender on Monday.

That evening, after dropping Danny off and putting Josie and Ralph to bed, Lil and I went out for a walk. After strolling a while, we stopped at a neighborhood bar, took seats in an isolated corner and slowly sipped our drinks. It was then that I broke the news to her. Since I had not mentioned this possibility before, she was plainly startled. "I think it's a mistake," she said, "Do you really expect fascism?"

"You know I don't," I replied. "But with the war still on in Korea, the atomic spy scare, the frenzy to outlaw the Party, we cannot exclude a further growth of reaction, which could succeed in driving the Party underground."

"How will it help things here, if some of you go abroad to a socialist country?"

"I don't expect to go to a socialist country. I intend to stay right here."

"But why you? Why not someone without young children?"

"I know, honey; I too would prefer someone else in my place. But I could not in good conscience object to myself. And if I did, how sure could I be that it wasn't just a cover-up for fear of undertaking a far more difficult and hazardous task?"

"I'm afraid we'll never be together again."

"We shall, we shall. The current hysteria can't last. Sooner or later it'll pass. When it does, we'll be together again. We must never lose sight of that goal—never."

Neither of us slept that night. I arose before the break of dawn, tiptoed to the children's room to take a long look at Josie and Ralphy sleeping so soundly, fought off the desire to give them a last hug and kiss, and then slipped silently out into the unknown.

COMPLETE NEWS—MAGAZINE SECTION—COMIC FEATURES

New York Post

HOME NEWS

Copyright 1949, New York Post Corporation
Entered as 2nd class matter at the Post Office at New York, N. Y.

BLUE FINAL 7 LATE SPORTS RESULTS

TWO SECTIONS | Sunny and mild. | NEW YORK, FRIDAY, OCTOBER 14, 1949 | Volume 148, No. 28[illegible] | 92 PAGE

11 REDS FOUND GUILTY

5 LAWYERS, DENNIS HELD IN CONTEMPT, SENTENCED TO JAIL

FBI READY TO MOVE ON 20,000 NEW YORK RED[S]

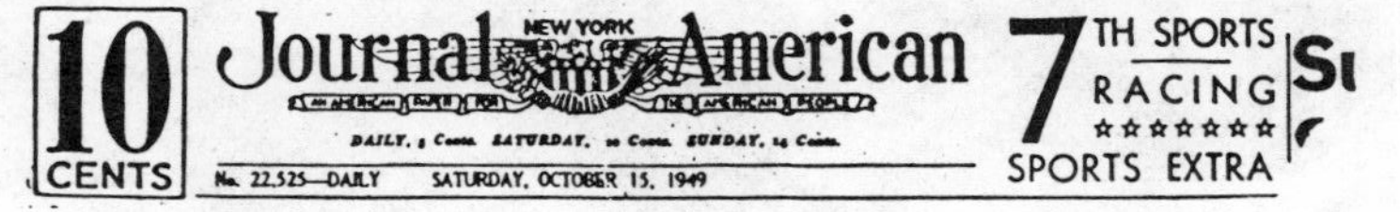
10 CENTS

New York Journal-American

DAILY, 5 Cents. SATURDAY, 10 Cents. SUNDAY, 15 Cents.

No. 22,525—DAILY SATURDAY, OCTOBER 15, 1949

7TH SPORTS

RACING

SPORTS EXTRA

One of many scare headlines that appeared during and after the Foley Square trial of the eleven Communist leaders. The one above was reproduced from the original newspaper, the right edge crumbled with age.

A June 5, 1951 headline in the same newspaper announced: FBI TO STRIKE AT 20,000 REDS.

Collier's

RUSSIA'S DEFEAT
And OCCUPATION
1952-1960

October 27, 1951 • Fifteen Cents

Preview of the War We Do Not Want

Robert E. Sherwood Hanson W. Baldwin Lowell Thomas Arthur Koestler Walter Winchell
Allan Nevins Edward R. Murrow Hal Boyle Stuart Chase Bill Mauldin Red Smith
J. B. Priestley Senator Margaret Chase Smith Erwin Canham Marguerite Higgins
Philip Wylie Howard Brodie Walter Reuther Chesley Bonestell Oksana Kasenkina

Collier's **magazine cover, October 27, 1951. Among those mustered for this notorious cold war issue were Robert E. Sherwood, Hanson W. Baldwin, Lowell Thomas, Allan Nevins, Edward R. Murrow, Stuart Chase, Bill Mauldin, Red Smith, J.B. Priestly and Walter Reuther.**

The caption began: "The bomb strikes Moscow, in retaliation for heavy attacks on UN cities. Seconds later, Kremlin (foreground) . . . was swept into oblivion . . ."

II——FUGITIVE!

1

Getting Away

Distraught at the realization that I would not be seeing my loved ones for years to come, I made my way slowly down the apartment house steps to the street below. The cool, crisp air roused me as my eyes focused to probe the pre-dawn darkness that Saturday morning. A cat scurried from a garbage can. Just around the corner to my left, I recognized the car I was expecting.

Ellen was at the wheel—a young woman who was a local trade-union leader and a Communist Party activist. When I had learned at the farewell party that I was not to appear on Monday to be jailed, I reached Ellen and explained the situation. She agreed to drive me to Chicago.

I reasoned that when the FBI learned that I had not turned up, it would begin its hunt where it last knew me to be, in New York. If I could reach Chicago before then, unnoticed, I might catch the sleuths off guard and win time to get myself properly settled.

Chicago was, of course, my preference. It was where I was born, grew up and had worked, the city I knew best. Chicago had a rhythm, tempo and spirit that made it different—at least for me—from any other place. I was well acquainted with its radical working-class traditions, the scope and characteristics of its present-day labor movement, its distinctly different communities and cultures, racial and ethnic, and the strength and influence of the progressive movement and the Communist Party. I also had numerous friends and comrades there on whom I could count.

And I had a personal reason. Although I well knew that I could not hope to see any of my family while I was being hunted, living in the same city would make it easier to learn how they were getting on.

Most important of all was the knowledge that an emergency setup had been established in Chicago to meet a contingency such as the one that had now turned into reality for me.

That such preparations had been made should not be surprising. Since the outbreak of the Korean War the year before, in June 1950, anti-Communist hysteria had ballooned and with it an ever-tightening repressive clamp on the Communist Party.

The Chicago offices of the *Daily Worker* and the Party remained open, but it was no secret that their walls were bugged, their telephones tapped and visitors monitored. Fewer and fewer people felt safe coming there. It became almost impossible to rent a meeting hall in the name of the Party or to distribute openly its leaflets and literature. Communist leaders were being tailed, whether visiting a worker's home, a union office, a Party club meeting, a relative or friend. The more they moved about openly, the more surely were they contaminating others with the FBI plague—adding ever new victims to the long list of people to be harassed or fired.

A number of Party leaders began to live away from home, conducting their activities in more discreet ways. They became known as the "unavailables" or the OBUs—Operative but Unavailable. Their numbers increased when it became known that federal grand juries were preparing new waves of indictments.

Workers who lost their jobs because of the witch hunt faced special problems. Often they were compelled to find work under assumed names and with new Social Security numbers.

I first met Bob and Sue, a young couple, during my lengthy sojourn as fugitive. Bob had grown up in a small Midwest town, played football in high school and entered college on a football scholarship. His father had been a coal miner. His sisters were hosiery-mill workers, badly exploited, with no union to protect them. The family was strongly pro-union, with a special affinity for the coal miners and their struggles, but none of them had ever been reached by socialist ideas. It was only when Bob was in the armed forces during World War II that he had met some radicals, one of whom read the *Daily Worker*. Later, overseas, he became acquainted with British Marxists. Back in civilian clothes, Bob went to work in a metal plant. Soon after, he joined the Communist Party.

Sue's background was different. She was from a town in New York State. Her folks were middle class, liberal New Dealers. The first Communist-organized meeting she attended was in support of the

Spanish Republic. Later she spent a week at a progressive summer camp in the Catskills. She shared a cabin with a group of young women, all of whom were involved in the labor struggles of that period. She became immensely impressed with the kind of human beings they were and what they were doing. Her interest doubled when she learned that they were all young Communists. She decided to join up.

During World War II, Sue worked in an arms-production plant. When the conflict ended, she decided to try her hand at Party organizing. She volunteered to go to the Middle West, seek a job, and help build the Movement. It was there that she and Bob first met, fell in love and married; soon they were the parents of a baby boy.

Suddenly, with no warning and for no apparent reason, Bob lost his job. He landed another—but then the same thing happened, and he noticed that he was being followed. Sue and Bob talked it over and decided that he should leave town to seek work elsewhere. She and the baby would remain behind until he found work. The same pattern repeated itself in the new town. This time, when he asked why he had been fired he was abruptly told, "You know the reason why."

Bob then decided to go to a big city where it would be easier to "get lost." He packed his bag one night and caught a bus to Chicago. There he applied for unskilled day-labor jobs, where he didn't have to show a Social Security card or leave an address. Later, he applied for a card under a new name.

Sue had left with their infant to join Bob at his rooming house in Chicago. But she soon found that her car was being followed. Determined not to lead the FBI to Bob, she sold the car to a dealer enroute, and with the money purchased a ticket to her parents' home in the East. There, sometime later, with the help of her sister, she was able to shake off her pursuers and join Bob without being followed. He was then working on a job under his new identity.

Our drive to Chicago was without incident. Ellen and I took turns, but she was always at the wheel when we drove into the rest areas and gas stations. Concerned about being recognized, I would feign sleep on such occasions, a cap slouched over my forehead. Ellen picked up coffee and sandwiches along the way, and we ate in the car.

Ellen was to drive straight back to New York as soon as she dropped me off. She wanted to be there in time for work on Monday morning and tried to catch a few extra winks when I was driving. Most of the time we talked about this and that, about people we knew, the situation in the labor movement, the problems arising from the anti-Communist hysteria and mounting repression.

Past midnight, as we came closer to the Ohio-Indiana state line, we realized that we would be arriving in Hammond, Indiana, my stopping-off place, in the early hours of the morning. We therefore pulled up along the side of the road and dozed for a few hours.

We were awakened by the first rays of dawn, continued on our way, and arrived in Hammond about eight o'clock Sunday morning. The streets looked deserted, the city still asleep. My rendezvous with friends had been set for that evening, but it was necessary for Ellen to leave me if she was to get back on time. So we stopped near a small park and square, in an area of the city where no one I knew lived.

I urged Ellen to drive carefully and to stop in the afternoon for a few hours of rest. We wished each other good luck, I expressed my gratitude, we embraced, and I stood waving goodbye as the car made its turn around the square and headed east.

Part of the morning I sipped coffee in a nearly empty cafeteria. Later I moved to a bench in the park, basking in the warm summer sun, my face partly hidden behind the pages of the Sunday *Sun-Times* and the Chicago *Tribune*. Still later in the afternoon, when the local movie house opened its doors, I spent several hours in an out-of-the-way seat near a side wall. I do not recall what the film was about. I do remember sleeping part of the time and awakening from a disturbing dream, induced as much by my own drama as by that being flashed on the screen.

That evening I was picked up by two friends, driven around for some time to make sure we weren't being followed, and then delivered to a spot on the South Side of Chicago. There I met another friend, who drove me to the place where I would be staying. It was to be my first home away from home.

At noon the next day I listened to the radio news. I heard that seven Communist leaders had begun serving their prison sentences that morning. They were: Benjamin Davis, Jr., Eugene Dennis, John Gates, Irving Potash, Jack Stachel, John Williamson and Carl Winter. Four others had failed to appear—Gus Hall, Robert Thompson, Henry Winston and myself.

I was now a fugitive.

2

The Hunt Begins

No sooner did it become clear that four of us had become fugitives than the FBI launched its massive hunt. To frighten the public into cooperating, stories were fed to the media about how dangerous we were. An example of this was a series of articles prepared "in cooperation with the FBI" and published by the Hearst-owned International News Service. They began:

> A nationwide FBI alarm is out for eight Communists—four of them bail jumpers, four of them evaders of arrest, *all of them classed with murderers, con men and kidnappers, as the government's most wanted criminals.* (Emphasis added.)
>
> These are the subjects of the most intense FBI searches in history.

The first of these articles (July 11, 1951), written by James L. Kilgallen, named the four "bail jumpers" in alphabetical order. It said we had been found guilty of "plotting to overthrow the United States Government." This, of course, was not the charge. We had been found guilty of a so-called conspiracy "to teach and advocate" a social doctrine.

Four others who had evaded arrest were also listed alphabetically: "Fred Fine, James Jackson, Jr., William Marron and Sidney Steinberg." These men were among the 21 Communists, tabbed by the press as "second stringers" who were indicted in New York on June 20, 1951, but had not been at home when the FBI showed up.

An introduction to the first article carried an appeal:

> Every citizen of the nation has been urged by the FBI to join in the intense manhunt for the eight Communist leaders. . . . You may be in a position to assist the FBI in locating and capturing the Red fugitives by reading the articles beginning herewith, giving detailed, intimate descriptions of the appearance, manner and habits of each of the hunted men.

Then the article dealt with me—my general appearance, height, weight, complexion. It even noted that my eyebrows were dark and heavy, "almost like strokes of a cartoonist's brush." Alongside this description were reproductions of mug shots, front and side views. Depicting my manner and habits, the article said I could most likely be found "where the John Does live and work." It added that "one would search too for a quiet intense man, one dedicated to the cause of Marxism ready to talk communism in taut, convincing phrases, interspersed with references to ancient jingles and modern history."

When the manhunt began, my brother Ben's youngest was seven years old. Kenny was a quiet, reserved, sensitive child. One day the children in his class were asked to relate what frightened them most. The answers were as varied as the children. One said he was frightened of thunder and lightning, especially at night. Another was terrified of a neighbor's dog. A third feared ghosts and goblins, and a few were scared of snakes. So it went until it came to Kenny. All he said was that he was afraid of "them." When asked to explain who or what he meant he repeated, "I'm scared of *them.*" No amount of coaxing could get him to say more.

Surprised at this unusual response, the teacher spoke to Kenny's mother about it. What was wrong? What childhood obsessions were causing this strange fear? Florence listened, troubled. She was not surprised. She knew there was nothing abnormal in Kenny's response. The abnormality lay elsewhere—in the circumstances that induced it. She thanked the teacher but told her not to be concerned. She well knew what frightened Kenny.

It was the FBI Kenny feared. Day and night, agents harassed the family, dogging their every step. Their apartment was bugged, their telephone tapped and an FBI car was always parked nearby. They knew that the apartment above their own was being used as an FBI listening post. Friends of Ben and Florence, who feared loss of employment or that they themselves would be hounded, ceased visiting them or even calling up. Neighbors were enlisted to spy on them. Some children in the community soon took on the attitudes of their parents, reinforced by the current TV fare of violence and crime, where the FBI and police are always the good guys and the others the bad.

Kenneth Green is now a young man, married, a father. He now says he never was scared and does not recall the school incident. He insists he had a good time; it was, he says, like playing cops and robbers. Billie, his sister, older by two years, married and the mother of three, vividly recalls the grimness of that time. She even thought it possible her parents would be arrested.

My own children, whose harassment was so much greater because their father was "you know who" and on the FBI's most wanted list, constantly lived in fear, although comforted by the courageous people who went out of their way, often at personal risk, to befriend them.

Kurt Vonnegut has observed that children's minds tend to empty at times of horror as self-protection from eternal grief. (The sons of Julius and Ethel Rosenberg refer to a similar experience. Blocked from their memories were some of the events in that most searing of human tragedies.) But mental blockage of this kind leaves its own kind of scar. The raw, open wound may be healed but scar tissue remains, often pressing on sensitive nerve endings.

I know that each of my three children was affected by the trauma of those years. And I am certain this is also true for thousands of other children whose parents were victimized during that shameful episode in our nation's history.

This does not invalidate Kenny's memory of the fun he had playing cops and robbers. My brother deserves much of the credit for this. Ben's marvelous sense of humor, his general optimism and high spirits, his deep inner convictions, served as a life-giving force animating all around him. Recognizing that fear and tension are at times best countered by ridicule and laughter, he devised pranks that would occupy the youngsters and stir their imaginations. In the games they played, the pursued and the tormented became the pursuers and the tormentors. The FBI's agents were cut down to size; they were seen as petty, mean, scrubby and sleazy snoopers.

Ben would have the kids scout the area for FBI cars, reporting their license numbers and the names of the occupants—that is, the nicknames the family gave them. FBI records report such counter-scouting activities, and of FBI agents concealing their faces while being photographed by Ben and the kids.

These are some of the things the children recall, but etched into their memories, so that they can never forget, is the cruel, vindictive war of nerves unleashed against the family by the FBI. But of all this I knew nothing, at least not at the beginning of what turned out to be a long odyssey.

3
Sanctuary

The people who had generously opened their home to me, with considerable risk to themselves, were strangers. The family consisted of three generations: Jim and Ann, the couple who had arranged for me to stay there; their beautiful children—Mary, three, and Paul, nearly two; and Ann's parents, who were always referred to by all members of the family as Grandpa and Grandma.

None were in the Communist Party, although Grandpa had been a member years before. Jim had been in the Young Communist League, having joined during the union-organizing drive at the Chicago stockyards where he worked. He left to fight for Loyalist Spain, however, before the yards were organized. Later, during World War II, he was in the U.S. Army. When he returned he was again a union activist but never joined the Party, although he considered himself a Communist.

Ann was not actively interested in politics, yet held staunch socialist views. These were inherited from her folks and reinforced by her own experiences. She had worked at many jobs: in a White Castle hamburger grill, a clothing factory, a brewery office, the telephone company, and alongside her mother at a large biscuit bakery. Her father, who still worked in a railroad repair shop, had been born in Czechoslovakia; Grandma, on this side of the big pond. Both avidly followed events in the old country.

Their home was on the pattern of many workers' homes: a two-story private dwelling, with the bedrooms on the top floor, and the kitchen, dining room and parlor (as it is called in Chicago) on the main floor. This entire floor was rarely used. Its shades were tightly drawn and its upholstered furniture carefully protected by plastic covers. Even the kitchen, immaculate, was seldom used.

The real living quarters were in the basement, which had its own stove, refrigerator, washing machine, television, table and chairs, and a small play area for the children. Here the family and friends gathered, entering through the basement back door. To be received on the floor above was to be told, even if not in so many words, that the visit was to be formal and brief. Only when some big family event took place was the first floor really put to use. Even then, to feel completely at home, close family friends would gradually inch their way downstairs.

I had witnessed this style of living in workers' homes many times. It seemed more common among families who were the first generation to own their own homes. Though even in rented apartments, the front room or rooms often were decorative and family living centered in the kitchen.

For a couple of weeks nothing of importance happened. Phil, who had arranged for my refuge, came to see me regularly, bringing news and books. We also spent time discussing problems in making our underground setup foolproof. I had known Phil, as well as his family, for years. A printer by trade, he had been a leader in the Young Communist League. He had a roundish, pleasant face and pitch-black hair, and was easy to get along with—a likeable fellow.

Actually neither of us, nor anyone we knew, had any real experience in this kind of undertaking. We decided to move slowly. We agreed that the home I was in could not be regarded as secure. It was okay for temporary use, but not for the long haul. The family was known as sympathetic to the Communist Party and we could not exclude that sooner or later their home would be spot-checked by the FBI.

I also sensed a certain unease on the part of the old folks. Nothing was said to me, my relations with them were excellent, the children and I got along famously, yet it was clear that my stay could not continue indefinitely.

An incident one night heightened this feeling. Grandma awoke with a piercing cry, frightened by a nightmare. When I asked her about it the next morning, she hesitated for a moment and then said, "It was about you."

"About me?" I asked, "What about?"

She hesitated again and then replied, "I dreamed that you had died and we didn't know what to do with the body."

Taken aback, I said, "Don't let that worry you, Grandma. I'm healthy."

We both laughed, but it was evident that my presence worried her. The dream was obviously a distorted reflection of her real fear—that I would be caught, and in their home.

As Jim had accumulated vacation time, we agreed that he and Ann would rent a cottage in the country where we could stay for a few weeks. This would ease the tension at home and give us time to make other arrangements.

Then something happened. A young woman who had been helping Phil reported that her apartment had been entered and ransacked while she was at work. We had no way of knowing whether this was a burglary, the doings of the FBI, or only a case of nerves on her part. But we could take no chances. All contacts with her were severed and it was agreed that I move elsewhere at once.

But where? A number of possibilities existed, each with drawbacks. One place was particularly suitable, if only we could be sure of the couple's reliability. Both were professional people. He, a writer, had been employed for many years by a conservative newspaper. She was a retired social worker. The husband had been attracted to Marxism while a student of economics at the University of Wisconsin. The wife had been drawn to the Movement by her contact with bruising poverty and social injustice. They had been members of the Party for some years but were quiet and unassuming in their ways, and few members knew them.

Could they be trusted? I finally decided on an expedient to help me decide, and I asked Phil to return the next morning for my decision. The books I was reading had been borrowed from this couple's shelves, and they bore the unmistakable marks of their owners' lifelong habit of underlining important passages and writing brief comments in the margins. One of the books Phil had brought me was Frederick Engels' *Anti-Duhring,* a brilliant polemical exposition of Marxist philosophy and economic theory.

That night I reread the books' marginal notes, trying to place myself in the mind of the person who had made them. I came away convinced that the person whose notations I read was honest, sincere, and deeply involved; I would put my trust in him.

Next evening I met Wilfred and Blanche. They picked me up in their car on a street corner quite some distance from their home. They had not known whom to expect and recognized me as the right person from a description Phil had given them. I had met Wilfred before, but not Blanche. Sitting in the back seat, I notice that Wilfred, at the wheel, was casting furtive glances at me in the rear-view mirror. "You know me, Wilfred," I said. "You know me." He took a sharp look, and from the changed expression on his face and the sudden acceleration of the car I knew that this time he had indeed recognized me, despite certain changes in my appearance. I now sported a mustache and wore a hat, as well as horn-rimmed glasses.

Many years later I asked Wilfred whether he had been nervous when he recognized me. "Well," he said, "I certainly hadn't expected *you*. I assumed you were somewhere else, far, far away, not on a Chicago street corner."

My new sanctuary was quite different from the one I had left. Instead of six people, there were only two. And this time I was truly underground—the only occupant of the basement, my bedroom having been the coal bin before the furnace was converted to oil.

Wilfred and Blanche were a middle-aged couple. They were gentle and considerate in every way. They possessed a superb library, and our animated after-dinner conversations ranged over a vast field. Wilfred had an encyclopedic knowledge of ancient civilizations and primitive cultures, had written fiction and plays, and had composed music. Blanche had taken to painting. It was first a pastime, then a passion, second only to her devotion to Wilfred, a love reciprocated in every way.

They accepted my living with them, and all the inconveniences and risks entailed, as a matter of simple moral duty. Yet they were understandably worried, more so at first than later. When I asked Blanche to take my soiled clothes with theirs to the laundromat, she felt it was hazardous, having heard of police dogs trained to pick up human scents. Not wanting to add to her worries, I told her I'd wash my own clothes, which I did for the months I stayed with them.

Wilfred was especially helpful to me as a writer. He corrected grammatical errors and clumsy constructions in articles I was writing, warned against the use of purple passages, and emphasized that the first objective of a writer is to communicate with his readers and that to this end clarity is the most important thing to strive for.

Both were extremely generous, contributing financially and otherwise to every worthwhile progressive cause. Yet they lived modestly, spending little on their own needs. I recall Wilfred going to work every morning with a brown-paper bag in which Blanche had placed a sandwich and an apple the night before. One day I asked, "Wilfred, aren't you tired of eating the same old liverwurst sandwich for lunch every day?"

"Oh," he replied, "is that what it is?"

For a moment I thought he was joshing me. The fact is he really did not know what was between those two slices of bread.

4

Family Is Target

In reply to my family's charge that the FBI was employing unconscionable methods to terrorize them, it could be argued that, after all, the FBI was only doing its job hunting down fugitives. But often their actions had nothing at all to do with the search and were even counterproductive. What happened immediately following my "disappearance" illustrates this.

When Lil and I took the children to New York, there had been an additional reason for the trip. Danny and Josie (Ralph was still too young) were to spend a few weeks at Camp Wyandot (formerly Wo-Chi-Ca), in New Jersey. We thought this would be good for them. Not only would the campers be children of their own age, but largely they would be from left-wing homes. To them, my children's relationship to me would be a badge of honor rather than of shame. Lil planned to stay in New York with Ralph until the older ones returned from camp. Then the four of them would return to Chicago together.

But things did not turn out that way. It seems that the FBI did not want the children to go to camp and exerted pressure on the camp management to bar them. This, according to a letter Lil received from the camp administration, included the threat to place the camp under constant surveillance if children of the "fugitives" were permitted to stay there. The camp management first wavered, then capitulated.

Danny and Josie—and Ellen, the daughter of Robert Thompson—were abruptly denied admission.

Danny and Josie had looked forward eagerly to camp. This cruel and unexpected rejection at the very last minute was a harsh and crushing experience for them. Danny, 13, was furious. "How can friends do something like this?" he wanted to know.

The camp management felt they had good reasons for their actions. They feared that massive surveillance by the FBI would arouse anti-Communist extremists in the community and could encourage acts of violence against the camp. Such threats had been made a year before, when Paul Robeson had been invited as a guest.

What could have been the FBI's motive, threatening to infest the camp area with agents unless the children were sent back home? What sense did that make in trying to nab me? If they actually thought I would be foolhardy enough to visit the camp, their course of action logically should have been the opposite—to lure me into a trap. Why did they want the children out of the camp? Was it to keep all members of the family physically together, to make surveillance easier? Or was it, as the family later charged, the first act of a war of nerves directed against them? (Jim and Esther Jackson's youngest daughter, Kathy, age 5, was also expelled—from nursery school!)

The answer to these questions is not to be found in the portion of my FBI files available to me. There is only a cryptic message sent by teletype to J. Edgar Hoover and marked "urgent." This told him that "Daniel and Josephine Green were refused admittance to camp because of fact they are children of [a] fugitive from federal justice." (Two lines in my copy of the message were blacked out.)

Early in the hunt, the FBI decided to make Lil its special target. Apparently she had used the words "fed up" (referring to her stay in New York) in a telephone call to Ben and Florence in Chicago, and the FBI interpreted these words as having a more general political significance. This, together with her request that Ben come to New York to help her drive the children back home, because she was too nervous to do so alone, led the FBI to believe she could be "broken." From then on, FBI agents repeatedly kept hectoring her for interviews: by phone, at the door, on the street, everywhere. Each time a special report was made to Hoover, ending up: "Further attempts at interview will be made."

Regular reports began to be sent to FBI headquarters about Lil's state of health and mental outlook. A New York informant, whom the FBI claimed to be an "employee of the State Party," was quoted as saying "Lillian Green was not happy about her situation." My mother was reported as bitterly complaining about continuous hounding of Lil. My aunt Clara was interviewed and quoted: ". . . the Green family is very nervous." My uncle was reported as speaking of Lil's "strained appearance." And at one point an FBI informant reported Lil as being in "low spirits."

Responding to the constant harassment, the family decided to make public the psychological war against them. Joining in this effort was Fred Fine's wife, Doris, who was undergoing the same kind of ordeal. The daily teletype report sent to Hoover on September 16, 1951, made first mention of this decision. It reported that Ben was even considering circulating a leaflet to "expose FBI intimidation." And on September 19 a teletype went to the "Director," informing:

> "DAILY WORKER" INSTANT DATE CONTAINS ARTICLE CHARACTERIZING SURVEILLANCE OF LILLIAN GREEN, WIFE OF SUBJECT BY AGENTS OF CHICAGO OFFICE AS A CAMPAIGN OF SYSTEMATIC INTIMIDATION AND NERVE WAR AGAINST WOMEN AND CHILDREN, DESIGNED TO CUT THE GREEN FAMILY OFF FROM THEIR FRIENDS AND NEIGHBORHOODS.

A reproduction of the full article followed. It quoted Lil, "If we go to the park, they sit down on a nearby bench. When I take the children to school, they are behind us all the way."

"We are being held hostage," explained Ben Green. "We have been condemned without a trial and deprived of every simple right guaranteed to citizens who are not criminals."

The article continued:

> Last week the FBI called the General Accident Insurance Company, and ordered them to cancel insurance on the cars driven by Ben and Lil Green.
>
> The following day, they opened a new campaign against Ben Green and the shoe store where he works. All shopkeepers in the vicinity of the shoe store were given an FBI poster describing Gil Green. They were also told about Ben Green, asked not to associate with him and to spy on his movements.
>
> At the homes of Lil and Ben Green, FBI squad cars are stationed constantly and conspicuously . . . .

"I don't know what the FBI intends to accomplish by these methods," Lil declared. "Neither I nor any member of my family has anything to say to them—and I'm sure even they realize it by now."

One day when Lil was alone in a summer cottage with "her brother-in-law's children and her own, two FBI agents suddenly entered and refused to leave when she ordered them to. 'We don't use guns much,' one of the agents told Mrs. Green, in front of the children, 'but sometimes a man we're hunting gets shot. Now you wouldn't want that to happen to your husband, would you?'"*

Several days after the first expose in the *Daily Worker*, a story about what was happening to the family also appeared in the Chicago *Daily News*, and was later reprinted in the Washington *Star*. The headline over the story in the *Star* read: Hunted Red's Family Carries On Alone In Silent, Hostile World. On the photocopy of this article in the FBI files, J. Edgar Hoover had penned in large bold script, "It is sickening how maudlin the press can get. I am surprised at the *Star*, for they write their own headlines."

As is verified by the above, I know that the FBI was far from indifferent to the public exposure of its methods. Shortly after these articles appeared, the FBI began a review of its surveillance policy. On September 27, 1951, the Chicago FBI office wired Hoover that "constant fisurs [physical surveillance] Ben and Lillian Green unproductive in developing pertinent leads for subject's apprehension. Green apparently aware fisurs since initiation and considered illogical physical contact between subject and family will be made while fisurs in progress." (Followed by twenty blacked-out lines, in my copy.)

On that same day a fuller memo was also sent to Hoover; it said, "The information available is that neither the subject's wife, nor his brother, Ben, are aware of subject's whereabouts." (Two blacked-out paragraphs followed.)

As a consequence, Hoover decided to replace the physical surveillance of Ben with "discreet spot surveillances," but insisted that "fisurs Lillian Green to continue."

Five months later, in February 1952, with public exposes still

*From an interview with Lil. See Albert E. Kahn, *The Game of Death, Effects of the Cold War on Our Children*, New York, Cameron and Kahn, p. 156.

embarrassing the FBI, and with an admitted eight full-time agents assigned to the surveillance of Lil, the Chicago FBI asked for a further policy review. In a confidential letter to Hoover, they evaluated the situation:

> As has been pointed out to the Bureau, Lillian Green is extremely surveillance conscious . . . [and] Informants have reported that the subject's relatives are limiting their contacts because of their awareness of Fisurs . . . *Therefore consideration should be given to the possibility that they will move more freely and be less guarded in their contacts if they believe coverage has been dropped. The purpose of the investigation to locate the subject would more logically be met by very discreet spot surveillances timed to Lillian Green's present routine and such other occasions as circumstances might dictate.* (Emphasis added.)

Hoover, however, disagreed. He replied (February 13, 1952), "It is not desired that the physical surveillance of Lillian Green be discontinued at this time." Despite the Chicago FBI's belief that direct physical surveillance was counterproductive and harmful if its purpose was to locate me, Hoover decided to continue it.

The psychological war against Lil was not limited to attempted interviews and close physical surveillance. On August 14, 1951, the Chicago FBI office informed Washington headquarters of the specific insurance carried on Lil's car. Shortly after, the family's insurance broker, an old friend, informed Lil that two FBI agents had visited his company's office, asking that her car's coverage be canceled. And it was.

With no other insurance company ready to issue a new policy for the car, Lil decided to sell it. A teletype to Washington (September 11, 1951), marked "urgent," informed the Bureau:

> Effort Ben Green continuing towards sale of Lillian Green's auto. All aspects of any transaction will be followed closely.

When Lil took a prospective buyer to look at the car, she found a large spoke imbedded in a tire. This could conceivably have been the deed of someone other than the FBI, but under the circumstances the family was convinced that it was only a part of what the FBI meant by "followed closely." This belief was reinforced when a would-be purchaser agreed to buy the car and left a deposit, only to call Lil shortly after to tell her he had been visited by the FBI, and to ask for his money back.

It seemed odd that the FBI not only did not want Lil to drive the car but also did not want her to sell it. It could be argued that if she did not drive, it would be easier to keep physical tab on her. But why would they want to stop the sale? If the FBI thought the car was going to be passed to me, the logical course would be to stay in the background and watch where the car went. Instead, what the FBI did made no sense at all, except, as the family charged, as part of a war of nerves.

But the family outwitted the FBI. Florence bought a used car from a friend, registered it in her name, then loaned it to Lil. FBI records report the transaction—Lil was seen putting 1951 license plates on an old 1941 Plymouth.

Stumbling blocks were also put in the way of Lil's efforts to earn a living. For a number of months after my disappearance, she worked for the Civil Rights Congress. This embattled organization could pay very little. Lil was eager, therefore, to find work where her salary would be sufficient to support the family. On November 5, 1951, a teletype informed Washington: "Lillian Green contemplates seeking a paying position in near future." Six lines of this message were blacked out.

Three months later (February 18, 1952), the Chicago Office expressed its concern to Washington over the fact that Lil and Ben "publicly and through the Daily Worker" exposed FBI efforts to block Lil's employment. "This may be an attempt on her [Lil's] part," the document said, "to obtain data for further publicity to the effect that this Bureau is preventing her from earning a livelihood by contacting her prospective employers . . . " Then came the words, "This may be a reference to the Bureau," but the rest of this sentence and five lines that follow are completely expunged.

The report asked Washington's advice on whether it should cease verifying "Lillian Green's application for employment at the various places she may contact." But whether Hoover responded to this request, and how, is not revealed in the pages turned over to me.

Doris Fine's efforts to find employment were blocked too. On one occasion Doris answered an ad for a wirer and solderer at a Chicago factory, a job for which she was qualified by experience. She was told when to report to work. But when she did, the personnel director who had hired her, impressed with her qualifications, now told her, "I'm sorry, the job's taken."

A lengthy memorandum covering FBI efforts to find me gives a dramatic account of a personal encounter between Lil and an FBI agent over the matter of employment. This states that on October 1, 1952, "T-17 of known reliability [known reliability is often an FBI euphemism for electronic surveillance] advised that Lillian Green was apparently employed on the seventh floor of the Rissman Building, 305 W. Adams Street, Chicago, Illinois."

Five days later, according to the memo, this fact was verified by an agent interviewing the "female elevator operator" of the building.

> After having made observations on the seventh and eighth floor at 305 W. Adams, Lillian Green was encountered shortly after she had entered the building to go to work. She recognized the writer and approached him with inquiries as to whether or not her present employer had been contacted and whether or not she was going to be fired from her job. Lillian Green stated that she had three children to feed and that while she could obtain employment at any time with the Civil Rights Congress she preferred to make her living through her own initiative.
>
> Green was advised that the FBI reserves the privilege of interviewing anyone deemed advisable in its efforts to locate her husband and it was pointed out to her that cooperation on her part would possibly assist in such efforts. Lillian Green then related that the FBI must be crazy if they think her husband would contact her at her place of employment, and further that she hoped she never saw him again. When questioned further concerning the latter statement, she explained that she hoped she never saw him again not because she did not wish to see him but because if she saw him the FBI would also probably see him and that she did not want her husband behind bars. Lillian Green was noted to be very nervous and distraught during this conversation.

The fact that she said anything at all to the agent indicated how wrought up she was at the prospect of once again losing a job.

5

Dry Cleaning and Cosmetic Change

When I first went underground, there were no guidelines to follow. Nor was it possible to compare notes with the other fugitives until some time later.

The families that I lived with first preferred that I maintain a low profile. Understandably, they feared that meeting other comrades would increase my risk of FBI apprehension. Would not the people with whom I planned to meet confide in others, until somehow the fact might reach hostile ears? Could we be certain that they themselves were free of FBI surveillance?

These concerns had to be given serious consideration, for more than my own safety was involved. If I were nabbed, and others' association with me became known, they could face prison terms for violating the Federal Harboring Act. At the very least, their lives would be disrupted, their jobs or professions imperiled.

It was important that those working with me remain undetected, for in some respects their risk was greater than mine. I was aware that even if I managed to elude the FBI net, the day would come when I would have to serve my prison sentence.

I recall one Sunday-afternoon chat with Wilfred and Blanche. We were seated on their back porch, at a wrought-iron, glass-topped garden table. The screen enclosing the porch shielded us from neighbors' eyes without blocking a splendid view of their back yard with its green lawn and bed of golden chrysanthemums.

Noting that another group of Party leaders had been arrested the previous week, Wilfred said, "I hope that what we're doing will at least save you from going to prison."

"Oh, no, Wilfred," I objected, "that's not how I see things. I do not expect the political climate to change that rapidly or completely. My hopes and expectations are more limited. I hope the Korean War ends without becoming enlarged, that the McCarthyite madness begins to recede, and that Gene Dennis and the others in prison are released. Then I can begin to do *my* time. As no one can say for certain how things will turn out, we have to continue with what we are doing. But when the political climate begins to change for the better, I shall surrender voluntarily. I have no illusions about dodging my prison sentence."

The only guarantee that McCarthyism would come to an end lay in the struggle against it, and I was determined to do what I could, hobbled as a fugitive though I was. Hence I resisted being put into cold storage. And I was reasonably confident that we could elude the FBI net.

The major reason for this confidence was the high caliber of the people working with me. Each had been carefully selected, based on proven reliability and record of leadership in state and local Party organizations. They bore the main responsibility for maintaining security in our setup, and they were superb. Even the slightest misjudgment of character could have proved our undoing. It is to their credit that when I finally turned myself in, nearly five years after my disappearance, the FBI, as I shall later show, knew nothing at all about where I had been.

Phil was the organizer of the setup when I first entered it. But he did not remain long at this post. He had bleeding stomach ulcers, which caused him unceasing pain and discomfort, and this assignment aggravated his condition, for tension was our constant companion. In addition, sleepless nights often made Phil late for appointments. Even when this tardiness was only by a few minutes, it violated our strict, self-imposed rules. Hence, for the benefit of Phil's health and the proper functioning of our small collective, a change was necessary.

Fortunately Sam, who had been working most closely with Phil, was able to replace him without a break in continuity. I had met Sam a number of times and learned to respect his judgment and integrity. In his middle thirties, and of medium height and build, he had brown hair, blue eyes and a bristling mustache. He and his wife, Shirley, had been Party leaders in a nearby state organization. Now he was working on a night job, which enabled him to meet people during the day or evening. But this was all too often at the expense of rest and time with his family. Nearly always short on sleep, he had acquired a remarkable ability to doze off even if only for a few minutes, when nothing was taking place. Nor did noise, no matter how high the decibel range, deter him. Yet, when he did have to be up and around, he would be completely awake and alert.

Sam was an excellent organizer. Although affable and easy to get along with, he was intolerant of carelessness and incompetence. He and I worked closely together and I always sought his views on the articles I wrote and on political issues under discussion.

Shirley had also held leadership posts in the Party, but was not actively involved in our underground work at first, although she knew that Sam was. Later, we drew her, too, into our active collective. She proved to be an extremely valuable addition. I got to know both of them well and became "Uncle Pete" to their two small boys.

I had certain natural advantages over some of the other fugitives in being able to function surreptitiously. I was not noticeably tall or short, fat or thin; not handsome, not ugly. I had no conspicuous disfigurements. I was an average-looking Joe, easily lost in a crowd. Gus Hall, on the other hand, with his large bold features, his six-feet-plus height, lumberjack's build and sailors' gait, could not so easily disappear. Even less so could Henry Winston, also over six feet, with a handsome, expressive face and dark-brown skin. Robert Thompson, too, was a six-footer, with unique features. Under the circumstances, my average appearance was of great help.

One day, however, when some of us were discussing our problems, my outward appearance came under critical scrutiny. Seated around a kitchen table, with our cups of coffee or mugs of beer in front of us, one comrade said to me, "Okay, it's true, you look like an ordinary guy, but there are still some things that make you more recognizable. Take your black curly hair; I think you should dye it."

For many years I had gone bareheaded, but I was now wearing either a cap or a hat whenever I went out. Under pressure, I became a redhead, but only for a while. I suspected that women might be more observant than men, and I feared that each time I sat down in a coffee shop or restaurant the waitress would notice that the roots of my hair were black. This might not identify me but it would call me to her attention, something I sought to avoid. Finally, my feeling of unease prevailed. I was given a reprieve and my hair returned to its natural color.

I did not grow a beard. At that time only old men—and not too many of them—wore beards. It would have singled me out.

"Your eyebrows stand out too much," was another complaint. I agreed to trim them with scissors regularly; tweezing would be too noticeable.

"Your cheeks have a sunken appearance and your nose is pinched," someone observed.

"What do you want me to do?" I jested, "Get a nose job or a face lift?"

"No," came the rejoinder, "that's too radical. I'll talk to Jerry about it, he may have some ideas."

Jerry did have ideas. He was a dentist and he came up with an ingenious invention, long before a similar one was used to transform the facial features of Marlon Brando in *The Godfather*. Jerry made a plastic removable denture that fitted over my lower back teeth and protruded a bit toward the cheeks. My facial hollows were now filled. For my narrow nostrils, he prescribed flesh-colored dental wax, molded by hand into small balls made to fit into each nasal cavity. The wax was pierced to allow breathing.

This worked admirably. I learned in the process that no two parts of the human anatomy are identical—one cavity was considerably larger than the other. But one fine summer afternoon, while swimming in Lake Michigan, I was mortified to see the two wax inserts defiantly bobbing up and down as they gently floated away.

A change was also ordered for my jutting ears. This defect, if it is one, would hardly be noticed with the long hair styles of today. But in the 1950s, when a close clipping around the ears was the mode, mine stood out noticeably. My resourceful friends had a formula for this, too. One of them had read in a motion picture magazine that movie stars with a similar problem simply used a special kind of mucilage. One drop would glue the ear back for a few hours. So now I had something in common with Clark Gable.

Recalling that I frequently recognized people by the way they walked, I began to insert a small, flat, smooth pebble in one shoe when I went out. It was enough to affect my gait.

These measures, together with the mustache and glasses I had acquired earlier, constituted the changes in my appearance. They were not enough to fool people who really knew me, but they were helpful in turning aside the more casual glance.

Often, even friends who knew me well did not recognize me; they simply never suspected that I could be in Chicago, walking its streets. They imagined me far away, perhaps in a socialist country, or in some spot off the beaten path.

We took this element into account, even tested it on some friends.

One of them I had known intimately for nearly two decades. He had come from Detroit to see me. He did not know where I was staying, so a member of our group met him and brought him to the house. On the way, my Detroit friend was told that something unforeseen had occurred; that in all likelihood a stranger who knew nothing about us would answer the doorbell. This was nothing to be perturbed about, he was assured, except that it was wise to just say hello and proceed to the rooms upstairs, where he would find me.

But when the doorbell rang, I answered it. My friend took a hasty glance at me, mumbled a few words of greeting, and then started to climb the steps. About halfway up I clasped him from behind. Startled, he turned around, gave me a searching look, and then, with a shout, returned the hug.

Sometime later, when I went to live with a new family in the rear of their small appliance repair shop, a similar experience occurred. Joe and Lois knew someone was coming to stay with them but not who it would be or exactly when the visit would take place. I had known them both as Party activists in Chicago. To see whether I would be recognized, I first made sure that no customers were in the store and then entered casually. As the chime rang, Lois came from behind the rear partition and asked, "Can I help you?"

"I have an old turntable that isn't working," I replied, "Do you do such repairs?"

"Yes, we do," she said, adding, "Did you bring it with you?"

"No," I said, "because I wanted to get some ideas of what it would cost."

"I can't tell you that without knowing what's wrong," she replied with unanswerable logic. "What if I have to replace a part? Bring it in and we'll give you an estimate."

"But if I do, I'll be stuck. You'll charge me whatever you like."

I saw the color mount in her face as she burst out, "I don't know what's wrong with you, mister, but if you want that turntable fixed you'll have to bring it in. I don't have time to waste."

As she turned to leave, I said, "Wait a moment, Lois, there's nothing wrong with me; it's with you. You don't remember an old friend."

Shaken at the mention of her name, she took one good look and then gasped, "Oh, my God, who would have expected *you,* and coming in like that."

In building our small collective, we neither overrated nor underrated the FBI's ability to apprehend me. We knew that their much-touted reputation for "getting their man" was highly exaggerated. Where they had a stoolpigeon they succeeded; otherwise they stumbled and fumbled, hoping that the wide spread of their net would catch something. Yet, with tens of millions of taxpayers' dollars to play with, and with thousands of agents on their payrolls (not to mention their countless paid and unpaid informers) we had to be on our guard. Consequently, we set up a number of strict rules aimed at foiling possible FBI penetration, and at precluding accidents or slip-ups that might result in our discovery.

To begin with, I stayed away from those sections of Chicago where the possibility of being recognized was greatest. This meant the Northwest Side, where my family lived, and areas where we had a relatively large Party membership or where Party and left-wing influence was considerable. As the former state chairman, I knew something of the Party's strength and the relative geographic distribution of its membership. It was not difficult, therefore, to select neighborhoods in which I would be least known.

To have some form of I.D. in case of accidental encounter, and a driver's license, I became Pete Golden. Pete is what I was called by the people with whom I worked, and I was "Uncle Pete" to their children. When I went out, I carried no other identity than that of Pete Golden, never anything that could be traced back to the families with whom I lived or the comrades with whom I maintained contact.

Twice the car in which I was riding was stopped by police. The first time was in Chicago. Sam was at the wheel, with me next to him, when we heard a siren and saw the blinking flashing lights of a police car just behind us. We pulled up and watched the police car stop. It was immediately apparent—since they did not stop alongside us with revolvers drawn, and only one officer began casually walking toward us—that this was about some traffic violation. We were told that our "left eye" was "blind," and were warned to stop at the very next filling station or garage to get the beam light replaced.

On another occasion I was driving alone on a highway in Wisconsin. It was dusk. Suddenly, I saw two highway patrol cars and a roadblock up ahead at the intersection. My first reaction was to turn around, but then I decided this would be foolhardy. As I approached closer, I saw the car ahead of me stopped and then permitted to continue; the road block had nothing to do with a search for political fugitives. I was politely asked to show my driver's license, then informed that on the road ahead, moving in the same direction, was a large road-paving machine that took up more than half the road.

Another precaution we took was that meetings I participated in were never held where I was living at the time. Moreover, I decided whom I would see and when. No one aside from those who had to have close contact with me knew where I was living at any given time, or how to reach me, except through established channels.

When I met someone, that person was first "dry cleaned;" that is, cleansed of any possible FBI contamination. He or she would be picked up by one of our skillful drivers, particularly adroit at detecting any signs of being tailed. Then, at some spot where a vehicle following them would have had to expose itself, there would be a switch to a second car. Sometimes there would be a sudden exit from the Outer Drive or some other Chicago speedway, and then an abrupt reentry going in the opposite direction.*

The last stage of the "dry cleaning" usually took place after dark and in such a circuitous fashion as to make it extremely difficult for the passenger to know exactly where he or she had been taken.

The "dry cleaning" squad consisted of ten persons, four of whom were not CP members. Those who were in the Party continued their customary Party club activities, confiding in no one about their political moonlighting. The non-members were, of course, sympathetic to the Party, and their main motivation was to do what they could to actively combat the growing political repression. None of them—whether in the Party or not—was told who was at the other end of their delivery service, nor did they inquire. If they suspected it was one of the fugitives, they kept it to themselves.

This was a remarkable group of highly dedicated people. Not only did they respond, no matter what time of day or night, but they even contributed financially to the endeavor.

Books, pamphlets, magazines and newspapers, particularly radical ones, would be picked up in small quantities, permitted to accumulate,

*Some of these methods were not unknown to the FBI. J. Edgar Hoover even issued instructions on how such cars could be detected—they would either be driving at high or low speeds, cross intersections at the last minute when the light was yellow, have people leave a car and walk in the opposite direction of a one-way street, make U turns on dark side streets, and so forth. What Hoover forgot was that millions of drivers do these very things—and every day.

and then brought to me by Sam. A friendly trade union leader collected labor periodicals, which were handled in a similar way.

Our readiness to put trust in non-Party people may come as a surprise to some. But it should be borne in mind that every crisis brings forth the best and the worst in people. In that frightful period of what is now known as McCarthyism, many shamelessly sold their souls to win absolution from the inquisitors. Others, however, found in themselves a courage they had never suspected. On two separate occasions , people at whose homes I stayed said to me with pride, "I never thought I had it in me."

One who cooperated with us was an extremely colorful personality, neither a Party member nor even, strictly speaking, a Party sympathizer. Lolly was middle-aged and upper middle class in background. She lived in an extremely well-to-do Chicago suburb and was well known in her community, involved in its politics, and a member of its school and library boards. We used her home to meet Party leaders from other parts of the country.

What motivated her was her implacable opposition to the witch hunt. She reacted to it with deep moral outrage. How could this be happening to *her* country! We saw the abnormality of what was happening as something inherent in societies torn by class conflict, but she did not. When she was asked to help, she was warned of the risks. She did not hesitate for an instant and gave no sign of fear. She acted as though her native roots, going back many generations, her white skin, ample means and "right connections" were enough to earn her immunity. I'm glad she never had to test that assumption.

6

Women, Children First

My mother was a special target of the FBI's psychological warfare. Taking advantage of her age and the fact that she still worked for a living—and aware of her love for her sons, and her anxiety about me—the FBI set out to frighten and intimidate her into "cooperation."

When they interviewed her, FBI agents stressed that it would be in my best interests if she cooperated. After all, they said, it was only a matter of time before I would be caught, but under what conditions that would take place they could not foretell. I *could* be shot down, they finally hinted, as they had to Lil.

Ma took this as a warning of what the FBI would do if she did not cooperate. Actually she knew nothing of my whereabouts, but the fear of my death preyed on her and became something of an obsession. An FBI teletype of a reinterview with her on September 8, 1951, gives some indication of this:

> Mrs. Williams [my mother's name after she remarried] was emotionally upset and expressed fears of subject being physically harmed if apprehended and was afraid he may have already been killed.

What that report failed to state, however, was how this agonizing thought had become planted in her mind.

In the months that followed, a number of FBI reports note Ma's emotional state and her fear that I would be killed or was already dead. An interview with my aunt Ida quotes her as having said, "Mrs. Williams is very upset emotionally over the disappearance of her son, is afraid he might be dead."

To add to this torment, my mother feared that the FBI would get her fired from her job. To deepen this anxiety, FBI agents began to interview her where she worked, a women's dress manufacturing firm. A teletype to Washington reports:

> Mrs. Williams interviewed at place of employment. . . . She denied knowledge of subject's whereabouts . . . stated that neither Ben Green nor Lillian Green know where subject is. . . . Mrs. Williams was not hostile, but uncooperative. Feared interview would jeopardize position.

The FBI kept an extremely close watch on my three children, especially Danny. Teachers, club and camp counselors, even other children, were enlisted in this effort.

On December 4, 1951, Lil was observed driving Danny to the Deborah Boys Club at Kimball and Ainslie Avenues in Chicago. A month later a counselor had been coopted. He promised to "carefully watch the activities of Daniel Green and determine who his closest associates were within the club [name deleted] stated that his inquiries would be made personally and discreetly through the staff at the club in order that the interests of the FBI would not be revealed."

On January 28, 1952, it was reported that Danny belonged to a group in the club known as the Naturals. "[name deleted] furnished a list of the members of the Naturals and related that among this group were [names deleted] close friends of Daniel Green."

On February 4, 1952, agents visited the home of one of these boys and obtained permission from the mother "to interview her son. [name deleted] was advised of the relationship between the subject and Daniel Green and was alerted for any information that might come to his attention concerning the subject's whereabouts."

The following day another mother was visited. She declined permission for the FBI to talk to her son, but said she would "discreetly" interview him "and furnish the information to the FBI."

On that same day a third home was visited and the parents granted permission for their son to be interviewed. "[name deleted] stated that he knew Daniel Green well and would remain alert when talking to him for any information concerning the subject's whereabouts."

Thus children were enlisted to spy on children. When Josie and her cousin Billie spent two weeks at the Abraham Lincoln Centre Camp at Milton Junction, Wisconsin, they, too, were spied on. It was reported that Josie had received no visitors and that she had told others that "her mother works in an office in Chicago and her father was working in an office in New York."

The main attention, however, was directed toward Danny. He was the oldest, and as such held a place of special responsibility in the family. FBI agents and informants reported everything about him, including his personal habits, even that on a trip to New York he was keeping "very late hours."

In May 1953, they reported that Danny, age 15, was the winner of the first prize for outstanding work in the field of biophysics. He had entered a Chicago citywide science fair and prepared an exhibit on "The Effect of Ultrasonics on Bacteria." On July 26, 1955, "that Daniel Green is now working at Price's Market Grill." On August 15, 1955, "Daniel Green was observed [name deleted] working at the above restaurant. It was also reported that he made $40 a week and tips."

The great importance attached to Danny by the FBI, especially as he grew older, is to be seen in the careful selection and training of an informant for one specific purpose, to pry out of Danny whatever information he might have. J. Edgar Hoover sent the instructions (September 16, 1955), when I was already missing for more than four years. He wrote [The first paragraph is blacked out]:

> In view of the above the Chicago office is instructed to give thoughtful consideration to giving the informant a specific assignment to obtain any and all possible information from Danny Green which might be of assistance in locating Gilbert Green. You are fully aware of the Bureau's desire to locate and apprehend this fugitive at the earliest possible date. The informant should be briefed on Green's background and should be impressed with the Bureau's keen desire to apprehend Green. [Then a paragraph of six lines is blacked out.]

The letter concluded by stressing that this matter should receive "preferred attention in the Chicago Office."

Who this special informant was, what special instructions he received, what information he turned over to the FBI, is not revealed in the files I obtained. The special concentration on Danny fared no better than those on Lil, Ben and my mother. None of them knew my whereabouts and thus could not confide anything, even to their closest friends.

7

Guilt by Kinship

Every member of my family, no matter how distant the relationship, was interviewed by FBI agents at least once. They were warned of the penalties for violation of the Federal Harboring Act and asked to cooperate in case they learned anything of my whereabouts. Their neighbors were also visited, shown photographs of me, and asked to report if I should show up or anything "suspicious" occurred. Each interview was then written up to become part of the FBI's forest of files.

Most of those interviewed, according to the FBI reports, promised to cooperate. Some apparently thought this the only way to get the agency off their backs. The chances of my crossing their path were extremely remote, so they felt they would never be called upon to deliver on the extorted promises. FBI agents understood this. Nevertheless, they thought it extremely important to get an affirmative commitment from each person interviewed. Clearly it was a psychological lever with which to pry loose further commitments.

My brother Harry, a year younger than I, and his wife, Sonia, who lived in Los Angeles, were the objects of special FBI concern. "Spot checks and periodic surveillances" of them were ordered, neighbors were asked to keep watch on them, and they were interviewed a number of times. At first Harry tried to reason with the sleuths, even to argue the pros and cons of the manhunt, but the agents were interested in but one thing: Would they, or would they not, cooperate? After dodging a direct answer several times, Harry and Sonia finally realized that it was best to give it to them straight. Harry said that they would not cooperate, while Sonia is quoted as telling them, "You can't make stoolpigeons of us."

Lil's brother, Ben Gannes, far removed from us politically, and with a life-style and interests quite different, also became a special object of FBI snooping. Not knowing exactly where he lived, the FBI sent out word to his friends asking that he contact them. When he did, Ben frankly told the agents that he never "believed in the ideas of Gil Green," and that he very rarely saw either me or his sister. But, he complained to the FBI agents, this did not stop the FBI from having victimized him. He had "not been permitted to work on a Navy project at Great Lakes, Illinois, during World War II *due to his relationship to Gilbert Green.*" (Emphasis added.)

Lil and I had never been told of this discrimination. We had no inkling whatever that someone as completely removed from us politically as he would be persecuted for nothing more than being related to me by marriage. It was guilt-by-kinship.

Stanley, as I shall call him, is the youngest of my many first cousins, about 15 years my junior. He grew up in Chicago in the years prior to World War II, when I lived in New York. When war came, Stanley enlisted in the U.S. Air Force, serving at bases in England and Italy. He flew 52 combat missions as a flight navigator and earned a lieutenant's stripes. When he returned home, he re-enlisted, having decided to make the Air Force his career.

After I returned to Chicago in 1945, I may have met him once or twice at some family gathering, but about this I have no firm recollection. I have no mental picture of what he looks like. Stanley soon moved to California, where he was assigned for duty. After that

I am sure that I did not see him at all. But he was a blood relative of mine, and this in itself was enough to put him under suspicion.

On November 14, 1951, a teletype to Washington informed FBI headquarters that inquiry had been made about Stanley at the Air Force squadron assigned to the Long Beach Municipal Airport. No derogatory information was found.

When interviewed at his home in Long Beach, Stanley told the agents that he believed "Communism is a national threat to the security of the United States," and that he had volunteered for the Air Corps and planned to make it his career. He added that he would "cooperate in every way to bring about subject's apprehension, but stated he has absolutely no knowledge of Green's whereabouts or where he might hide."

The investigation continued, with Air Force Intelligence also brought into the picture. On July 13, 1953, the Los Angeles Office of the FBI "advised that there would be a security hearing on the question of the revocation of First Lieutenant's [name deleted] commission in the United States Air Force *because he is a first cousin to and was in touch with the subject in 1947.*" (Emphasis added.)

The climax came a few months later. The weekly summary teletyped to Washington on November 13, 1953, advised that Stanley had been "released from active duty with the USAF *for the convenience of the government.*" (Emphasis added.)

His commission was not taken away. His record both in war and peace was too unblemished for this. Instead, he was summarily kicked out. Again, guilt-by-kinship.

A final FBI report on this squalid episode told how Stanley, his hopes of an Air Force career now shattered, was trying to sell his Long Beach home and find other ways to make a living.

8
Kidnapped in Mexico

Not until late in October, 1951, were steps taken to link up the fugitives. Up to then each of us had been very much on his own, working with a small circle of comrades in his particular setup. For a number of them, I later learned, the circle was very small indeed, and being cooped up or underground was more than a figure of speech. Under the circumstances, however, it was wisest to feel our way forward slowly, and for this decentralization was imperative. It enabled us to gain experience and to ensure, to the extent that it was possible, that if FBI penetration occurred in one setup it would not spread to the others.

We fugitives held no face-to-face meetings. Nor was there any direct contact with comrades in the Party's national headquarters. During those first months, the people I met with were members of our own setup and, from time to time, one or another Party activist in the Chicago area. From them I learned how things were going and also received news about my family.

Those first months were a period of accelerated political repression. As we had foreseen, the Supreme Court's upholding of the Eugene Dennis case convictions (June 1951), had led to a new wave of anti-Communist indictments and FBI raids. Of the second group of twenty-one Party leaders indicted in New York on June 20, 1951, only seventeen had been apprehended, and the FBI struck again a month later, at the other end of the continent. Twelve prominent California Communists were picked up, and shortly after, three more. William Schneiderman, the California State Chairman of the Party, was seized in New York City. (He had been chosen to be the temporary General Secretary of the Party during the prison absence of Gene Dennis.)

In early August, twelve more Communist leaders were arrested in Pittsburgh, Baltimore and Cleveland. And toward the end of August, seven were seized in Hawaii. Among them was Jack Hall, the Hawaii leader of the International Longshoremen's and Warehousemen's Union.

Obtaining reasonable bail for Communists, never easy, was now made more difficult. For some, bail was set as high as $75,000 and $100,000. This was justified on the ground that four convicted Reds had jumped bail and that the Supreme Court's decision in the Dennis case had laid to rest whatever constitutional issues were involved.

Seizing upon this as pretext, the Government set out to cripple the entire bail-raising effort, ordering the trustees of the Civil Rights Congress Bail Fund to disclose the names of all contributors. When they refused, on the ground that this would turn over the names of thousands of additional people for persecution, they were cited for contempt. As a result, Dashiell Hammett, W. Alpheus Hunton, Frederick V. Field and Abner Green were sent to prison.

Those newly indicted were compelled to spend weeks in jail—some even months—before bail was reduced to more reasonable amounts. And now contributors to the bail fund were required to appear in person, give proof of ownership of cash or securities, and specify for whom the bail was intended.

The arrests were only one aspect of the mounting repression. An increasing number were being fired from jobs and blacklisted. Foreign-born militants were rounded up and held for denaturalization and deportation, many without trial or judicial review. The House Committee on Un-American Activities was riding higher than ever, bullying, "Are you now or have you ever been . . .?" and demanding the names of still others to be hauled up before the Committee.

Passage of the McCarran Internal Security Act in 1950 had opened up a second heresy hunt. A Subversive Activities Control Board (SACB) was established and held star-chamber proceedings to determine whether organizations that were deemed "Communist-action" groups by the Attorney General, or their members, should be compelled to register as foreign agents of a criminal international conspiracy or face long prison terms and heavy fines.

Not to be outdone in anti-Communist zeal, state governments were busy setting up their own "little" Un-American Committees. Criminal syndicalist laws that had gathered dust since the notorious Palmer Raids of 1920 were reactivated.*

*In a sedition trial in Pennsylvania, Steve Nelson, James Dolsen and Andy Onda received 20-year sentences.

Riding the crest of the repressive wave was the press. Cashing in on, and intensifying the hysteria, *Collier's* (a magazine now defunct), dedicated its October 27, 1951, issue to a "Preview of the War We Do Not Want." Its 137 pages described "Russia's Defeat and Occupation—1952-1960." A full-page painting illustrated the effects of the atom bomb dropped on Moscow. The caption below read:

> Seconds later, the Kremlin (within enclosure in background) was swept into oblivion, Red Square (surrounding avenue) was heaped with rubble, St. Basil's Church (bulbous towers on the right) was gone.

Eighteen prominent Americans described this one-sided atomic war and its consequences. They related how the U.S. occupation forces brought the American way of life, girlie shows and all, to the sex-starved, culturally deprived Soviet people.

In this increasingly hostile climate, the Communist Party's operational leadership functioned under very trying conditions. Many of the Party's national leaders had been arrested in the second wave of Smith Act prosecutions, among them Elizabeth Gurley Flynn. Some were still in jail awaiting the outcome of the bail fight. With each new series of arrests, difficulties mounted. It became ever more necessary, though much harder, to raise large sums for bail, court costs, lawyers' fees, and to reach the public with the issues involved.

Those in open leadership positions faced constant harassment from the press, received crank phone calls and threats of violence, and had the FBI agents stalking their every step. Paradoxically, those of us who were fugitives had certain advantages. Since the FBI did not know our whereabouts, we could not be followed. Nor were we subjected to the same kinds of financial crises and administrative headaches. Consequently, even though handicapped by being in the underground, we could pay attention to some aspects of the Party's work that the open leadership could not.

As confidence grew in the ability of our separate underground setups to survive, so also grew the need for some form of coordination. How were the others doing? Which of them needed assistance? What was our collective estimate of events and how did we see the path to ending the nightmare of Red Scare and McCarthyism? And lastly, how could we establish regular contact with the national Party leadership not in prison, without endangering our own decentralized, underground functioning? These questions could only be answered in a face-to-face meeting of fugitives.

A tenuous link did exist by which we could reach comrades in New York concerned with leadership-security problems. On two occasions Phil had gone east to discuss these issues. On his return from his second trip, in September 1951, he had brought me a sealed envelope containing a typewritten message—something like—"Suggest you make arrangements to move to Mexico City as rapidly as possible." It also informed me how I could make contact there.

This proposal took me by surprise; my reaction was one of consternation. As the note was unsigned, I did not know who sent it. But since the message was delivered by Phil, I took for granted that it was authentic. I assumed it came from either Gus Hall or Henry Winston, or had their approval. Without delay I sent off a reply, which a comrade took next morning to New York, stating that I was in total disagreement with the proposal and citing my reasons. I said I did not believe that the repression in the country had reached a stage warranting refuge in a foreign country. I believed such a move was unnecessary and inadvisable. I was certain that I, at least, could function more effectively with less risk in the United States rather than in Mexico or elsewhere. As for going to a socialist country, I felt that would cut me off completely from the ongoing struggle here. I asked that the proposal be reconsidered and wrote that I was awaiting a prompt reply.

None came. A month later, in October, I was shocked to hear on the midday radio news that Gus Hall had been arrested at a motel in Mexico City and was being brought back across the U.S. border. (My recollection is that I had no advance knowledge that Gus was contemplating this trip, but in discussing this episode more recently with Phil, his recollection is that I did know and that he had informed me of it.)

Since then I have had occasion to ask Gus Hall why he went to Mexico. He said that he, too, had objected to leaving the United States. "Why then did you go?" I asked.

"The pressure was too great," he replied. "The comrades in the national office were insistent. They thought my staying here was unsafe. So finally I went along with the idea."

Another comrade who was involved in helping to organize Gus Hall's trip, says that the possibility of our going to Mexico, and even to a socialist country, had been discussed among members of the national leadership even prior to our becoming fugitives.

Gus had entered Mexico by swimming the Rio Grande and then

had made his way to Mexico City. The raid on the motel came in the early morning hours. He was awakened to find the place swarming with heavily armed uniformed police and plainclothesmen. By their appearance and accent, Gus quickly recognized some of them as coming from the States. Powerful floodlights bathed the outside area. Handcuffed and shackled in leg irons, Hall was thrown in the rear of a car, which immediately began the 800-mile drive to the U.S. border. Two cars preceded and two followed the entire way.

"From the manner in which orders were given it was clear to me," Gus later related, "that FBI men controlled the entire operation. But when they approached the border checkpoint they faded out of the picture to make it appear as a purely Mexican immigration action."

On the U.S. side of the border, a DC-10 was standing by. Hall, guarded by about fifteen FBI agents, was flown to Texarkana, Texas, the site of a federal prison. From there he was taken by auto to the Federal Penitentiary at Leavenworth, Kansas. Soon after, he was flown to New York to stand trial for bail-jumping.

Hall's kidnapping evoked a storm of protest in Mexico. Within a few days a demonstration of ten thousand people took place in front of government buildings in Mexico City. The kidnapping was seen as an imposition of U.S. power upon a country with a proud record of political asylum. One year earlier, Morton Sobell, later sentenced in the Rosenberg trial to a thirty-year prison term, had been seized in the same way. In both cases the purpose was to bypass Mexican courts and prevent the granting of asylum.

How Gus Hall was apprehended we do not know. Evidence points to misplaced confidence in a person who had helped in the border crossing.

With Hall's arrest, it became even more urgent that the fugitives arrive at a common understanding among themselves and with those in the Party's national center, particularly with its national chairman, William Z. Foster.

Before making definite plans for such a meeting, we first had to eliminate the possibility that Gus's arrest had left clues leading to us. I was reasonably certain it had not. Each setup was completely sealed off from the others, and it didn't seem likely to me that the FBI would have waited to put their hands on Hall in Mexico had they been able to do so earlier in the States.

When finally Henry Winston and Bob Thompson were contacted,

they too agreed that the time had come for a meeting. There was also agreement to limit this first meeting to the three of us, excluding for the time being—solely for reasons of security—the other four fugitives.

Aware that Winston, because he was Black, would have more difficulty traveling than we, it was agreed that we would meet in Brooklyn, New York, where he was living.

How was I to get to New York by the first week in December, 1951? Up to that point I had stayed close to Chicago and its environs. Phil, Sam and I went into a huddle. We immediately ruled out as too risky the use of any form of public transportation. Who was trustworthy who also owned a car good enough to travel in snow and ice?

The choice fell on a couple I did not know. Several days later Phil and I came to dinner at a modest flat on Chicago's North Side. If Jack and Vera were astonished to see me, they gave no indication. Their nervousness showed in other ways. Vera talked compulsively all evening. I wondered what it would be like traveling to New York and back with her. However, both were intelligent, knowledgeable people, staunch in their convictions and completely trustworthy. I was sure that Vera's nervousness, as well as her volubility, would taper off.

Phil accompanied us on the trip. He and Jack sat up front, Vera and I in the back. We wore hunting caps and short winter coats, the proper attire for the rural North at that time of year. Had we been stopped and the car searched, we would have appeared strange hunters indeed, with not a gun among us!

While the car was sturdy and dependable, it had seen better days. Once on the road, its speedometer conked out. Since we did not want to stop for repairs, we worried about keeping under the speed limit and yet getting to New York on time. This turned out to be no problem at all. Vera's musical ear was so finely tuned that she could judge the speed of the car by the pitch of the wheels. She would call out from the back seat, "Step on the gas, Jack, you're doing only about fifty-five," or, "Hold it, baby, you're hitting over seventy."

To me this was a remarkable feat. With my poor hearing, a legacy of mumps, measles, chicken pox or scarlet fever (or the combination—all at age six) it was hard to believe that anyone could have so sensitive an ear.

Vera and Jack had come to the Communist movement in the mid-Thirties. They had been stirred by the Spanish Civil War and the great labor upsurge of that period. "Everything was alive then," Jack said. Vera recalled that even during the heyday of anti-fascist unity her World War II activities in behalf of Russian War Relief had led to an investigation of her brother.

In time I got to know them well and their home became a place where I could meet others.

9

Fugitives Get Organized

Despite the difficulties with the car's speedometer, we managed to get to New York City with time to spare. After we had cruised the area, I was dropped off at a previously designated street corner in the Bath Beach section of Brooklyn. There I was picked up by a member of Bob's group and taken to the apartment where the meeting was to be held. It was dusk. The circuitous route the driver had taken made it impossible for me to judge exactly where I was. The home was that of an ex-seaman, now the building's super. Bob and Winnie were already there.

After warm greetings and inquiries about health, we exchanged news of our families. It wasn't good news. The pattern was the same: a conscious FBI policy to make their lives unbearable.

Then, after a bite to eat, we talked about Gus and his arrest. I informed them of the note I had received proposing that I make arrangements to move to Mexico, and what my response had been. We agreed that it was a mistake to seek refuge outside the U.S. and decided to send word to that effect to Bill Foster and to others in the Party's national office.

Our more substantive discussions began the next morning. These included a review of events in the five months since we went underground, new developments in the labor movement, and more important, how we, even though handicapped as fugitives and forced to continue functioning in our decentralized fashion, could be of assistance to the Party's leadership.

In reviewing the general situation, we noted that negotiations to end the Korean War were at an impasse, with pressures from the extreme right and the military opposing a settlement. It seemed to us that with the growing unpopularity of the war, the Truman Administration would like it out of the way before the 1952 elections. But the Administration was paralyzed from acting to end the conflict for fear of being held responsible for "losing" the war. This explained their ambivalence, their veering between the poles of negotiated settlement and further escalation. We agreed that McCarthyism was still riding the crest, with most liberal and labor leaders groveling before it. Yet here and there new voices of opposition were being heard. We saw the new wave of Smith Act indictments as serving a dual purpose: further appeasing McCarthy and simultaneously trying to decapitate the Communist Party by chopping off layer after layer of leadership.

We concluded that the key to future developments depended on bringing an end to the Korean War and the building of a broad-based movement against McCarthyism. We were also in accord that special measures be taken to thwart the FBI's ability to pick off Party leaders at will.

Our discussion of the labor movement centered mainly on the damaging effects of the cold war. The unity around immediate goals that had characterized the CIO in the years of its greatest advances was now shattered. Instead, paralleling the Government's actions, a wholesale purge of "Reds" in labor leadership was under way. Many unions had adopted constitutional provisions barring Communists from office and, in a number of instances, even from union membership.* At the same time conservative-led unions were engaged in a wholesale raiding of progressive-led unions, often in collusion with the Government and employers.

In my remarks, I gave examples of what was happening in the Chicago area, an important outpost of unions under progressive and left influence. At the very time that farm-equipment and metal-fabricating plants were closed by workers engaged in long drawn-out and bitterly-fought strikes, their unions were being raided, to the delight of and with the connivance of the companies.

Two interrelated problems confronted militant unionists: first,

*Before the witch hunt was over, 59 percent of unions barred Communists from office and 40 percent from membership.

how to keep the progressive-led unions from being dismembered and destroyed; and second, how to build the unity of workers around their urgent needs in the *entire* labor movement, despite the cold-war, splitting policies of many in labor leadership.

During the months prior to our meeting I had spent time studying the situation in a number of important unions and was impressed with both the gravity and complexity of the problems faced. I became particularly interested in developments in Detroit's River Rouge Ford Local 600 of the United Auto Workers, the largest plant local in the world, with 65,000 members. In a recent local union election, a "unity coalition" slate of progressive and left-wing workers, with Black workers playing a prominent role, had swept into office. What was particularly significant about this election was that Walter Reuther and the rest of the UAW top command had actively opposed the Local 600 unity slate. The lessons of this victory were therefore important for the struggle in other unions as well.

I had begun work on a series of articles discussing problems in the labor movement, and proposed to Winnie and Bob that I make direct contact with comrades in Detroit intimate with the situation in Local 600, in order to get a first-hand view of that development.

Winston and Thompson agreed I should continue to work on the articles I had begun, and also delve more fully into the lessons of Local 600. This however, raised the question crucial to all we had been discussing: What good were our deliberations if we had no effective way to reach the Party's Center with our views or to arrive at a common outlook? In fact, what purposes would my articles serve if there was no assurance they would appear in print?

As this touched on the central reason for this first meeting of fugitives, our discussion rapidly moved to these related questions. We agreed that a summary of our thinking and proposals would be written up after the meeting was over and submitted to those in the Party's Center as well as to the other four fugitives. I was asked to write the summary.

In discussing our place in the structure of Party leadership, we proposed that the seven fugitives be considered a separate, yet integral, grouping within a united national leadership; that we should meet regularly, convey our opinions to the Party's Center and, in turn, receive suggestions on how we could be of greater aid. To facilitate such an ongoing relationship, we proposed that a leading comrade be chosen from those who were in the "unavailable" category, who could meet with us regularly and be our link with the Party's center. We further proposed that another person be selected to act as a go-between for the fugitives, to help coordinate their work and to provide organizational assistance to any fugitive setups that needed help.

This last suggestion was particularly urgent. Henry Winston and Jim Jackson, the two Black fugitives, faced incomparably greater obstacles than the rest of us. If they lived in Black ghetto communities, which were subject to far more rigorous police surveillance, accidental discovery was obviously a greater possibility. Housing conditions in Black communities were also more crowded, with fewer families enjoying the luxury of a spare room. Yet if Winston or Jackson were to live with white families, they would be trapped indoors.

These difficulties, we agreed, had to be overcome. We would not permit underground considerations to stand in the way of the very closest relationship between us. Black-white participation as equals had to be ensured.

To weld such close ties among us, we agreed that the three National Board members should live, if at all possible, in a contiguous area. For this we chose the Chicago region. We urged the immediate assignment of a Chicagoan familiar with the Party's membership in the area to help get Winston located there as rapidly as possible. We also urged special organizational assistance to help strengthen Jackson's setup.

The meeting with Winston and Thompson marked a turning point in our underground activities. Our proposals were approved by the other fugitives and accepted by Bill Foster and the Party's Center, including an understanding that we could submit articles to *Political Affairs,* using pseudonyms.

I completed my first article a few weeks later. Before sending it off I asked Sam to reread the manuscript for any final suggestions and to affix a pen name to it. He chose John Swift. It was under that name that articles appeared for the next four years.

The other fugitives also wrote under pseudonyms. Henry Winston became Frederick C. Hastings; Bob Thompson—Alex E. Kendrick; Jim Jackson—Charles P. Mann; Fred Fine—Mark Logan, and Bill Norman Marron—Frank Brewster.

My first John Swift article, "The Parasitism of the U.S. War Economy," appeared in March 1952. Its aim was to disprove the strongly held view at the time that ever-increased military spending was a necessary evil, even a blessing in disguise. Such outlays were portrayed as an antidote to economic depression and a guarantor of good times. President Truman said it was the way to "defend the free world" and "to achieve a material well-being never before known." In my article I contended that increased war expenditures would lead to the opposite results: growing inflation, lower living standards, a gradual impoverishment of the country and, in time, a major economic crash or some unimaginable war.

I believe this general analysis has held up. Yet, in one specific and important respect, it erred. It tended to see another Great Depression as close at hand. It was a reading of the Fifties from the scrolls of the Thirties. Events have once again shown, however, that no two decades are exactly alike. Thus it has taken thirty years and another terrible war (in Southeast Asia) for the baneful effects of the war economy to make themselves more fully felt. But unfortunately, even as this is being written, the insatiable appetites of the Pentagon and the huge corporations that profit so greatly from military orders, grow with ever new momentum.

In a plane hurtling through space, one looks down at the green fields furrowed into checkerboard squares and they seem to recede in slow motion, at a snail's pace. So it often is with social change. We are hurtling through the greatest revolutionary age in all history, yet things often appear to be standing still or barely moving at all.

Several weeks after the Brooklyn meeting, I met Chris. She had been chosen to coordinate our fugitive activities. I had heard of her, but had not known her before. She had been borrowed from the West Coast organization shortly after the outbreak of the Korean War and had become a part of the Party's national reserve team in case of a complete clampdown on the Party.

We spent a few hours talking things over. I gave her my views of the problems we faced. She, in turn, filled me in on conversations she had already held with some of the others.

Chris was tall, attractive, in her early forties but looking younger. She was energetic, yet soft-spoken, with a quiet manner and a warm smile. When I later asked her how she had come to the movement, she replied, "I was virtually born into the socialist tradition." Her forebears were from Germany, a great grandfather having fought on the barricades in Saxony during the 1848 Revolution. Her maternal grandfather had emigrated to Hawaii as a contract laborer. Only after working for ten years to pay off his passage did he move to California, in the early 1880s. Chris grew up in a socialist home, reading the famous weekly *Appeal to Reason,* the socialist paper from Girard, Kansas, to which Eugene V. Debs was a regular contributor. Her father had been a member of the Socialist Party, in the same branch with Jack London, in Oakland, California. She remembered how her father kept her spellbound with adventure stories he had heard London read to his Socialist local for "audience response."

Chris was a well-balanced, down-to-earth sort of person. She was not given to rhetoric or flights of fancy. Shuttling regularly from one fugitive setup to another, aware at all times of the dangers involved to herself and others, she was ever on the alert. Yet no one could have guessed the burden of her responsibilities, either from her appearance or her demeanor. If she had to say no to some request, she did, but in such a way that no one could take offense.

Chris would bring not only tidings, good and bad, but also more palpable things: a jar of homemade chili from Claude Lightfoot, my good friend in the leadership of the Illinois Party. Or a sweet potato pie, as only Henry Winston knew how to bake. And once I received a beautiful turtleneck sweater handknitted by Geraldine Lightfoot, Claude's wife, and a favorite in our family.

Such small tokens of affection meant a great deal in our austere existence, and Chris went out of her way to make their delivery possible.

10

Toothless Rufus

There is little doubt that the FBI's search for me and the other fugitives was thorough, but it was also thoroughly wasteful, stupid and vindictive. With tens of millions of taxpayers' money, and accountable to no other governmental body, they were free to follow every conceivable gumshoe clue, no matter how ridiculous. FBI activities did stir up a lot of dust and gave the appearance that they knew what they were doing. But without a live stoolpigeon to give them a *real* lead, the FBI got nowhere.

My family's soiled clothes came in for careful scrutiny. Every laundry and cleaning store in the community where the family lived was visited and alerted—the World Laundry, Lake City Cleaners, Checkers Cleaners, Sun Ray Cleaners, and the Magic Cleaners. It was as if they thought I was sending my dirty duds home!

On October 4, 1951, an urgent teletype was sent to Washington analyzing the contents of a bundle of soiled clothes picked up the day before by World Laundry. The report contained a number of vital "clues." First, the bed sheets carried the marking CL-214. Then, two hospital gowns from Mount Sinai Hospital were found, as well as a towel labeled "Hotel Graystone Buffalo." And lastly and most important of all—a scrap of paper in a pocket of Danny's trousers "with the name C. Rattne or C. Pattne on it."

The FBI went into action. Here were real clues! The markings on the bed sheets led nowhere. The hospital gowns netted the fact that the only family member who had been to that hospital was Ralph, as an outpatient. The hotel towel was traced to my stay at the Graystone, in Buffalo, one night in 1944. A check of the hotel telephone log showed that I had made two local calls. Thus, they now had two more names to add to the growing list of people to be watched and questioned.

As for that important piece of evidence in Danny's pants' pocket, the answer came a month later. A check at Chicago's Roosevelt High School "advised that Cecilia Rattner teaches English in Room 212. The original scrap of paper "2 by 5 inches" had borne the message "Green from 212 to 237—11:20," and was signed "C. Rattner."

FBI files are filled with evidence of how far afield the hunt went, and how far back in time. Lil was born in Cleveland, in August 1910. A report verifies the birth, that it took place at her parent's home on East 29th Street, that she was the fifth child, and that the attending physician was a Dr. Edward. They actually tracked down Dr. Edward, who acknowledged a birth by that name, but knew nothing of the family since then. The neighborhood was then scoured for someone who had lived there way back in 1910, but without success. The investigation did not end there, however. The Cleveland FBI wired, "Will continue to check informants."

The FBI also checked out my birth record and birthplace, on Maxwell Street in Chicago. I learned from the report that my mother at the time was 21 years old, my father 24. I, too, was delivered at home. Once again the FBI set out to find the attending doctor and anyone who had lived in the neighborhood in 1906. I also learned that my father had come to this country from Yanova, Lithuania in 1902.

In 1929 I had worked as an assembler at the Keen Hair Waving Machine Company on Hudson Street, near the mouth of the Holland Tunnel in Manhattan, New York. The FBI soon found that the company was no longer in existence. It had been owned by three people, all members of the Unger family.

The FBI located one of the Ungers at his home in Brooklyn. He explained that his father had run the business but was now dead. The only other person who would have known the 50 or 60 people employed in the machine shop was John Metz, the foreman. He, too, was dead.

How tenaciously the FBI dug into my past can be seen in the resurrection of a person I had all but forgotten. I had known Rufus briefly in 1925.

About a year after I became active in the Young Workers League, three of us—my brother Harry, another young fellow and I—decided to start a modest summer camp for children of poor working-class families. Our aim was to help them escape, even for a week, from the sultry heat of a Chicago summer.

But how do three young people without funds or means go about organizing a summer camp?

First we made the rounds of left wing labor and fraternal societies to sell our idea and to solicit funds for the project. We also placed an appeal in the columns of the *Daily Worker*. Then we borrowed an old Model-T Ford and began to search for a suitable campsite. We found one near Argo, Illinois, near a stone quarry. It was owned by a farmer, who would let us use the plot in exchange for a promise to buy farm produce from him. We then bought four or five secondhand army tents, and with about $300 in our treasury, we were ready to open camp for fifteen to twenty children a week. My younger brother, Ben, was in the first group. That we avoided illness and accidents and kept the camp going, for the four or five weeks of its life, is nothing short of a miracle.

The cook for this nonprofit venture was none other than Rufus. He was an itinerant farmhand and had experience slinging hash for farm laborers and working off and on in greasy spoon restaurants on Chicago's skid row. He was affable, liked children, and could enthrall them with real or fictional adventure tales. Most important of all, he agreed to work without pay. He had lost his front teeth in some brawl and was lovingly called Toothless Rufus by the children, a monicker he accepted with good humor.

How the FBI heard of him and located him, and what they thought they could learn from him so many years later, is a mystery. But he was an apparition from my past, and to them a possible lead. When questioned, Rufus was kind enough to describe me as "of good character insofar as his contact was concerned," that I was "courteous and easily met," but he "could furnish no information or assistance in the location of the subject."

Of course not! We had not seen or heard from each other in more than a quarter of a century.

11

Grim and Farcical

The closer relationship in the underground made it easier for the fugitives to consult on policy matters, to assist one another in case of need, and to swap anecdotes. A few of these come to mind:

A comrade was to make contact with one of the underground groups for the first time. The instructions were explicit—appear at a specified street corner on a designated evening and time, carrying a six-pack of beer and smoking a cigar. The comrade, a woman, had no alternative; she stood at the street corner conspicuously and nervously displaying a cigar in her right hand and a six-pack in her left.

There was also the story of an "unavailable" who had come to Chicago and found work as a waitress in a Loop luncheonette. One day two people sat down at a table, each carrying a crumpled brown manila envelope. She had never seen either of them, but immediately suspected they were friends. "Sometimes business or professional people come in with manila portfolios," she explained later, "but only Communists carry *crumpled* ones."

We had our share of health problems, too. Fred, one of the fugitives, had to have an emergency hemorrhoid operation, which was performed on a Ping-Pong table. It must have been the first in medical history.

One day, when Jim Jackson came to Chicago for a meeting, he complained of a toothache. Our good friend Jerry was equipped to handle such emergencies with his portable dental drill. But not this time. A quick glance at Jim's teeth made that clear. An appointment was made for Jerry's dental office late that night. Some hours later, Jim was the possessor of ten new fillings. Also a record.

Winston's dental problems were also taken care of by Dr. Jerry. As we did not want Winnie to travel too late at night, it was agreed that he stay over at Jerry's home until the following evening. Then something unforeseen occurred. The family had just moved into a new apartment and a close friend arrived unannounced, eager to look it over. Nora, Jerry's wife, did not know how she could explain Winnie's presence, or even who he was. So, after some awkwardness, she told her visitor that she didn't want her to see the place until it was in proper order. Hurt and shocked at this apparent discourtesy, her friend left, angry and perplexed. It was not until some time later that she got the full story.

Jim Jackson had a scary experience while living in Kinloch, an all-Black town just outside St. Louis. He was awakened one night by screeching police sirens and blinding searchlights concentrated on the house where he was living. Convinced that he had been discovered, he hurriedly began to burn every scrap of paper. But before he had finished, a knock came at the door. It was Charlene Mitchell, with baby Stevie in her arms. (Jackson was staying with the Mitchell family.) "Don't worry, Chubby" Charlene said. "No one's coming here. It's next door."

There had been a bank robbery in St. Louis that day, reportedly the first by Blacks in the city's history. Twenty-five thousand dollars had been taken. To celebrate the occasion the robbers had stopped on their way home for a quart of whiskey. It was their undoing. In the middle of the night the police found them, asleep, next door to Jim's "retreat."

When Winnie was preparing to move to Chicago, there was the

problem of concealing his identity enroute. Black travelers who crossed state lines by car were frequently subjected to being stopped by highway police. Ruth, a comrade who worked with him, came up with an idea. She went to the pastor of her church in Harlem. She told him that "a brother" was traveling across the country and needed a disguise. She asked the reverend to give her a clergyman's frock and a document indicating that the bearer was a man of the cloth. The minister, who had confidence in Ruth and knew her politics, agreed without asking any questions. So Winston wore a dark coat and reversed collar all the way to Chicago.

I, too, was involved in serio-comic incidents. Suddenly I developed difficulty in swallowing. My throat didn't ache and I had no fever. But I felt listless and had trouble getting solid food down. A week or ten days of this led me to a nearby doctor. Sam accompanied me. The physician was a total stranger.

After examining me he asked, "Have you been under tension recently?"

Somewhat taken aback, I replied evasively, "Well, doc, who nowadays is not under tension?"

He said he thought that was precisely the trouble and wrote out a prescription to relax my throat muscles. I was to place a small pill beneath the tongue before each meal and let it dissolve completely. But only ten times.

Three days went by but I felt no better. When we returned to Chicago several days later, Sam took me to another doctor, a friend. One brief look brought the diagnosis: strep throat.

"How can that be?" I asked, "the throat is neither sore nor do I have fever."

He insisted, gave me a shot, a sleeping pill, and strict orders to get to bed as rapidly as possible and to sleep for at least twenty-four hours. Within two days I was back to normal.

(I told this incident recently to Harry Epstein, a wonderful doctor and friend, who said, "In my opinion, the first doctor's diagnosis was correct. It *was* caused by tension. But the second doctor knew how to treat it. You were cured by twenty-four hours of continuous sleep.")

I had been staying at a summer cottage with one of the families befriending me. Driving past the local bait store one morning, I decided to inquire about the best lures for fishing in the nearby lake. I was shown a lure with six hooks on it, each large enough to catch a whale, or so it seemed to me. "You don't mean to tell me," I said, "that this lake has fish large enough to go after that?"

"Oh, yes," was the reply, "it's our most successful lure." Still incredulous, I nonetheless paid a dollar and took the lure.

On my way to the cottage I stopped at the lake's pier for a cast or two just to get the feel of this big lure. On my second try I felt a sharp pull. It was a strike, a beautiful largemouth bass. Slowly I reeled it in, wondering how to land it without a net. Seeing a rowboat moored to the pier, I maneuvered my catch to the side and with a flip cast it into the boat. As the bass flapped wildly against the boat's bottom, I tried to figure out how to get it onto the pier without losing it.

By this time quite a crowd had gathered and I thought I heard a voice shouting, "Gil! Gil!" Momentarily stunned, I simply stood there. Then the voice came in more distinctly: "The gills, the gills, grab it by the gills!" Vastly relieved, I stepped into the boat and did exactly that.

Getting to the car, however, was another matter. Someone had rushed out of a cabin with a hand scale for weighing my catch. I then learned about the local newspaper's weekly contest for the largest fish caught. They were sure I would win it. All I needed was a witness, the exact weight of the fish, and a photo of myself proudly holding it up. Somehow I managed to stay out of that contest.

The bass weighed a little over five pounds. That night we had a feast. Stuffed and baked, the fish was devoured by five adults and four children, all ravenously hungry.

12

"Informants of Known Reliability"

When one considers the many cases of mistaken identity involving individuals certain they had seen me, it is shocking to think how many innocent people may be languishing in prison on the basis of similar false identifications.

Hundreds of reports about me came from all parts of the country and from all walks of life; from highly respectable citizens and from those not so respectable. Most were affected by the anti-Communist paranoia of the time, when every stranger, or person who seemed strange, was a subject of suspicion.

In March 1954, in a full-page ad in the Hearst press, Ulysses A. Sanabria, President of the American Television Corporation and an adviser to the Government's Munitions Board, would say:

> We must know who that smiling stranger is who moved in next door—across the street—who opened a little shop down the block . . . EVERYONE must be investigated and accounted for. The atom mine may come riding down the street in some innocent appearing lad's home-made jalopy . . . or under the pile of rags in the junkman's rickety truck . . . or be distributed among several of those suitcases on that bus, or street car, to be quickly assembled in some sub-cellar in the dead of the night. . . . Our only salvation . . . if indeed the nefarious plan has not already been accomplished . . . is immediate total policing, full security measures and a nationwide dragnet . . . But what is done must be done TODAY! Tomorrow may be too late!

There were also those who sought some form of personal glory, and were not overly concerned about how they got it. If they guessed right, they could achieve it instantaneously. But even if they guessed wrong, they would still be the center of a brief moment of excitement and attention.

There were other motives as well. Wily con men, adept at extracting personal gain from every situation, did not let this opportunity pass. Some saw their chance to pay off personal grudges. The CIA and State Department also joined the act, and it became a mass pageant for mentally deranged people.

Once, "approximately eight persons," according to an FBI report of November 9, 1951, "identified" me and two others [names deleted] as the three men sitting in an auto. On another occasion, in a Brooklyn cafeteria, four separate individuals identified me as the dishwasher who had worked there. In these, as well as other instances, the persons so identified did not resemble me in the slightest.

Typical of the hysteria that had people seeing Reds everywhere was a letter sent to FBI Director Hoover (July 5, 1951):

> Dear Sir, my family do not like publissity therefore do not want to be mix up with other people affairs. However I feel you would like to know a place that the eleven convicted reds use to meet. . . . I will wager they are in this apt or the people know where they are . . . These lousy reds have been meeting there for two years. Sincerely,

The communication went on to describe the location of the apartment. The FBI found it and reported back to Hoover (July 10, 1951): "No info could be furnished by neighbors concerning Communist activity of occupants. . . . no further action being taken."

A letter sent to Hoover by a more literate informant from Onaway, Michigan, also points a finger at a neighbor family:

> Dear Mr. Hoover: These are my reasons for writing. I am quite sure that Gil Green was in our town in August . . . I am also quite certain that I saw Henry Winston and that he was visiting at Mr. Sugar's home in Black Lake.*

Then came a revealing indication of the woman's state of mind:

> [name deleted] has worried for some time about how easy a group such as the Communists could tie up all railroad movements in this country and would like to talk to someone with authority. (September 27, 1951.)

Hoover responded thanking the lady for her information (October 11, 1951). He also instructed the Detroit FBI to investigate and to report back "action which you anticipate taking."

Patriotic prostitutes likewise offered their services. One wrote to Hoover: "I'm writing to let you know about this man, Gilbert Green. I know where he is . . . I would have went out with him one night . . . I could tell you more. But not on paper its too long."

Another informant was described as a "20-year-old, sex deviate, who identified subject as unknown male with whom he had a 'street pickup date'."

One letter was addressed familiarly "Dear Edgar," and concluded, "Henceforth, I will call myself Madame X." She, too, wrote, "I'm quite sure this is the guy you want." Her obsession with the fear that Communists were everywhere was so great that she had refrained from calling the FBI office in New York lest I be the one at the switchboard [!]. "Who knows, eh?" she wrote.

The FBI stamped this letter: "Expedite processing, February 14, 1952." And a note of thanks was sent to Madame X, signed "John Edgar Hoover, Director."

On January 11, 1956, a letter to Hoover informed that Henry Winston and I could be found working on the third floor of a factory [name deleted], in which just about everyone—from the supervisors

*Maurice Sugar, of Detroit, was legal counsel to the United Auto Workers in its formative years. He was also a legal advisor to us in our Smith Act trial.

down—were "reds." But more: "This intellectual nerve gas they use on the people, working there. They also use dope—by means of rubbing it with their fingers—it tends to make you dizzy and affects your eyesight. . . ."

Just as weird were those who used the FBI manhunt to settle some personal scores. On October 18, 1951. for example, Hoover received a copy of an airmail, special delivery, registered letter—postmarked Arlington, Texas—which had been sent to the FBI office in San Antonio. This anonymous letter told of a "beautiful blond" [name deleted] who could tell "whereabouts of Gil Green." It said she was an experienced airplane pilot, made regular flights to Mexico, and is "very clever and doublecrosser." The writer promised to give more information later if it was needed.

On the basis of this letter, all Bureau indices were checked. The FBI laboratory examined the letter and envelope for latent fingerprints. The investigation that followed included cities as far apart as New York, Buffalo, Chicago, Dallas, San Antonio and El Paso. The conclusion of the FBI: She was blond, a licensed pilot, also clever. But the letter had been sent by an irate ex-husband "to cause her trouble."

Bizarre too is the story fed the FBI in Phoenix, Arizona, by a "confidential informant of known reliability, whose identity must not be divulged," on September 28, 1953. According to this character, he had met Winston and me at the Kentucky Hotel, Juarez, Mexico, on or about July 9, 1953. He said we were engaged in running narcotics across the Mexican border. On one occasion, he added, such packages were "personally taken across the international border by Winston and mailed at downtown street corner mailboxes, El Paso, Texas."

The informant described Winston and me in detail: the kind of clothes we wore and our personal habits. He claimed to have been our confidant and said we had told him who we were.

For nearly a month the FBI pursued this hot lead from its "confidential informant of known reliability." But, on October 23, 1953, Phoenix discontinued all contact with him. "Information furnished was found to be completely fictional and appeared to represent an effort on the part of the informant to secure some degree of clemency insofar as a violation of the Narcotics Drugs Import and Export Act on his part was concerned."

13

Underground at Work

After Winston settled down in the Chicago area, we began to meet regularly, but never all seven fugitives together. Those not present at a meeting were informed of our talks—and of the conclusions we reached.

Our relations with the Party's national office and with the "unavailable" sector of leadership were coordinated by Max. He attended many of our meetings and contributed to our deliberations. Several years younger than me, Max had joined the YCL in 1927 while attending James Monroe High School in the Bronx. Later, at the College of the City of New York, he had continued his League activities. A member of a poor, working-class family, Max worked after school as a waiter. He was of medium height and build, and blond. Extremely reserved, Max was a diligent student of Marxism. With a voice that was barely audible, he was more at home on the podium of a lecture hall than as a speaker at a protest demonstration. Yet the issues of the time and his social conscience impelled him toward struggle and militant leadership. I had known Max from our days in the leadership of the YCL, and we had become close friends.

Now Max's responsibility was to help bring about a synchronization of views and a coordination of policy. Differences were inevitable under our conditions of physicial separation, so his assignment was both delicate and difficult.

In time, something of a natural division of labor developed among the fugitives. During most of 1952, I continued giving close attention to problems of the labor movement. Two of my four articles dealt with the situation in River Rouge Ford Local 600. UAW President Reuther had summarily removed the elected leadership of the local, charging it was "Communist-dominated." In a new election held some months later, the progressive unity coalition was swept back into office and with a much larger majority.

Bob Thompson, who had been the State Chairman of the Party in New York, continued to keep tabs on the situation there, even from afar. He had established his own system of communication with a few people in the New York Party leadership.

Winston, while concerned with all aspects of Party work, concentrated much of his attention on developments in the fight for Black equality, with special emphasis on the South. For this purpose he kept in close touch with Jim Jackson and with others working in the South.

Jackson had been Southern Regional Secretary of the Party before he became a fugitive. For all practical purposes, he retained that function. His style of work was not all that different. Conditions in the South even prior to the witchhunt had never made possible the open functioning of the Party. Our strong stand for Black equality was anathema to a southern system based on the discrimination and oppression of Black people. Even in the best of times, CP organizers worked in the South at their peril. And the 1950s were the worst of times. But some things were different. With a Federal warrant out for his arrest and the FBI hunting him, Jim could no longer live at home with his family or move freely, even in the North.

My first meeting with Jim in underground conditions took place at a small cottage outside of Gary, Indiana, where Winston was then living with a Black family. We referred to it as "Winnie's farm," for across the road a poor Mexican family had turned a vacant lot into a vegetable garden.

One of the chief purposes of our get-together was to hear Jim's observations about the situation in the South. He described the process of industrialization, the vast changes in agriculture, with cattle farming replacing cotton, cotton becoming mechanized, and the massive forced migration from the land to the urban ghettos of the South and North. He reported that Black people were being kept out of the newer industries, such as aircraft and chemical, but were trickling into some of the older industries. Conditions were thus being created for a growth of Black-white working-class unity. He also spoke of the stirrings among Southern Blacks, especially over the issue of the right to vote, and of the growing repression by those in power—an alliance of McCarthyism and Dixiecrat racism.

Jim also told about a Southern Peoples Common Program he was drafting. He had already discussed its main ideas with Winnie. When I met Jim again sometime later, still in the underground, the Southern Program had been drafted, discussed by comrades in the South, and edited into final form. Advocating socialism as the eventual goal, the Program placed its main stress on building the widest possible unity around immediate common objectives.

Much later I learned from others in the South of the resourceful manner in which the Program had been circulated. Aware that under prevailing conditions relatively few copies could be distributed by hand, the 24-page Program was printed to fit into a large letter-size envelope. Local Party clubs in the South compiled lists of people they thought should receive the pamphlet and raised money to defray the cost of the mailings. Then a day and hour were chosen—April 1, 1953, at 4:30 p.m.—using the mailing chutes in large office buildings. This was to foil any tampering with the mail by the FBI or local authorities; the Program envelopes were part of the avalanche of mail deposited in the chutes near the end of the business day.

The 1952 elections reinforced the reign of McCarthyism. Now its victims included not only the politicians who had stood up against this scourge (such as Senators James E. Murray of Montana and William Benton of Connecticut) but also erstwhile liberals whose own advocacy of anti-Communism had helped pave the way for these inroads.

At the Republican nominating convention in July, McCarthy had received a hero's welcome, wildly cheered when he accused the Democrats of "treason." Eisenhower did not sink to this level; nonetheless he campaigned with McCarthy and chose as his running mate Richard Nixon, whose only claims to distinction were his dirty campaigns against Jerry Voorhis and Helen Gahagan Douglas, and his success in jailing Alger Hiss.

In response to the McCarthy onslaught, the Truman administration once again set out to demonstrate its patriotism. On September 17, in the midst of the election campaign, the FBI made raids in three more states. Five prominent Communists were seized in Michigan, six in Missouri (including William Sentner, regional leader of the United Electrical and Machine Workers Union), and six in the Pacific Northwest.

This activity did not, however, save the Democrats from a "soft on Communism" label. McCarthy charged Adlai Stevenson with being a Communist stooge, and Nixon inveighed against the "Truman-

Stevenson gang's toleration and defense of Communism in high places."

With the Democrats striving to out-McCarthy McCarthyism, and Eisenhower promising in the last days of the campaign that—if elected—he would go to Korea to end the war, the outcome was fairly predictable. The GOP presidential ticket was swept into office, and McCarthy handily won reelection to the U.S. Senate from Wisconsin.

The campaign over, our group met to take stock. We gathered at Jack and Vera's on Chicago's North Side. Max joined us.

Bob Thompson analyzed the election gains of the pro-McCarthy candidates and forecast a more reactionary regime in Washington under constant pressure from the extreme Right. At the same time, Bob noted, the coming to power of a Republican administration for the first time in twenty years would frighten working people with the specter of a return to the days of Herbert Hoover, thus stiffening mass resistance.

Thompson urged a shift in the CP's electoral tactics. He maintained that it had been focused almost exclusively on getting a larger vote for the Progressive Party's presidential ticket,* but had virtually ignored the meaningful contests between anti-McCarthy and pro-McCarthy candidates in the established party lines.** He argued that the single most important task for anti-fascists was to halt the spread of McCarthyism, and that this meant administering defeats to its candidates. He pointed to a number of election races where CP efforts might have tipped the balance in favor of candidates opposed to the cold war witch hunt. If far-right candidates continued to win elections, as in the past two elections, it would be impossible to turn the tide against McCarthyism, he contended.

There was general agreement with the main direction of Bob's views, as well as with his assertion that signs were lacking of an imminent mass breakaway from the two-party system. The Progressive Party could be a vital catalyst on issues, Bob said, but to see it as a base for a new mass party was a delusion.

Winston urged a more realistic grasp of why people vote the way

*In 1952 the Progressive Party vote, with Vincent Hallinan and Charlotta Bass as the standard bearers, had dwindled to less than one hundred thousand, from over a million votes for Henry Wallace in 1948.

**Senator Thomas Benton (D-Conn.), for example, had introduced a resolution to expel McCarthy from the U.S. Senate, and Senator James E. Murray (D-Mont.) had voted against the Internal Security Act sponsored by McCarran of Nevada.

they do. As example he referred to the votes of Black people in 1948. He pointed out that they had not voted for Henry Wallace, even though his stand for racial equality had been far in advance of the other presidential candidates. Black voters recognized, Winnie said, that Wallace had no chance of being elected and that the Dixiecrats had fielded their own Presidential ticket to help the Republicans win the election. Black people therefore feared that a Republican administration would wipe out the gains of the New Deal period and intensify racial oppression. That is why, Winnie said, they voted for Truman—not as their preferred choice—but as the practical alternative to those they feared more.

We spent a day drafting a resolution embodying our estimate of the election results. Max brought it to Bill Foster and others in the leadership. Considerably amended and much expanded, the resolution appeared in the December 1952 issue of *Political Affairs* for discussion by the Party membership.

14

Paul Robeson in Peoria

Searching through its past records, the FBI found that on April 23, 1947, "informant T-2 learned that Gil Green had just been in an automobile accident around Peoria, Illinois, and had two teeth knocked loose." This set into motion a new line of inquiry and action.

The story of the accident was accurate, its details were not. On the way to Peoria my car had skidded on a sharp turn and wet pavement, ramming its nose into an earth embankment. My mouth met the steering wheel with such impact that three upper teeth were broken, leaving only jagged roots. The car itself fared slightly better, enabling me to arrive in Peoria in time for an extremely urgent meeting.

A telephone call that afternoon had informed me of a highly explosive situation developing in Peoria. Paul Robeson had been scheduled for a concert in the city's auditorium. But a few days earlier the mayor had canceled the use of the hall, and right-wing racist groups were threatening to "get" Robeson if he attempted to perform elsewhere in the city.

How the FBI viewed this is indicated by a letter from J. Edgar Hoover to "Director of Intelligence, War Department, *The Pentagon*" on May 3, 1947, and delivered by "special messenger."

The letter opens: "Subject: Racial Unrest Created by Paul Robeson's Scheduled Appearance at Peoria, Illinois." Note that what Hoover chose to call "racial unrest" he says was "created" by Robeson's scheduled concert, not by violent racist efforts to prevent it. Holding the victim responsible for his own victimization, Hoover quotes Robeson as saying he would not be "bullied," and that Peoria citizens, "in their own way," and "feeling as I do, will demonstrate their own feelings against the un-American assault."

Many Peoria citizens, particularly those in the Black community, were demonstrating their determination to hear Robeson. "The Ministerial Association of Peoria," Hoover wrote, "has invited Paul Robeson to appear in Peoria at some future date and he will be allowed the use of a church to make a speech allegedly against 'Peoria Racism.'"

Hoover's message further informed the Pentagon that "through a reliable and confidential source," which a second document of the same date identified as "microphone surveillance on the Communist Party headquarters, Chicago, Illinois," it was learned that William L. Patterson had told a meeting that "he saw more guns down there [in Peoria] 'among our people' than he had ever before and that they expected violence."

"It is not known," continued Hoover, "if Patterson referred to Communist Party members when he used the words 'among our people,' or whether he referred to negroes [the lower-case *n* is Hoover's] in Peoria, inasmuch as Patterson is a negro."

Sending all these details by special messenger to the Pentagon, the FBI was implying that Communists and/or Blacks might be armed and threatening violence. But Hoover knew very well that all the violence was coming from the other direction. It was while I was rushing to Peoria to help *prevent* violence, to do my part to protect Robeson from it, that my car accident occurred.

Once the Chicago FBI learned of my dental mishap, they set out to find where I had gone for repair. On

May 8, 1952, they reported to Washington that Dr. I. H. (Jiggs) Shapiro had made a denture "for upper right three front teeth of subject." Shapiro, however, had "no records or copies of X-rays" of the work done.

Wanting to alert the entire dental profession to watch for someone with a similar dental deficiency, the local FBI office teletyped Washington asking that the Bureau "consider advisability of contacting American Dental Association in an effort to determine their attitude towards publishing identification order descriptive data as well as the information concerning subject's denture in their official organ." On May 12, 1952, Hoover wired permission.

Next day another teletype told Hoover that [name deleted] of American Dental Association "displayed a very cooperative attitude." The American Dental Association Journal circulated about 80,000 copies and the deadline for the July issue was June 12. What was required were "brief facts, glossy print for preparation own mat, and description including dental deficiencies." Hoover wired authorization to send such material.

The article appeared in the July issue under the head, "FBI Seeks Information on Communist Fugitive," and began "The Bureau of Investigation has called on dentists to assist in locating Gilbert Green . . . one of the Communist leaders convicted of violating the Smith Act." Then followed a description of me and a request to look for "an upper removable partial denture to replace three upper right front teeth." There were also reproductions of my FBI mug shots.

So important did the FBI regard this dental-journal assist that Chicago's SAC (Special Agent in Charge) proposed to Washington that "a letter be directed to [name deleted] over the Director's signature, expressing the Bureau's appreciation for his splendid cooperation in this matter."

But the FBI had goofed. They were looking for a man with a removable denture. I was equipped with a permanent one.

15
Two Must Die

Our fear about having an army general in the White House had proved somewhat excessive. Despite initial steps to expand the war in Korea unless the other side became "reasonable," the Eisenhower administration moved toward ending the conflict. The fact was that the war had become too unpopular and the five-star general who was now President was aware that the war could not be won without escalation into a more dangerous conflict. What a Democratic administration had feared to do because of McCarthy's "twenty years of treason" charge, a Republican administration felt safe in doing. The result was a gradual softening of war rhetoric and a greater accommodation to world realities. Even before the signing of the Korean armistice in July 1953, the outcome was predictable.

The election results, however, had made Joseph McCarthy more arrogant than ever. He was named chairman of the U.S. Senate Committee on Government Operations, and appointed himself chairman of its Subcommittee on Investigations. He was now in a strategic spot from which to harass and threaten anyone and everyone, including those in government departments and the Eisenhower administration itself.

Continuing to build up a network of informants within the government (which he euphemistically termed a "loyal American underground"), McCarthy announced: "I have instructed a vast number of federal employees that they are duty-bound to give me information even though some little bureaucrat has stamped it 'secret' to defend himself." At the same time, he challenged the Administration's policies in Korea, its relations with the United Nations and the NATO countries, and the nomination of Charles E. Bohlen as envoy to the Soviet Union. By the end of 1953 he was publicly indicting the

Eisenhower administration for failing to fight Communism, and launching a "twenty-one years of treason" charge.

In the face of McCarthy's melodrama, to which the press pandered with scare headlines and daily sensations, Eisenhower sought to turn the tables to his own advantage. Thus, with the first sign of improvements in foreign relations (especially with the USSR), he intensified anti-Communist witch-hunting here at home. Nixon, now vice-president, boasted: "We're kicking the Communists and fellow-travelers and security risks out of the Government . . . by the thousands." Eisenhower followed this up later with a proposal to Congress that Communists be deprived of citizenship. More FBI raids were ordered. Communists were seized in Philadelphia, Boston and Atlantic City. And on June 19, 1953, there took place the most monstrous crime of the McCarthy era, the legal murder of Julius and Ethel Rosenberg. The late Jean-Paul Sartre called it fascism, "a legal lynching that has covered a whole nation with blood." Eisenhower, who refused clemency, said that his army experience taught him that executions have a "salutary" effect.

I shall never forget that day. Sam, Shirley, their two youngsters and I were driving to Connecticut where I planned to attend a Party conference. We had left Chicago in the morning, arriving at the Indiana-Ohio state line late in the afternoon. It was a perfect day, with only a wisp of white clouds against a crystalline sky. The children were restless, the fresh air invigorating, so we decided to call it a day. We found lodgings at nearby Pokagon State Park. There we swam, bathed in the sun, and relaxed as the two boys wrestled in the sand like carefree puppies. We had no premonition of tragedy.

For many months, from the time of their arrest in the summer of 1950, and especially after their trial the following spring, I had agonizingly followed the legal moves to save the lives of the Rosenbergs. Massive demonstrations were taking place worldwide. We fugitives kept abreast of developments and discussed what possible steps could be taken. In October 1952, the U.S. Supreme Court refused to review the case. The following February, Eisenhower turned down a clemency appeal, and on May 25 the U.S. Supreme Court for a second time refused to go into the issues of the trial. The Rosenbergs were scheduled to die on Friday, June 19, 1953.

Two days before, on June 17, a final plea was made. With the Court recessed for the summer, a brief was submitted to Justice William O. Douglas, citing new legal grounds and asking for a stay of execution until the full Court could hear argument. Douglas granted a stay, and millions throughout the world greeted his courageous act (which brought demands in some quarters for his removal from the bench). Now the Supreme Court would review the case when it met in the fall.

But this was not to be. Apparently fearing that further delay would intensify world clamor for justice and mercy, and determined that the Rosenbergs must die, the Administration, in an unprecedented move, prevailed upon Chief Justice Fred Vinson to call a special session of the Court. On June 19 the stay ordered by Justice Douglas was vacated, in time for the executions to take place that same day. The switch was pulled just before sundown; the Jewish Sabbath had not been desecrated!

We were unaware of these last charged hours, still under the impression that the Supreme Court would act in accordance with tradition, and that nothing new would occur until the fall. The grim news reached us that evening. The Rosenbergs were dead.

We sat speechless, in agony and anger, struggling to accept the finality of it. My grief was heightened by a feeling of guilt—that I could have thought this accursed day lovely and frolicked on a beach while the "salutary" execution was being carried out.

I had lived through the tragic murders, some also in cold blood, of comrades and friends. Harry Sims, 21, had been killed while walking a railroad trestle in Kentucky; he had been organizing coal miners. Joe York, also 21, had been shot down by Ford-plant gunmen while marching in a peaceful demonstration for jobs in Detroit. Both were active members of the Young Communist League in the 1930s.

Earlier, I had lived through the tragedy of the execution of Nicola Sacco and Bartelmeo Vanzetti, two immigrant Italian workers, put to death in 1927 by the Commonwealth of Massachusetts. They were immigrants and radicals; that was their sole crime. They were made-to-order victims for the anti-Red crusade of the '20s.*

The murder of the Rosenbergs was not an act of passion, not a momentary flareup, not committed by a cop or a hired thug. It was an

*They have since been pardoned posthumously in a proclamation by Governor Michael Dukakis of Massachusetts—more than half a century after their deaths.

organized, premeditated judicial murder of two young parents; its consummation involved the very highest levels of Government, and it was not deterred by three years of unprecedented national and international outcry against it. The case had begun at the height of the Korean War, yet the Rosenbergs were executed when the fighting had ceased, a month before the final armistice was signed.

16

Guatemalan Hide-out

The New York *Sunday News* and the Chicago *Tribune* of March 1, 1953, published an article by Stanley Ross, datelined Guatemala City, Guatemala. Ross, the *News's* special writer on Latin American affairs, reported (as contained in FBI documents of March 3 and April 30, 1953) that Henry Winston and I were "hiding out in Guatemala" and that the "Communist controlled" government had given us jobs in the Santa Maria Generating Plant, located on the Samala River about 20 miles from Quezaltenango.

Ross also said that the secret police and the anti-Communist networks of the Mexican, Salvadoran and Dominican Republics had cooperated in tracing our flight from the United States to Guatemala. According to his findings, we had first gone to Mexico, later boarding a steamer in a Pacific port which transferred us to a launch that took us to Puerto Berrio, Colombia. Later, Ross reported, we met with Jose Manuel Fortuno, General Secretary of the Guatemalan Communist Party and "chief advisor" to President Jacobo Arbenz. It was Fortuno who had decided to hide us at the Santa Maria Plant, according to the dispatch.

The FBI immediately set out to check all this. On March 3, 1953, Ross was interviewed by agents at the New York *Daily News* office. He stated that his information had come from a tip given him by [name deleted]. He indicated he was friendly with this person and had past associations with him, involving events in Central and South

America. Ross's informant did not indicate "where in Guatemala the fugitives might be located," but that "he [Ross] might get a good story if he went there."

So Ross was dispatched to Guatemala on February 17, 1953. He remained there a week. His first contact in Guatemala City was with the U.S. Embassy. Then he was reached by someone—how he did not indicate—"by [name deleted] who was employed by [name deleted]." This person told Ross that he was in temporary hiding "as the Communist forces in Guatemala were looking for him."

Later, Ross went on, he was contacted by still another person who had "heard from two of his members who were still in the hills that there were two Americans at the government plant at Santa Maria, and that these members indicated that one was a Negro and one was a white man named Greenberg, who was employed as an electrician, and that these individuals resembled two of the photographs [name deleted] had supplied them."

This, Ross told the FBI, was the basis for his sensational discovery. He admitted he had not checked our alleged whereabouts, "inasmuch as it would take several days for them to get back to Guatemala City." But he was so convinced of the reliability of his informants, and that we were the men, that he had left Guatemala to file his story.

Whether we were or were not in Guatemala continued to elude the FBI for more than a year. I, too, was perplexed, having read the first article when it appeared on the front page of the Chicago *Tribune*. The story seemed to be an FBI plant. But why? I had no idea that the FBI was as confused as I was.

On February 7, 1954, the mystery deepened even further. The 6:45 PM newscast on New York's WPIX television station (owned by the *Daily News*), reported from Guatemala: "Recent visitors at a labor meeting included Henry Winston and another convicted U.S. Communist, Gilbert Green." The same report was also broadcast the next morning. Once again the FBI went into action.

An FBI summary, dated February 25, 1954, gives us a clue to what this was all about, in a February 5, 1954 teletype news dispatch from Guatemala:

> The expulsion this week of two American newsmen from Guatemala, here, focused growing United States attention today on the tiny Red dominated "banana" republic. . . . Senator Alexander Wiley of the

> Foreign Relations Committee termed Guatemala "the bridgehead of Communism in Latin America" despite repeated denials by Guatemalan President Jacobo Arbenz. Just last week the country was host to some top international Reds at the Second Congress of its General Labor Confederation. And reports have it that Henry Winston and another convicted U.S. Communist, Gilbert Green, have found safe refuge in the Latin American country. Bananas, too, added to Guatemala's differences with America. Arbenz' government has expropriated the holdings of the American-owned United Fruit Company. The latest manifestation of Guatemala's growing totalitarianism was its order yesterday that all foreigners residing there "illegally" get out within 48 hours. . . . Here in the heart of the Western Hemisphere the classical Communist pattern was emerging in tough little Guatemala.

Four months later, on June 27, 1954, the democratically elected government headed by Arbenz was overthrown by an outside armed force that invaded the country. John S. Knight, publisher of the Chicago *Daily News,* the Detroit *Free Press,* the Miami *Herald,* and a string of other newspapers across the country, wrote an editorial in which he referred caustically to this armed overthrow as a "brilliant diplomatic maneuver" for the U.S. State Department. Knight's star reporter, Edwin Lahey, who covered the event in Guatemala, described it in these ironic words: "Thus ended a revolution that came about because these squares in Guatemala didn't know that left-wing governments had gone out of fashion in the Western Hemisphere, and that sooner or later they were going to be knocked off by Uncle Sam, directly or indirectly."

The prolonged fakeries about our alleged stay in Guatemala, and the related journalistic inventions seem to have been part of a larger purpose: to prepare the public mind in this country for the need to overthrow the Arbenz regime. Our names were merely being fed to the news media as part of the overall intrigue of the CIA and the State Department, while the FBI was kept waiting.

Among my FOIA documents, there is a copy of a letter addressed to "The Honorable J. Edgar Hoover," dated October 18, 1954. It is a reply to an inquiry Hoover sent to the U.S. State Department March 18, 1953. The reply reads:

> With the recent change of government in Guatemala it became possible for the Embassy to make checks in the files of the [a number of words are deleted]. Utilizing this new channel, efforts were made to ascertain

> whether any information was available concerning communist fugitives. . . . A reliable source within [deleted] states that there is no record of any kind on either of these men.

Note that Hoover's request for definitive information about us, written in March 1953, was finally complied with 18 months later, in October 1954, after the Arbenz regime had been overthrown.

17

Connecticut to High Sierras

The conference in Connecticut was considerably different from any other I had yet attended as a fugitive. It had more than twenty-five participants and its scope was national, with heavier attendance from eastern and midwest states. The majority were "unavailables"—that is, those in operative leadership positions but not living at home. I was the only fugitive.

Convening so large a gathering of leading activists, and with someone in my legal situation present, was clearly hazardous. Yet we felt the need for it was urgent, and we were confident it could be organized with full regard for security.

The Korean War had ended, and evaluation of the changed situation required careful collective judgment. True, Korea remained cut in half, but the imminent danger of world war had subsided. This made it more difficult for McCarthyism to terrorize and stampede the nation toward an American form of fascism. Yet the influence of McCarthy on domestic policy seemed to be greater than ever. The execution of the Rosenbergs was the most horrifying example. Consequently, the Administration seemed to be moving simultaneously in opposite directions.

This state of affairs, we were convinced, could not continue indefinitely. The scales would inevitably tip, one way or the other. Either full-scale McCarthyism would reverse the logic of the Korean armistice, or this first meaningful move away from cold war confrontation would prove to be the beginning of the end of McCarthyism.

What happened in the immediate months ahead would therefore be crucial. Just as growing popular opposition to the Korean War had been a paramount influence in bringing it to an end, so now, it seemed possible to help create a groundswell against McCarthyism itself. The mounting divisions over policy within the Administration and in big business circles would also help, we believed.

The conference was carefully organized. No one except those directly responsible for the arrangements knew where it was to be held. Each person was thoroughly "dry cleaned" before being brought there, a process that took several days. No one could leave before the conference was over. Delegates went as they had come, on a staggered schedule. Thus there was no concentration of cars to indicate the number of people within, and no out-of-state license plates to attract attention.

The meeting took place in a large frame house. There was ample sleeping space for about half our number; the rest made do with blankets or sleeping bags on the floor. I was the last to arrive. Only the very few directly involved in the decision knew that I would be there. I did not make a report, limiting myself to speaking in the discussion. I had, however, helped prepare the general analysis as well as the proposals to be submitted.

When our underground collective had discussed the need for a conference, it was felt that the presence of someone from the elected National Board of the Party would be helpful. It would indicate that what was being proposed represented the thinking of the Party's top leadership. Neither Foster nor Elizabeth Gurley Flynn was able to attend, and since Winston—the most authoritative member of our group—would face great difficulties in making the trip, the choice fell on me.

The principal report to the conference was made by Max. The Party membership, he began, is fully aware of the dangers facing the country. What is needed, however, is "consciousness of the new possibilities which are emerging." These, he said, are "only the beginnings of a new situation." (This report, under the pseudonym of Andrew Stevens, "New Opportunities in the Fight for Peace and Democracy," was later published in pamphlet form. It also appeared, in two installments, in *Political Affairs.*)

Two other reports were made: Claude Lightfoot's on the status and problems of Party organization, and Ed Strong's on developments in the struggle for Black equality.

For me, this conference was an exceptional opportunity to renew acquaintance with good comrades and friends, many who had, like myself, come out of the ranks of the Young Communist League. In meeting breaks, at meals and late into the night, we talked. I heard firsthand news of Lil and the children, and how each was doing. I also learned about what was happening elsewhere, about the mood of the people, and the state of the Party organization. When I finally stretched out, utterly exhausted, sleep evaded me. At the first sound of movement in the house, I was up.

I vividly recall the images of many of those I talked with and some of what we talked about. But I also recall something utterly trivial: Instead of old-fashioned cow's milk for our coffee, we were served some new-fangled chemical substitute euphemistically labeled "non-dairy cream."

I had been the last to arrive and was the first to leave. Without the formality of a goodbye, I slipped out. It was late Sunday night. By the time my absence was noticed I was far away.

Our confidence in being able to outwit the FBI soon received a severe shock. A bare few weeks after our conference, in August 1953, a remote cabin in California's High Sierra was raided by about fifteen FBI agents armed with shotguns. Among those seized were two political fugitives—Bob Thompson and Sidney Steinberg. Thompson, veteran of the Spanish Civil War, and bearer of a Distinguished Service Cross for exceptional bravery in World War II, was kept chained to a tree under the blazing sun for more than three hours.

At the time of the raid, Steinberg had been living in California for about a year, but Thompson had just arrived. When our fugitive collective discussed my attending the conference in Connecticut, Bob had proposed that he go west for a similar purpose. He was confident that he could make the trip without mishap and that Sid's setup was safe.

No hard evidence is available as to how the FBI learned of Bob and Sid. However, Steinberg has told me that some weeks earlier, while he was living in San Jose, he received a frantic message to move out, as someone working in their group had noticed he was being followed. The very remoteness of the cabin may have been a factor in Bob and Sid's capture. Generally speaking, the greater the isolation, the greater the chance of being noticed and arousing curiosity, if not suspicion.

The best place, probably, to be undetected (all other factors being equal) is among people, so long as nothing is done either in appearance or behavior that flouts local customs.

Shortly after Bob's arrest, the FBI made known some of the stops he had made on his way to California, implying that he had been followed. But an FOIA document dated November 19, 1953 makes clear that the FBI had not had prior knowledge of Bob's whereabouts. It was only after obtaining the identification papers he and a companion, Sam Coleman, had used, along with their car license number, that the FBI had been able to trace the stops they had made, most of them at "small out-of-the-way fishing lodges."

Bob's absence from our deliberations created a real void. He, Winnie and I had become a closely knit group. On several occasions Winnie and I had sharply disagreed with Bob, once over an article he had written which we believed expressed an exceedingly narrow view of Party-trade union relations. We implored him to hold that article until major changes were made in it. But Bob was adamant. Only after it had appeared in *Political Affairs* and caused something of a storm from trade unionists, did Bob acknowledge that he had been in error. Bob was neither subjective nor vindictive. If convinced he was wrong, he readily admitted it.

The Cold War pursued Bob into prison. In October 1953, while standing in the chow line in the Federal Detention Center in New York City, where he was awaiting trial for bail-jumping, Bob was struck from behind with an iron bar by a Yugoslav fascist who was being held for deportation. His skull fractured, Bob underwent three operations. He survived, but with a metal plate under his scalp. The injury tormented him for years and contributed to his untimely death.

With Bob jailed, the relationship between Winnie and me, always close, became even more so. By this time he had moved into Chicago, only a few blocks away from where I had grown up on Chicago's West Side, now a Black ghetto community. This enabled us to see each other more frequently.

Early in 1953, recognizing that change was in the air, the Party asked me to begin work on a new Party Program. Its aim was to describe the situation at hand in plain words, and to avoid abstruse statements of general principles good for all times and places.

Before I had anything I thought worthy of showing anyone, my wastebasket was filled to overflow. Finally, the work took shape. After a number of discussions in our own collective, then in the operational leadership, the document was mimeographed and sent to members of the National Committee for consideration and criticism. About three hundred specific amendments came back. These were carefully considered by a small drafting committee, of which I was a member. The Program, still in draft form, was then published in *Political Affairs* (April 1954) for the consideration of the entire Party. Along with it there also appeared a reprint of a letter I had written in the name of the drafting committee explaining to the members of the National Committee our reasons for rejecting some of the amendments.

I also wrote an article for the program discussion under the name of John Swift—"The Working Class and the Two-Party System." An article by Winston, "A Reply to Some Harmful and Incorrect Views," appeared under the name of Frederick Hastings.

After further changes in the draft, to take into account the widening discussion, the Program, "The American Way to Jobs, Peace, Equal Rights and Democracy," was adopted at a National Election Conference of the Party in New York, August 7-8, 1954. The Conference participants were informed that 650,000 copies of the Program in its draft form had already been circulated.

18

"Have You No Sense of Decency, Sir?"

The year 1954 saw the turning point in the battle against McCarthyism. It opened with McCarthy riding high. He had been appointed to the Senate's all-powerful Rules Committee and funds were voted to continue his inquisition. The year ended, however, with McCarthy's censure by the U.S. Senate. Two events signaled the change: the Army-McCarthy hearings in the spring, and the Congressional elections in the fall.

The Army-McCarthy hearings erupted out of a rather bizarre incident. One of McCarthy's young staff members, David G. Schine, (a pal of the comittee's chief counsel, Roy Cohn) was being drafted into the U.S. Army. To obtain special treatment for him, deferment or an army commission, McCarthy resorted to his usual tactics. He hurled accusations at the Army leadership for being less than zealous in weeding out subversives. After taking this abuse for some time, Robert E. Stevens, Secretary of the Army, finally lashed back. He declared that he would not accede to Army personnel "being browbeaten and humiliated." Significantly, the announcement was made from the Eisenhower White House.

Thus, the Administration belatedly made known its intent to stand up to McCarthy. Apparently it believed the time was ripe for this. The end of the Korean War had begun to alter the country's mood. Further, McCarthy's offensive had taken a new tack. It was now aimed at the Eisenhower administration itself.

To accuse the Democrats of being "soft on Communism"—even of "treason"—was one thing; to abuse the U.S. Army and an administration headed by a five-star general, now President, was quite another. McCarthy evidently had gone too far; he had to be slapped down.

The hearings began in March and continued for two months with the familiar McCarthyite charges, rantings and posturings. They were avidly watched on TV by millions of Americans, their interest kindled by the frequent clashes between Joseph McCarthy and Joseph Welch, two quite dissimilar personalities.

Welch, a native of Iowa, a Republican, an old-school conservative and a senior partner in a prestigious Boston law firm, was the Army's counsel. He was soft-spoken and courteous, with none of the histrionics often associated with courtroom lawyers. MCarthy, on the other hand, was the typical blustering, menacing ham, playing to the worst prejudices of his presumed fans.

The climactic encounter betwen them occurred when McCarthy began to bait Welch for having had on his preliminary staff a young man who, while a student, had joined the National Lawyers Guild. Outraged by this backhand attempt at character assassination, Welch turned on his inquisitor: "Little did I dream," he exclaimed, his eyes fastened on McCarthy, that "you would be so reckless and so cruel as to do injury to that lad." McCarthy gleefully persisted in his attack. At last the attorney, with mournful eloquence observed: "Senator, you have done enough. Have you no sense of decency sir, at last? Have you left no sense of decency?"

These words, heard by millions, had a telling effect. They seemed to symbolize for many what was really involved: not a choice between Right and Left (for certainly the Army general staff was far from the Left) but between simple decency and ruthless demagogy.

Years later a friend, Roger, who had been on the Party's Southern Regional Committee during that period, told me of an experience that illustrated how rapidly people's views changed during the course of the hearings. To make it easier for Roger to visit families in both white and Black communities without arousing suspicion, he sold home fire extinguishers door-to-door. In one town he frequented, he usually stayed overnight in a small hotel, a stopover for railroad trainmen. Awaiting their scheduled departures, they would gather at the television in the hotel lobby to watch the "Washington Spectacular." At first they sided with McCarthy. Then, almost overnight, the outrageous performer lost his audience. "It was then I knew," Roger told me, "that McCarthy was finished."

Several months later, in July, Senator Ralph Flanders (R-Vt.) introduced a resolution calling for censure of McCarthy for conduct "unbecoming a member of the United States Senate." A committee was named to sift the charges.

The committee dallied until the Congressional elections of November 2, in which, for the first time since the Wisconsin senator's meteoric rise, a string of pro-McCarthy candidates went down to defeat. Six days later the committee unanimously recommended McCarthy's censure. But he refused to concede that the jig was up. He delivered still another blast in which he quoted (as proof of a Communist plot), a headline in the *Daily Worker*, "THROW THE BUM OUT."

The Senate didn't go quite that far, but on December 2, 1954, by a vote of 62 to 22, McCarthy was officially censured. His political demise was swift.

I followed these developments with a feeling of relief, even of joy. Now I was certain that the tide had really turned. Now, at last, the end of my lacerated existence as a fugitive seemed in sight. I began to think of the next stage of my long odyssey.

The thought of going to prison would, of course, make anyone's heart sink. I could also assume that additional time would be given Winston and myself for jumping bail. Gus Hall and Bob Thompson had been sentenced to three additional years; it was unlikely that we two, who had successfully outwitted the FBI for so long, would get more lenient treatment.

And Winston and I were determined not to be apprehended in the remaining time, but to walk into prison with heads high, in full public view, without apologies, and at a time and place of our own choosing.

I had spent nearly five months behind bars during the Foley Square trial, so that being jailed was not something utterly unimaginable. I was confident that I could get along with the other men, although I was realist enough not to exclude the influence of McCarthyism, even behind prison walls. Bob Thompson had been attacked in prison by a self-styled Red-hater, and William Remington, a liberal caught up in the witchhunt of the Fifties, had been murdered in prison under mysterious circumstances.

These risks existed. But there were risks in the outside world as well. I therefore tried to give them little thought. Could anyone foresee then that Winston's imprisonment would end in his total blindness?

Prison presented itself as a long, dark tunnel that I knew I had to pass through if I was to reach sunlight again. In my particular circumstances, going to prison had one important benefit—it would enable me to see Lil and the children from time to time and to communicate regularly by letter. I had received snapshots of the family, via the grapevine, but I yearned to *see* them—to touch and embrace them, to hear their voices, learn their thoughts, keep in touch with their daily lives and, I hoped, share their dreams.

Lil and I had a means of reaching each other with written messages, but for obvious reasons we had used it sparingly. Our missives were addressed as if to another person, and type-signed as though by someone else, and we could not reveal our innermost thoughts.

Each year on Valentine's Day I would have a bouquet of red roses sent, one for each year of our marriage. They never were sent from the same florist twice, nor from the same city. Gifts would also reach the children on their birthdays, without any personal messages.

Once, when Josie visited family friends in Detroit, a conversation was taped without her knowledge. It was brought to me by Sam some weeks later. I listened to it alone, and wept as I heard her voice again and got some glimpse of how the family was faring.

A number of those working closely with me were parents of bright, lively and lovely children, all of pre-school age. This was a real blessing. I would play with them, bounce them up and down on my knees, ride them on my back, and sing ditties about Dunderbeck and Old MacDonald's Farm, sometimes changing the lyrics to include them. But the very love I bore these children only deepened my longing for my own. The more I showered them with affection, the greater was my sense of guilt that I had deprived my own of a father's presence and love.

Often I joined in outings—to the woods, a lake, an ice-skating rink or pond—and sometimes I would see a youngster at a distance who resembled Danny, Josie or Ralph. My heart would beat faster until reality sobered me again. With the passing years I no longer knew exactly what they looked like. I could only visualize them as they had been when I left home.

Hence the prospect of my going to prison was like entering on the home stretch, difficult and dangerous though it be, of a long journey. The sooner the better.

19

Closing Out

So shortly after the 1954 elections, Winston and I began to discuss the advisability of closing down our underground center. We talked this over with Jim Jackson and Fred Fine, both of whom had been pressing for an end to their own fugitive status. They realized, of course, that they would almost immediately face trial on their original Smith Act indictments, but felt that the changed political climate would be to their advantage.

The evil associated with McCarthy's name and career lingered on, however, even after his downfall. At the very time the resolution offered by Sen. Flanders to censure McCarthy was being debated in committee, the U.S. Senate voted into law the Communist Control Act of 1954, "An Act to Outlaw the Communist Party." A single senator, Estes Kefauver of Tennessee, had the courage to vote against it. That much-touted liberal, Hubert Humphrey, was one of its most active sponsors.

In January 1955, a new chapter in the Smith Act prosecutions began. For the first time a Communist was convicted under the membership provisions of the law. Claude Lightfoot, the leader of the Illinois Party, was indicted in June 1954. He spent four months in the Cook County Jail while fighting for reasonable bail. When convicted, Lightfoot was sentenced to five years in prison, and a $5,000 fine. Other Smith Act indictments followed. Nor did the Government halt arrests under the "conspiracy" provisions of the Act. Five Massachusetts Communists were seized as late as January 1956.

These signs of continuing repression stirred some doubts that the time had come to disband the underground. Some in the Party's National Center pointed to the fact that Elizabeth Gurley Flynn and the other defendants convicted in the second New York trial had now begun to serve prison sentences. Nor was it certain that Gene Dennis and the other Board members would actually be freed or be permitted to engage in Party affairs after their scheduled release in March.*

It was also feared that the rash of new Smith Act membership indictments, particularly the conviction of Lightfoot, could mean that the Government was preparing to try those soon to be released on still-pending membership indictments.

In view of all this, it was felt that nothing precipitous should be done; let things remain the same until Gene and his comrades came out. March was only a few months off, so we reluctantly agreed.

I had given thought for some time to writing a book. I had even chosen its title and discussed its theme with friends. Now that some months of waiting loomed ahead of me (exactly how many I could not know), I began in earnest.

The book was to serve two interrelated purposes: to explain why the Red Scare had struck this country with such vehemence and lasted so long, and how to prevent it from recurring.

I thought it important to deal with this issue because the virus that produced McCarthyism was still very much alive, even though now

*The March 1955 date represented the maximum time they could be kept in prison, for they had earned eight days statutory "good time" for each month of their five-year sentences. The balance of time—with the exception of the last six months—would have to be done "on the street," under parole supervision.

somewhat under control. There could be no assurance, therefore, that it would not turn virulent again, perhaps with even more devastating results.

In some respects the witch-hunt had made no sense at all; it appeared irrational. The United States had emerged from World War II as the most powerful, the dominant capitalist country in the world. U.S. capitalism faced no threat of revolution, whether peaceful or violent. Nor was it menaced from abroad. True, the very existence of the Soviet Union presented the challenge of a contrasting social system, but it was not a military threat. Why then such hysteria, when other capitalist states, much smaller and weaker than ours, with borders much closer to the Soviet Union and with powerful Socialist-Communist movements, had not become hysterical?

The witch-hunt served the interests of those who sought to undo the gains won by labor and progressive forces in the New Deal era; to snuff out labor militancy and radicalism; to intimidate the nation into accepting a staggering armament burden, and to win acquiescence for U.S. intervention anywhere in the world.

The Red Scare had this purpose long before anyone ever heard of Joe McCarthy; he merely carried the frenzy to its insane extreme. To the extent that the American people allowed this to happen, it was because they had been misled into losing sight of their real foe, right here at home, focusing instead on a fictitious foe abroad. The real foe was U.S. monopoly capital.

It was this thought that gave my proposed book the title, *The Enemy Forgotten.* Actually, the real enemy had been more obscured than forgotten, pushed back into a secondary place by the anti-Communist and anti-Soviet hysteria.

I thought it important to trace the conflict between the Many and the Few as it had raged in bitter struggles throughout the history of our country. Whether called "vested interests," "propertied interests," "economic royalists," "robber barons," "trusts," "monopolies," "corporate powers," "Big Business," or later, "multinationals," the few who hold wealth and power have always been the foe of the laboring millions. The struggle against their ever-growing concentration of wealth and power is part of the great American progressive and democratic tradition.

This struggle inspired the poetry and prose of some of our greatest literary and humanitarian figures: Walt Whitman, Frederick Douglass, William Sylvis, Mark Twain, John Swinton, Frank Norris,

Eugene V. Debs, Edward Bellamy, Theodore Dreiser, W.E.B. DuBois, Upton Sinclair, Carl Sandburg, and many others. Edgar Lee Masters caught its spirit:

Arise! Do battle with the descendants of those
Who bought the land in the loop when it was waste sand,
And sold blankets and guns to the Army of Grant,
And sat in the legislatures in the early days,
Taking bribes from the railroads! . . .

Or, two decades later, Stephen Vincent Benet:

Many, yet few they robbed us in broad daylight,
Saying, 'Give us this and that; we are kings and titans...
And, after them, the others,
Soft-bodied, lacking even the pirate's candor,
Men with paper, robbing by paper, with paper faces,
Rustling like frightened paper when the storm broke.

When I first mentioned the book project to Winnie, he encouraged me to go ahead. So did Fred Fine. By that time I had already spoken with those in my immediate setup and received a promise of their full cooperation, indispensable in helping me do research and giving me the benefit of their critical judgments.

Sam and Shirley assumed major responsibilities. Sam took charge of gathering research material, spending hours in libraries, borrowing books for me, excerpting from others, and frequently finding rich new sources we had been unaware of. Shirley worked tirelessly culling official statistical reports and checking carefully for factual errors. They were the first to see copy as it came out of my typewriter, and more than once they raised questions for reconsideration.

As the first draft of a chapter was finished, it was passed around to some other members of the collective for fuller discussion and treatment. One such chapter, "Process of Political Realignment," dealt with the peculiarities of the American electoral system that make it so difficult to break out of the straitjacket of a corruption-prone, corporate-dominated, two-party system.

Another subject that came up for animated discussion was the perspective in the struggle for full Black equality. At the time— especially after the U.S. Supreme Court decision against school segregation*— there was great optimism that racial discrimination

**Brown v. Board of Education,* 1954

was now completely on its way out and that by the 100th anniversary of the Emancipation Proclamation (January 1, 1963), all major forms of racial prejudice would be eradicated. In fact, the National Association of Colored People had set that as its target date. Its slogan was "Free by '63!" We, too, were optimistic, but warned that the struggle for full equality would not be won so rapidly, and that a reversal in the trend could also occur.

Winnie and I met frequently during these last months, usually at his apartment in an old walkup building in the Lawndale district on Chicago's West Side. We discussed the rough-draft chapters of the book, and it was with his assistance that I framed the chapter on the struggle for Black equality, "Freedom for the Freed."

While I was writing *The Enemy Forgotten* I lived at the home of a middle-aged couple. Leo had been born in Brooklyn of working-class parents. Six months of high school completed his formal schooling. He had worked on many different jobs—in shipyards, in a slaughter house, as a laborer with pick and shovel, as a hackie, on a truck as a moving man, and at odd jobs in the clothing industry. Finally he got a break and learned to be a cutter of men's garments, a job that required considerable skill. He was head of the cutting room in his factory when Marcia and he were asked to pull up stakes and move to the Middle West.

Marcia had been born in Hungary of a Catholic peasant family. Her formal education added up to five years of elementary school. Arriving in the United States in the mid-Twenties, her first job was that of a domestic worker. Two years later she went to work as a fur pointer. The fur industry being highly seasonal, she finally settled on the craft of machine operator in an upholstery shop.

Although all their relatives were in New York, and both had seniority on relatively good jobs, they agreed to start all over again in a strange city in the Midwest, where they knew not a soul. Much later I asked them whether they had been nervous when they learned that I was to be their boarder, and whether they were aware of the federal law against harboring fugitives. Leo replied that in view of the repression in the country, he had to consider such a risk as "part of the struggle." Marcia, however, admitted to a degree of nervousness, "Not at the possibility of a prison term," she said, "but that I might do something wrong that would endanger others."

When I moved in with them in Chicago, they were living in a four-room, second-floor flat in an area of the city where there were few, if any, Party members. (Sam had helped them choose the general location.) Leo had found a job, not a skilled one, but (as Leo put it), "a job." He was doing heavy physical labor in the shipping department of a large plant.

This was not the best kind of work for a man in his middle fifties, but Leo was in good physical condition and was managing. He was affectionately known on the job as "the old man," but was able to keep up with the youngest. He became good friends with the "guys at work" and was invited to their picnics, weddings and other gatherings.

Leo came home dead tired, often after hours of overtime at his backbreaking job; yet he never complained. Still, we found time to talk, usually at dinnertime or on a weekend, and I kept him and Marcia abreast of what I was writing and got their reactions to parts of my book-in-progress. I learned a great deal from their practical down-to-earth approach to problems, which stemmed from decades of earning a living in a variety of situations and in both union and non-union workplaces.

Marcia liked to paint. She would seat herself at the front window, where the natural light was best and her subjects were close by: a vase of flowers, a bowl of fruit, the house across the street, the tall stately elm at the corner. Or, sitting under an umbrella at the lakefront while Leo and I swam, she would try to capture the spirit of sky, sand and rolling tide on paper or canvas. She reminded me of other working people I had known; often, during long-drawn-out strikes, they suddenly discovered artistic talents they never suspected they had. Some wrote poetry, others composed songs, still others took to pen or brush.

Everywhere I stayed I made it a practice to assume some household chore. I would help paint an apartment, tile a bathroom, or shovel a load of coal down a basement chute. I rarely cooked, because that was not my forte. There was one chore, however, that I always took on: dishwashing. Wherever I stayed, whenever I was invited out to dinner, I would insist that the dishes were my province. "You do the skilled work," I would say. "Let me do the unskilled."

After my first meal with Leo and Marcia, as the table was being cleared, I put forth my claim. But they would hear nothing of it. At first I thought it was their customary courtesy toward a guest, so I said, "Look folks, my doing the dishes may not be helpful to you, but it is to me. It helps salve my conscience."

Finally sensing my determination, Leo looked at Marcia and said, "If that's how Pete feels about it, let's not argue." But I noticed that Marcia was unhappy about this capitulation.

That evening, after the dishes were washed (I thought I had done a good job), Leo slipped quietly back into the kitchen and remained there for some time. When I went in, there he was, doing the dishes all over again. Embarrassed, he explained, "Marcia is peculiar that way. She wants the tableware scoured after each meal. She's also fussy about the pots and pans. They must shine like mirrors inside and out."

Humbled, I watched the master at work. In *this* household washing dishes was not an unskilled job—it was an art! But I learned. In time I was even able to win Marcia's approval.

Of all the people I met with, only two knew where I lived—meetings with comrades were held elsewhere. Only Sam came to the house regularly, but sometimes it was Shirley, or the two of them, and occasionally they brought their two tow-headed youngsters along. When the children came, it was a special treat.

When I left the house for a meeting that might last for a day or more (as often occurred), I tried to stay away a bit longer, particularly if there was open space in which to roam. During the heat of summer I would disappear for a longer period, giving Marcia and Leo some time to themselves. One place I went to at such times was a cottage at a small lake about forty miles north of Chicago.

Joe and Lois lived there with their two small children. Lois was the young woman who had failed to recognize me when I turned up in Milwaukee at their repair shop without prior notice.

I had lived with them in back of that store during the winter of 1952-53. We spent many a Sunday ice-skating on the pond in Brown Deer Park. Later, when Joe's father became critically ill, they gave up the shop and went home to visit him. They were reincorporated into our setup with new identities, after we had made sure they were "clean." It was then they moved into the country cottage, for Joe had found work in a nearby foundry.

Joe and Lois were Chicagoans, both university graduates. Joe held a master's degree in electrical engineering. Lois was first attracted to the Communist movement during the struggle on behalf of Republican Spain. Joe had become involved during the Henry Wallace presidential campaign in 1948. What appalled Joe was the sudden cold war switch from fervent praise for the Soviet Union and its heroic role in World War II to reviling it as the enemy. When a fellow engineer invited him to hear Elizabeth Gurley Flynn, Joe went. It was then he had joined the Party. As a result, he and his friend were fired from their jobs as "security risks." Unable to find work in his profession, Joe wound up as an appliance repairman.

Joe, and even more Lois, had been harassed constantly by the FBI. Agents would visit their home, ask questions about others, try to get Lois to talk. In one of their cruder efforts, a fellow showed up one day, representing himself as a promoter for Camel cigarettes. He gave her a sample carton and offered to send one to each of her friends. Then he asked for their names and addresses. Of course, he didn't get them.

Joe's work at the foundry, with its unbearable heat, was very hard, especially for one unaccustomed to that kind of toil. But his youth and determination carried him through.

Lois, with two small children to care for, stayed at home. Donald, the two-year-old, was a fearless daredevil, a constant candidate for first aid. Roslyn, a year or two older than Donald, was his opposite in temperament; a lovely little girl. Lois always kept them spotless. The washing machine seemed always to be whirring, and clotheslines crisscrossed the house, fully laden when bad weather made outdoor drying impossible.

We also had fun. In winter we skated on the lake and tried our hand at ice fishing. It was at this cottage that the big bass I caught had been baked and enjoyed. And it was there that, after a meeting to edit the Party's draft program, we had watched the last part of the Army-McCarthy Senate hearings on TV.

20
An Obsession

With each passing year the manhunt became more and more a personal challenge to Hoover, and in time, an obsession. No resources were stinted in the compulsion to attain his objective.

As far back as April 1952, according to a six-month roundup report of FBI efforts, more than 3,280 investigations of separate homes and employment places of active CP members had been made in New York City alone. This search for us included inquiries "to secure sources of information in each neighborhood." Neighbors were to be used to spy on neighbors. Although the FBI report does not indicate the homes that were surreptitiously entered and searched (a number of paragraphs of the copy given me had been completely deleted), it is now known that the FBI engaged in illegal entries—"black bag jobs"—on a wholesale scale. One former FBI agent, W. Wesley Swearingen, who had been assigned to the Chicago FBI office, testifed that from 1952 to 1963 he personally took part in "about 300" of them. (Chicago *Sun-Times,* Feb. 2, 1979.)

To bolster its efforts, the FBI held a special, secret one-day national conference on March 21, 1955. The specific purpose was to relate experiences in Party infiltration and explore how these could be utilized in the hunt for us. An FBI document of March 29, 1955, sums up the conference as having been "highly effective in affording the Bureau and the field an opportunity to exchange ideas and resolve investigative problems."

In a memo of September 30, 1955 (perhaps as a result of the conference) a new "concept" was outlined. FBI investigative activities up to that point, the memo said, had concentrated on persons known or suspected to be active Party members. However, those who—according to FBI files—had dropped out of the Party over the years and ceased being active were no longer "the subjects of security investigations." Is it not likely that many of those listed as dropouts are really "sleepers," asked by the Party to lie low and be available for "special assignment"? These individuals, the memo concludes, might very well be the crucial ones for the FBI to investigate.

From this general hypothesis a more refined deduction was made. Since Henry Winston and James Jackson had considerable experience in the South, the FBI suggested "that southern [FBI] officers review closed security cases and check out all subjects who were active Communists and whose cases were closed because they suddenly and for no apparent reason ceased Party activity."

The memo then called for a check on every person who, according to FBI files, had dropped out of the Party from 1940 to 1955. To indicate the scope of this effort, the FBI memo lists the approximate number of cases to be investigated in six select southern cities: in Atlanta, 6,000; Charlotte, 9,000; Richmond, 9,000; Norfolk, 5,000; Mobile, 1,500 and Miami, 13,000. A total of 43,500 persons in only a half-dozen southern cities!

What is utterly fantastic about all this is that the Communist Party in the years of its peak strength (1943-45) never had more than a handful of members in cities like Atlanta, Richmond and Mobile. With the terror that existed in the South against Communists (long before the witchhunt of the 1950s), the Party never had a membership in that entire region of more than two thousand. Even given a high rate of turnover, the figures cited by the FBI bear no relationship whatever to actual Party membership.

Who then were the 43,500 listed for security checks? They must have been persons who in one way or another had spoken out on social issues: against lynchings and the poll tax, in support of the CIO's organizing efforts; or they may have been associated with the Southern Negro Youth Congress or any other liberal-progressive group of the New Deal period. But perhaps FBI agents, knowing Hoover's passion for adding ever more names to his security files, were padding them at random to show what a "good" job they were doing. If so, how many tens of thousands of names were put on the FBI's "active" lists?

In a letter dated October 6, 1955, Hoover ordered the FBI in twelve southern cities to begin this investigation and to report on progress being made on the fifteenth of each month, "commencing Oct. 15, 1955."

If the number of cases listed for only six cities is any measure of those in FBI security files around the country, these total must have been hundreds of thousands. This explains why, as late as 1959, when the anti-Communist hysteria had waned, there were still only four FBI agents in New York City assigned to combating organized crime, but "upwards of 400 agents in the same office were occupied in following domestic Communists." (The *Valachi Papers* by Peter Maas and Volume I of *Robert Kennedy and His Times* by Arthur Schlesinger, Jr.) No doubt a similar allocation of FBI personnel and resources existed in other areas of the country.

The FBI's anti-Communist crusade did not cease with the end of the McCarthy era; just took on a new and in some ways even more perverted twist. Counter Intelligence Program (COINTELPRO) became its secret name. Not until years later was COINTELPRO exposed as a massive effort to destabilize the Party and to disrupt peoples' lives by the vilest means possible.

Attempts were made to disrupt Communist Party conventions, to defame its leaders, to manufacture rumors to turn wife against husband and husband against wife. An attempt was even made to incite Mafia violence against Party leaders by sending forged letters accusing the Mafia of responsibility for the repeated bombings of Party headquarters.

One of the more shameless aspects of Cointelpro was initiated by a letter from J. Edgar Hoover to the New York SAC [Special Agent in Charge] dated Oct. 29, 1959. This suggested that consideration be given to the use of "some new strategy or techniques to bring Communist Party leaders under suspicion as being FBI informants, revisionists or secretly engaged in some phase of anti-Party activity."

In response, the New York FBI began to review Party leaders with an eye to framing one of them "as an FBI informer." Who that person should be, and the methods to be employed, were discussed in memoranda between Washington and New York over an extended period of time.

A letter from J. Edgar Hoover to the New York SAC (2-19-60), discusses possible methods to be used. Before "definite plans can be made," he wrote, "the New York office must first obtain a great deal of information concerning [name deleted] such as whether or not he uses a typewriter on a regular basis or uses longhand in his correspondence." Then Hoover explains why the forgery of handwriting is to be preferred in this case;

> The Document Section of the Laboratory Division advises that in order to simulate two pages in the handwriting of an ordinary individual it would take approximately 24 hours continuous work . . . *To alter a typewriter to match a known model would require a large amount of typewriter specimens and weeks of laboratory work. It is not felt that this technique of altering a typewriter should be considered in this connection.* (Emphasis added.)

This is an explicit admission—by J. Edgar Hoover himself—that forgery by typewriter was well within the purview of the FBI, even though rejected in this particular frame-up. Thus, what seemed incredulous to many when Alger Hiss charged that he had been framed-up by typewriter, must now be given credence.

In choosing its victim, the FBI sought "the highest leader possible," as this would "create the greatest disruptive effect." Ben Davis, Jr., former New York City Councilman and an extremely popular national Party leader was considered first. But he was dropped because he was too big to tackle and because the FBI did not have enough samples of his handwriting "to make possible the preparation of a spurious informant report."

Then Arnold Johnson, the National Legislative Director of the Party, came under consideration. But Washington demurred, urging caution "so as to insure success and avoid embarrassment to the Bureau, [for] if we attempt such a technique and the Party becomes aware of our efforts such action will have the opposite effect of unifying the top Party leaders who will band together to fight the common enemy, the FBI." This was coupled with an admonition "that this technique must be carefully planned and perfectly timed [for] it can be used only one time and it must be successful that one time." The letter to Hoover concludes: "The following is offered for the Bureau's consideration and comment." (The two paragraphs taking up a full page are blacked out.)

Unable to agree on who should be framed-up in the top leadership, the FBI began to cast its eyes on the next lower rung—individuals in the New York State leadership. One memo indicates that for a while Clarence Hathaway, then State Chairman of the Party, was marked. After deliberation, he was passed up, too.

In the summer of 1964, a letter ostensibly handwritten by William Albertson, State Organizational Secretary, was found in a car in which he had been riding. The letter dealt with recent decisions made by the state office regarding personnel assignments. The letter also requested more money and was signed "Bill."

Photostats of this letter, with accompanying samples of Albertson's handwriting, were sent to three separate handwriting authorities. Each responded that the letter written was indeed that of Bill Albertson. Faced with such seemingly irrefutable expert opinion, the Party leadership expelled Albertson from its ranks and branded him publicly as a government stoolpigeon. But the new information contained in FBI files raises the question whether Albertson was the victim of the FBI's "new technique."

21

Back to Foley Square

Gene Dennis and the six other members of the Party's National Board who had entered prison in July 1951 were released in March 1955.* Before being freed, each had to post a $5,000 bond on pending indictments for Party membership.

Once they were out of prison, Winston and I began to press for a rapid end to our fugitive status. But those in the Party's Center, including the newly released Board members, did not agree. We were told to wait until November; our proposal would be considered when those just released would be free of all federal parole restrictions.

With more time available, I began to enlarge the scope of the book I was writing. I also wrote a number of letters to Dennis, with whom I had had a close personal relationship over many years. In these letters—in the course of discussing various problems confronting the Party and the movement—I also argued for an end to the procrastination over our fugitive status. I urged that a decision be made imme-

*Irving Potash, the furrier's union leader, had been released a few weeks earlier. He had earned extra "good time" on a prison job. Ben Davis, Jr., was taken directly from the federal penetentiary in Terre Haute to the Pittsburgh county jail. (see p. 239).

diately that when November came we could end our existence as fugitives.

The replies I received were evasive. The merit of our point of view was granted, but we were urged to be patient. One letter even quoted a member of the Board as questioning the "propriety" of Communists surrendering to the authorities voluntarily. This specious argument angered me. The Board members who had served their time had also "surrendered voluntarily," if such a term could be used. We were not proposing to leave the struggle, only to participate in it more effectively by getting our prison sentences behind us. Such a step, I felt, was also in the best interests of the Party's battle to gain its full legal rights. What, after all, was the alternative? To wait until the FBI nabbed us? Or were we to be doomed to this nether world eternally?

Finally it was agreed that Jim Jackson, Fred Fine and Bill (Norman) Marron, the three who had been indicted in the second New York roundup, should come out into the open in November.* As for Winston and myself, we were to wait and see what happened.

Winston and I reluctantly accepted this delay, but we were convinced it could not be a long one. By the end of the year, Winnie and I began to make our own plans for what we facetiously referred to as our "coming-out parties." The first question we faced was whether to surface in Chicago or New York.

Chicago seemed the logical place, for we were living there. But we knew that if we surrendered in Chicago we would be taken in handcuffs and leg irons by prison van to New York, to be turned over to the jurisdiction of the court where we had been tried and convicted. Obviously, we preferred heading to New York on our own.

We thought it advisable, however, that I be first to appear at the Foley Square Courthouse, and Winston some days later. We feared that rampant FBI racism, encouraged and abetted by Hoover, could result in violence being used against Winston if he were seized before reaching the courthouse. I would go first, to make sure there would be a procedure established which the authorities then would be constrained to follow with Winston.

Once agreed on this, we each began to plan for the trip east. We were to make contact when we arrived there.

Just about this time, as my mind dwelled more and more on the day I would finally see my family again, an article appeared in the Chicago

*Sidney Steinberg, the fourth of this group, had been seized with Bob Thompson in August 1954 and was serving a three-year sentence for "harboring."

Daily News that disturbed me greatly. It had been written by Edwin A. Lahey, chief of the Washington Bureau of the Knight Press, which included the Chicago *Daily News,* Detroit *Free Press,* Akron *Beacon,* Miami *Herald,* Charlotte *Observer,* and others.

I had become acquainted with Lahey when he covered our long trial at Foley Square. He was a friendly, likeable fellow and we soon found we had some things in common. He too came from Chicago and its West Side, but from the Irish area. In his youth he had been interested in the radical movement and had sympathized with the I.W.W.; he was in contact with the *Catholic Worker* group led by Dorothy Day.

Lahey was opposed to the Cold War, and in 1948 had supported Henry Wallace's bid for the presidency. He had even toyed with the notion of leaving his newspaper job to work full time in that campaign. "But," as he told me in his amiable, self-deprecating fashion, "I didn't have what it takes; the good life and I were getting along too well."

There were apparently two Ed Laheys: one the person appearing in print, the other the man with warm human concerns. Lahey wrote in an easy, witty, breezy style. He circumvented the censorship that exists on all publications by concealing his real thoughts and concerns under a veneer of "nothing is sacred." Yet in real life Ed was acutely troubled by social injustice, although rarely involved in combatting it.

The article I found so upsetting was about me and my family. It began by telling me that if I had spent more time in pool rooms and less time in libraries, I would not be in my present jam. But what hurt me deeply was the callous, cruel way Lahey poured salt on our wounds. Writing during the 1955-56 Christmas—New Year season, he implied that I, and other Communists, lacked "normal, human sentiments . . . especially during the holidays when men like to be with their families."

What distressed me even more was that the article would certainly be called to Lil's attention, and most likely also to Danny's and Josie's. I knew the mental anguish it would cause them. Lil, at least, knew me well enough to understand how deeply I felt about her and the children. But what would the children think?

Troubling, too, was the fact that the article included our home address. This would once again focus on the family the attention of the rabid and deranged, would encourage new threats and harassment.

Unable to sleep, I felt I had to respond—and immediately. I sat down at the typewriter and banged out a lengthy reply. But before I had a chance to mail it the next morning, I was persuaded to wait for the day I came out into the open. To mail it now would unnecessarily inform the FBI that I was somewhere in the Chicago area. I knew it would only be a matter of weeks before my emergence, so I placed my letter to Lahey in a separate folder and filed it in the rack that held the chapters of the book I was working on.

A week before I went public I added a sentence to the letter, giving the exact day and time I would appear at Foley Square. The Chicago *Daily News* carried the letter on page 1 in its issue of February 24, 1956. One part read:

> As for human sentiments and the capacity to love one's own kin, I give ground to no man. And in rejecting your caricature of myself, I likewise reject it for all Communists.
>
> What I did five years ago arose from the very greatest love—for those closest and dearest to me, my own flesh and blood—and the human family of which we all are members. Nor can I separate one from the other.*

After synchronizing our plans with Winnie's, Sam and I began to dismantle our underground setup. We wanted to make sure that there would be no loose ends when we left.

On a wintry morning during the first week of February, Sam and I left Chicago for the trip east. I took with me only the things I would need for the remaining time and the two documents still to be mailed—my letter to Lahey and the manuscript of my book.

We drove through the city's streets, Sam at the wheel, I in deep meditation. How long would it be before I returned? What would things be like? Was Thomas Wolfe right that "you can't go home again?" At a stop light I read the curb warning: "Wait for Green." Would Lil wait? And the children? Would I be a stranger to them?

Sam's voice broke into my introspective mood, saving me from sinking into self-pity. The day was crisp and bright, the highway clear. We drove straight through, reaching our destination the same night, at the home of a young couple in eastern New Jersey. They

*For the full text of letter to Lahey, see Appendix.

were unknown to us, except for what we had learned from Irma, a comrade who had worked closely with both Chris and Max and who had been of great help to us. This home had been a haven for Fred when he was a fugitive.

Herman and Millie, our hosts, were in their mid-twenties. Born and raised in New York City, they had joined the Communist movement in their teens. Herman had entered the YCL when only 13, and at 16 was in the Party. He had inherited his socialist views from his parents, together with a love for Jewish culture, language and tradition. At 18 he became a writer on a left-wing periodical.

Herman had been drafted during the Korean War, but was soon confined as a "security risk" to the Fort Dix army base in New Jersey. He was discharged from the army near the end of 1953. But the FBI did not let up, preventing him from finding work at his craft. Wherever he applied, his political record soon followed. To free themselves of the FBI curse, the couple moved out of town, changed their names, and acquired new Social Security numbers. Later, Herman found work in Manhattan, but he commuted, and sedulously avoided old friends and haunts. Once he was recognized, but brazened it out by saying, "You must have me confused with someone else."

It was in this setting that they agreed to the use of their home as a place of refuge.

I remained with them for nearly three weeks. A few more things had to be taken care of before I could conclude this chapter of my life. First of all, we had to make sure that Winston had arrived safely in the East and coordinate last-minute plans with him.

Then, too, the manuscript of my book had to be gone over for the last time and completely retyped, so that none of its more than 350 pages would have anyone's fingerprints but my own. Herman had editing experience and his heavy black pencil was put to use. Every evening when he got home from work, he would read another chapter and propose ruthless trimming and cutting.

When this mayhem was over, the edited copy was given to Irma, who had come to help us finish up. She would don rubber gloves and keep everyone out of the room she worked in. Before the entire manuscript was retyped I wrote a short foreword that explained why and under what circumstances the book had been written.

Winston and I did not see each other after we left Chicago. With

Sam acting as our intermediary, we decided that I would appear at Foley Square on Monday, February 27, at noon. Winnie would follow a week later, on March 3.

Five days before my scheduled appearance I sent a letter to Lil, and another to newspapers and wire services. This alerted them to my planned appearance, my reasons, and the precise day, time and place. These too, bore no fingerprints other than possibly my own.*

Still one more thing remained to be done: a personal message to the wonderful people who had worked so closely with me for nearly five years. Since they could still be prosecuted for violation of the federal harboring law, I could not address them personally or send messages by mail.

I had often facetiously referred to myself as "the man who came to dinner," so I wrote to them in the form of a closing theatrical announcement of the famous play by that name. It read:

> *THE MAN WHO CAME TO DINNER* is terminating its nearly five-year run. Appearing at the Subway Theater—left of Broadway—the play has been a center of controversy since opening night. Severely panned by all professional critics, called indecent and unethical by some, it has miraculously defied all prophecies of an early demise. In fact, it has broken all previous records for this kind of performance on the American stage.
>
> While the play has been attacked by its critics as injurious to public morale, it has been defended by its supporters for encouraging resistance to tyranny and conformity. The majority of the public, however, did not become directly involved in this debate, feeling none too strongly one way or the other. It is this latter factor which partly explains the show's long and continous run. Had the public indicated a strong dislike for the play it is doubtful it could have survived.
>
> Despite the raging controversy which surrounded it, the show had the unwavering loyalty and passionate support of all its participants. Never has a show—and we choose our words carefully—been blessed with men and women of greater devotion and readiness for self-sacrifice.
>
> Although the performance of the leading character was on the mediocre side—with the single exception of his true-to-life portrayal in the dishwashing scene—the acting of the supporting cast was superb. Considerable credit for the success of the show must go to those involved in management, public relations, research, technical work,

*My FOIA files show that as soon as J. Edgar Hoover learned of my letters to the press he asked for originals so that the FBI laboratory could try to detect fingerprints.

finances, and musical score. Tribute must also be paid to the artists who painted the scenery and the stage hands who skillfully set up the props.

The producers wish to take this opportunity to thank all who helped make this theatrical venture a success. The man who came to dinner wishes to express his personal gratitude for the help, kindness and friendship which came his way. He desires to convey his deepest personal regard and affection for all those who were part of this important experience. He apologizes for any rudeness he may have displayed and does not excuse this on grounds of artistic temperament.

Our leading man is leaving for a command personal appearance which he has put off for some time. How long he will be gone from the haunts left of Broadway is not yet known. He hopes not too long. When he returns he expects to renew his acquaintance with the close friends acquired during the run of the play, although he joins them in hoping that it will not be in any return engagement of the present show.

After the command performance is over he intends to participate in some supporting role in the greatest drama of all time—"Mammon Remembered." This ambitious production requires so large a cast, and so skilled and devoted a group of performers that there is room in it for all Friends-Never-to-be-Forgotten.

There have been pressures to prolong the present engagement. These have served no useful purpose. They have been met by a Swift rejoinder—"For Pete's Sake!?" (Whether the exclamation mark or the question mark is the correct punctuation, only time will tell.)

So our curtain lowers on still another show while the greater one continues—for the show must go on!

[signed] Pete.

With all arrangements made and my work finished, we found time to chat and relax at the New Jersey retreat. Back of the house was a large open space. It was February, but there were days when I could exercise in the sun and even sunbathe. A nearby pond invited ice-skating, weather permitting. But it was unseasonably warm and I could use it only once or twice.

As the day of my departure approached, I hoped for at least one more ice-skating spree to make up for the years of deprivation ahead. Sure enough, on the last day—Sunday—my opportunity came. I do not recall that anyone else skated, but I know I had a glorious time, with the cold air beating against my face, while my body was so warm that gloves and coat had to be discarded. And as I skated, the thought in back of my mind was: Would I still be young enough to enjoy skating when I came out of prison?

Our young hosts did everything possible to make my stay pleasant. Before I left I felt as though we had been friends for a long, long time.

Much later I was to ask them whether they had been frightened at the possibility of imprisonment for harboring. Millie said that she had been more frightened when tormented by the FBI. "I felt so morally justified in what I was doing," she said, "so outraged at what was happening—especially the execution of the Rosenbergs—that it would have been an honor to go to prison for that cause." She had been upset about another matter: a sense of guilt for leaving a young sister, ten years her junior, and her father. (Her mother had died some time before and she had been like a mother to her sister.) Others I worked with expressed similar feelings of guilt.

Herman said that it was a time when he felt he was risking jail in nearly anything progressive he did—working for peace, distributing literature, refusing to cooperate with the House Un-American Committee. "After all, when someone as prominent as Dr. Du Bois was being prosecuted for sponsoring the Stockholm Peace Petition, who could claim immunity?" Under these circumstances, he said, "Going to prison carries with it a badge of honor."

Monday morning. It was time to embrace Millie and Herman and thank them for everything. I promised to see them when I came out. Sam, Irma and I left by car. Under my arm was my manuscript, securely wrapped and addressed, to be mailed when I got to New York. My letter to Ed Lahey had been mailed the week before. As we approached the entrance to the Hudson Tubes, Irma gave me a gift, a pen, hoping I would be allowed to keep it in prison. We said goodbye; I embraced them and made my way alone to the Tube entrance. It was about 11 AM.

The trip to Manhattan was all too brief. The first thing I did was drop my manuscript into a mailbox. Then, shortly before noon, I hailed a cab and asked to be taken to Foley Square. On the way I told the cabbie who I was, why I had been on the lam, and why I was now turning myself in. I asked him to drop me off punctually at noon in the courthouse driveway, at the foot of the stairs. I added that if he did precisely this, I had a ten-dollar bill that was his, for he would need it more than I, where I was going.*

As the church chimes tolled twelve, the cab entered the driveway, and I emerged directly into a waiting crowd. Coming toward me were Lil and the children. In an instant we were in each other's arms.

Minutes later I was in custody.

*My FBI files show that, as soon as I surrendered, J. Edgar Hoover ordered that the cab driver be found. A few hours later he was located, and FBI agents asked him to give them whatever money I had given him. He told them that the fare had been seventy-five cents but that I had given him a five-dollar bill. This may only mean that over the years, with the rampant inflation we've had, my memory has exaggerated my own generosity.

Fugitive since 1951, former Illinois Communist leader Gilbert Green mounts steps of U.S. Courthouse in New York to surrender. He is greeted by crowd including (l. to r.) his daughter Josephine, 14; his son Danny, 18; Mrs. Green and another son, Ralph, 10. (AP Wirephoto)

Gil Green Gives Up In N.Y.

Gilbert Green, 49, Chicago-reared Communist leader, surrendered in New York to begin serving a five-year prison term.

Asked by reporters where he had been hiding from the law since 1951, Green replied Monday:

not seen any of them since he vanished from his Chicago home at 3143 W. Eastwood four and a half years ago.

There was a tearful reunion between Green and his kinfolk, as curious persons milled about, before he went into the court-

he had written a book, "The Enemy Forgotten," and sent it to a prospective publisher.

Among those who greeted him in New York was Benjamin Davis, former New York councilman who was among the 11 convicted

Green was rumored at various times to have fled to Central America after his conviction. He was president and valedictorian of the 1924 class at John Marshall High School here.

As he embraced his wife, Lillian, Green told reporters:

"Now the Federal Bureau of

—1950—

Ralph, Josie, Dan and Lillian Green try to peer through bars at West Street jail.

The five Smith Act case attorneys. Left to right, Abraham Isserman, George C. Crockett, Jr., Richard Gladstein, Harry Sacher and Louis McCabe. Inset, John Abt, General Counsel for the Communist Party.

One of many demonstrations against the Smith Act prosecutions.

Henry Winston and Gil Green in custody.

III——LEAVENWORTH

1

West Street Again

The West Street jail was a detention center for those awaiting trial or being transferred to Federal prisons across the country. Sometimes prisoners who had sentences of a year or less were permitted to do their full time here. Eugene Dennis served his contempt sentence here in 1950 for challenging the House Un-American Committee.

Although I had already been given a five-year sentence, I still faced trial on a contempt charge for failing to surrender in 1951, so I could expect to remain at West Street for several weeks.

A few days after arriving, I read that Winston would be surrendering the following Monday. This did not come as a surprise to me for it had been part of our previous understanding. Apparently stung by criticism for having allowed me some leeway, the FBI made sure that Winston would have none. He was not permitted even a brief moment to embrace his family, greet his friends or be interviewed by the media. As soon as he was spotted approaching the courthouse steps he was seized. He became my cellmate that afternoon and until we were separated two months later, enroute to different prisons.

Neither of us was a stranger in what we sardonically referred to as our "exclusive men's club." We had also shared a cell at West Street before, during the nearly five months of our trial, but that had been a large one with occupants in its more than a dozen bunks.

Not much had changed; the overcrowding was somewhat worse, and the din a great deal more so. The loudspeaker blared incessantly, from wake-up to lights-out. A TV set had been added. The cacophony every evening was maddening. Numbed though we were by this endless shock treatment, we learned how to communicate.

Our cell was centrally and strategically located. We had been placed in it for easier surveillance. It had a wall on only one side; we were separated from the surrounding corridors on the other three sides by bars. The resemblance to a cage in a zoo was extremely close. We were set apart from the other cells, as if to draw special attention to the zoo's prize exhibit of two reputedly dangerous criminals.

To emphasize this special status, we were kept under lock and key night and day. Our food trays were passed in to us. We were let out only for a periodic shower or to the visiting room. Thus we could not mingle with the other men, could not leave our cell for mess, work assignment, roof time or recreation. We were in a prison within a prison.

The official explanation was that this was for our own "protection." We were reminded that Bob Thompson had had his skull crushed at West Street two years earlier. But why wasn't Sid Steinberg being kept in isolation? Sid had been arrested with Bob Thompson in the California Sierras and was serving a three-year sentence for harboring, but he had been sent back to West Street to await his own Smith Act trial, and he was there when we arrived.

Sid was a skilled butcher and maybe he was needed in the kitchen. In any event, the fact remained that he was admitted to the general population but we were not. Winnie and I wondered whether we were getting punitive treatment for having eluded the FBI hunt.

At any rate, we were opposed to any treatment that would set us apart from the others, even if it were for our own "protection." Our best security, we believed, lay in letting the men get to know us as human beings. While there was no guarantee this would shield us against possible violence, we were convinced that any action on our part that could be interpreted as seeking or accepting "protection," or as seeming to fear the other prisoners, would not be in our best interests. The fact is that we did not fear the men, had gotten along well with them while here in 1949 and felt certain we could do so again.

We therefore decided to press for our right to be in the general population, choosing to concentrate on one specific aspect of this prison discrimination: the denial of open-air time. We wrote "copouts" (intraprison letters) to Warden Kenton, Acting Captain Maines and Parole Officer Franciscus. We also enlisted the aid of our attorney, John Abt.

About two weeks later we won this skirmish. Our efforts also led to work assignments. The prison library had no librarian at the time, so I volunteered for the job, and my offer was accepted by the authorities.

Most of my thoughts during those first weeks of imprisonment were, of course, of my family. My total physical separation from them seemed to have lasted for an eternity, and had opened a gaping chasm that could be bridged but never completely closed. The children's memory of me had dimmed, yet the grim facts continued to haunt their daily lives, so that forgetting me was impossible. When I appeared in the flesh again on the courthouse steps of Foley Square, I asked my son Ralphie, "Do you recognize me?" and he replied, "I think I do, Dad;" but if he did it was probably only because he was expecting me.

In my first letter to Lil after I had surrendered, I wrote, "The children have undergone a remarkable transformation. Danny—a young man; tall, handsome and quite mature. Josie—worlds apart from the skinny little tomboy who used to climb trees better than a monkey. She has become a fragrant flower whose petals are only now opening up. Ralph—no longer a small boy, but not yet a big one. He has the same tenderness and wistful charm he had as a child."

Lil looked much the same, and when our eyes met we knew that we had the same feeling for one another. Yet her eyes also told me something else—the terrible strain she had been under. And when she raised a hand I noticed a slight tremble that I had not observed before.

I wanted desperately to become a living part of their lives again. But how, when the accursed separation was not yet over? Still, we could now keep in close touch and see each other regularly.

With visiting hours more lenient at West Street than at a penitentiary, and not knowing how long it would be before I was shipped out or where, we decided to make the most of the opportunity. This was not easy for Lil; it entailed considerable travel and expense. She was working a fulltime job, so she could visit only on weekends. This meant flying to New York, and back to Chicago in time for work on Monday morning.

Lil decided, however, to visit me every Saturday as long as that was possible. She did so for a full month. I was uneasy about so demanding a schedule, yet was happy to know she wanted to see me as much as I did her.

The visiting room was hardly conducive to either privacy or intimacy. Even the presence of a loved one could not induce a feeling of respite, for the physical setup emphasized even further the cruel reality of separation. A long row of prisoners faced another of visitors across a table, divided by a high glass panel. Hence to touch, or to catch a whiff of the other's body fragrance, was impossible. Voices were also distorted, for conversation had to take place over a telephone. And to top it off, a guard sat so close that he could monitor both sides of the panel and observe every move. Each visit was eagerly awaited, followed though it was by bitter frustration.

Danny, Josie and Ralph each came to see me during that first month, as did Ben and Florence. My brother Harry had come from Los Angeles to greet me when I turned up at Foley Square but could not make another trip so soon after. My mother, who was so eager to see me (and I her), was prevailed upon to put if off for a time. We feared it would be too much for her frail health, particularly so soon after my reemergence.

In my conversations and correspondence with the children I tried to catch up with the changes that had taken place in each of them. I wanted to know what was happening at school, what subjects they liked best, what they were hoping to do when they grew up, what they did in their spare time, about their friends, and how they had stood up to the terrible ordeal. I wanted to get to know them intimately again and for them to know me.

Danny was more loquacious than the younger two. We had known each other better. He was now in college, studying electrical engineering. He told me of the jobs he had held after school and his determination to continue his studies while working to defray his expenses. Josie, in high school, was far more taciturn than Danny, both in her conversation and her correspondence. The dark years had definitely been tougher on her. Ralphie was in grade school. When he visited with Lil he had to be encouraged to open up. Then his talk poured out like a torrent. But while Lil and I talked, he kept staring at me as if to try and fathom this strange man who, he knew, was his father. It wasn't long, however, before he wrote asking me to fulfill a paternal duty—to "get Danny to stop picking on me." They shared a bedroom, and the eight-year age difference made for frequent incidents.

In my letters to the family I tried desperately to become a part of their lives again. I offered advice, tried to intervene in family disputes, and sought to influence the children's likes and dislikes. I wanted to know if they enjoyed ice skating, and if not, why not; if they liked a certain book or author, and if not—why not. I even tried to persuade Lil that what she needed was time out for physical exercise. But what "time out" could she find, employed on a fulltime job, burdened with daily family chores, playing the role of both mother and father, visiting me regularly, writing frequent letters, and speaking at public meetings about the injustice of our imprisonment?

Ben undertook to keep me abreast of political developments. Unable to receive the *Daily Worker* or any other Movement publication—not even the liberal *Nation*—I was eager to find out what was happening in the Party and on the Left generally.

My approved correspondence list was limited to close family members. I knew, however, that I could have at least one non-family correspondent if that person were approved by the Prison Board. My preference was for a knowledgeable person who did not necessarily have to share my own political view. But who would agree to correspond with me, and perhaps take the heat for so doing? I thought there was an off-chance that Ed Lahey would. Not wishing to embarrass him by submitting his name without prior agreement, I asked John Abt to sound him out. Ed's reply was not long in coming:

> I would be delighted to correspond with Gil Green while he is doing that long stretch in the stone crock. I wish you had advised him, however, that while I have my own personal views about the law under which he was convicted I am a dyed-in-the-wool cynic.
>
> If Gil needs someone whose cynicism is open to assault I would be glad to be his pigeon and would promise to keep up with my end of the correspondence.

There was a postscript "Will you tell Gil that his wife Lillian wrote me at his request to thank me for the publication of his letter. I felt uncomfortable about answering a letter from a woman facing such a long separation from her husband and solved my problem by letting it go."

On March 16, 1956, according to my prison files, I submitted a request to Mr. Franciscus, the Parole officer, that the name of Mr. Edwin A. Lahey be added to my approved list of correspondents. However, it took a good deal more than this to make him acceptable to the prison authorities.

I had my second day in court on March 19, 1956. The first lasted nine months, but this one took a little more than an hour. The charge against me, contempt for failing to surrender when ordered, was heard by Judge Archie C. Dawson.

Paul W. Williams, U.S. Attorney, set out to prove but one thing: that I had known of the court order and wilfully disobeyed it. His evidence was the letter I had sent to the press and my interview with reporters on the courthouse steps. A newsreel of that occasion was shown. What appeared particularly incriminating to the prosecution was my reply to a reporter's query about where I had been. I said it was "in People's Town, U.S.A., at the corner of Constitution Avenue and Bill of Rights Street." To him this was both evasive and "contemptuous."

John Abt, my lawyer, stressed the obviously discriminatory nature of the proceedings. In all the history of the United States, no fugitive had ever been charged in a federal court with contempt, until Gus Hall; his had been the first such prosecution. The second involved Bob Thompson and my case was third. The proceedings, we were convinced, were obviously political persecution for our unpopular beliefs.

Winston's trial took place a week after mine, also before Judge Dawson. We were both found guilty and sentenced to three additional years in a Federal penitentiary. Prior to sentencing us, Judge Dawson likened us to "arbitrary dictators." He said we had set ourselves above the law by refusing to surrender upon court order. The judge was apparently unaware of American history—about the Underground Railroad to protect runaway slaves from the Fugitive Slave Law; about the period when workers' efforts to form unions were considered "illegal conspiracies against free trade"; about the decades when striking workers were compelled to defy court injunctions; and about what was happening in the South at that very moment—a massive civil-disobedience movement against racist, Jim-Crow laws. Our actions were in keeping with that tradition.

I wrote Lil: "How things get turned upside down. The Constitution is violated by sending men to prison for their political beliefs, but it is the victims of this contempt for the law who are themselves accused of contempt!"

2

Enroute to the Big House

Two days after we had been sentenced, the Justice Department asked Warden Kenton for an evaluation of how Winston and I had "adjusted." And on April 6 the warden was informed that "by direction of the Attorney General" Winston was to be sent to the Federal penitentiary at Terre Haute, Indiana, and I to Leavenworth, Kansas. Within two weeks there were enough transits to fill a bus and we were ordered to gather all our belongings.

We didn't know how long the trip would take, by what routes we would travel, or what stops we would make. Before entering the prison bus, we were told to line up in pairs to be handcuffed. When Winnie's and my turn came, the driver took one look and said, "You guys will have to separate, we don't seat Negro and white together." We insisted that we were friends, had been convicted together, were harming no one, and that if a prison regulation was being "violated" we had already done so—we had shared a common cell. After consulting with Acting Captain Maines, who was supervising the contingent, the driver reluctantly manacled us together. "They're Commies," he explained to the guards in the bus.

The vehicle in which we traveled was old. It huffed and puffed as it climbed hills, its bones creaking loudly with every move. In addition to the driver-guard there were two other guards each in a wire-mesh cage and armed. One cage was in the center of the bus, on the right; the other, in the rear. All three men had access to separate exit doors. It might have been a scene from Kafka: We, the prisoners, appeared to be free; it was our keepers who were the caged!

Using the toilet at the rear left of the bus required considerable dexterity, depending on which wrist was manacled. If it was the right, both partners shuffled over to the center cage, where the guard, through a small aperture, could unlock the handcuff. But if it was on the left wrist you proceeded directly to the rear, dragging your partner with you. Then he waited outside, still attached to you, with the toilet door slightly ajar. These goings and comings were closely observed by the guard in the rear, and only one couple could rise at a time.

Once on the road, we were informed that our first stop would be the federal prison at Lewisburg, Pennsylvania. But the driver took his time, zigzagging from one inferior highway to another. If his intent was to keep the bus from being followed, or from being ambushed along the way, he was more than successful. Sometimes it seemed as though he didn't really know where he was going. At lunchtime, we stopped near a roadside diner, in which the guards took turns eating, while we sat in the bus munching on previously prepared baloney and cheese sandwiches.

The jolting and jarring were as bad for our backsides as they were for our nerves. Yet Winston and I were glad to be on our way, however sorry that we would have to part company soon. As we rode, our eyes devoured the unfolding vista through the barred bus windows. Spring was in the air, from the rolling plains and carpeted earth to the craggy mountains in the distance. With a feeling blended of joy and sadness we watched children at play in schoolyards, tulips emerging from tenderly cared-for lawns, women strolling with baby carriages or rushing home with shopping bags, and laborers returning after a day's work. We alone seemed out of place, hurtling toward dungeons to be buried alive.

We arrived in Lewisburg in time for dinner. Here Winston and I were separated, he shunted to a Black cellblock, I to a white. After being given coveralls to mark us as transients, we were marched single file toward the mess hall, hugging the right-side wall of a wide corridor. A line of Black prisoners was moving in the same direction along the left side. Suddenly I glimpsed Winston passing by in the opposite line. On the spur of the moment, I dashed to the other side and got into line directly behind him. We then filed into the dining room and took seats next to each other at a table with other men, all Black. If they were surprised at my being there, they did not indicate it. We introduced ourselves and began to eat.

Our maneuver had not passed without notice, however. Men at other tables were pointing to us. Soon a guard appeared and I was ordered to move. Winston and I protested that we were friends, had traveled together, and that we saw no harm in eating together as well. Noting that we were being observed by other men in the hall, the guard decided to cut the exchange short. I was ordered to move to a white table.

We remained at Lewisburg for nearly a week, waiting for a bus to fill up for a trip to our next stop. Each time we filed to the mess hall we were closely watched. The scene in the dining room became a matter of general discussion. There were some whites who disapproved, but from the greetings and smiles of Black prisoners, I knew that my action had met with their approval. (When we were in West Street in 1949, we had succeeded in breaking down the segregation there, but six years later this aspect of racism was still rampant in the rest of the Federal prison system.)

Another incident of our stay at Lewisburg deserves mention. This, too, took place in the mess hall. While at breakfast the morning after our arrival, a prisoner brushed up to me and whispered something about "gifts from Jerry" and to keep my eyes on the floor. A few minutes later a pack of Camel cigarettes came my way, I swiftly snatched it up and soon there was another pack. This was followed by two large chocolate bars delivered in the same efficient manner.

Jerry was V. J. Jerome, also known as "V.J." He was an old friend and comrade, who for a number of years had been editor of the Party's theoretical magazine, *Political Affairs.* He had been convicted in the second of the Foley Square trials, had been sentenced to three years, and was doing time at Lewisburg. He was a gifted poet and author of the novel, *A Lantern for Jeremy.*

He had not been at the same mess with us the evening before, but had learned of our arrival via the prison grapevine. Knowing that we would not be able to buy anything in the commissary while enroute, and remembering that Winnie was a cigarette smoker, Jerry organized the under-the-table rapid delivery service with some of his prison friends as his way of greeting us.

We, of course, knew Jerry was in Lewisburg and wondered how he was getting on. We were especially concerned about him because we knew him to be a person more at home in the world of books than with people. Jerry was an authority on Cervantes, a student of English literature, of history and the arts, and an erudite Marxist. He also had the reputation of being rather absent-minded. A story was told that one day he called his office and asked his secretary why he was at the Grand Central railroad station and where he was to go.

But Jerry was doing okay. He was looked upon by the other men as something of a one-man encyclopedia and, even more importantly, as a warm, sensitive human being to whom they could come with their problems. We got to see him once—on the day we were permitted outdoors for a spell, not in the main yard, but in a smaller area reserved for men in isolation or in transit. Jerry was on the other side of the wire fence that separated us from the larger yard. He was spearing discarded candy and cigarette wrappings and papers blown by the wind, depositing them in a large cloth bag hanging from his shoulder. This was his prison assignment. As he told us in the few minutes we had together, this job had been given him as a form of punishment. "But," said Jerry, "it has a good side to it; I'm in the open air."

We left with a warm feeling about Jerry. He could cope.

A letter I sent home on April 24, 1956, described the way I spent my time at Lewisburg:

> I am kept in complete isolation. I have a cell to myself. There is no chance to talk through cell bars, for the cells are walled off. Three times a day I leave the cell to go to the mess hall. When eating is over, I return. Once we were let out in the yard and once, thus far, to the library. Last night we also saw a movie. Other than that I've had to keep myself company. I can spend my time in two ways—either reading or listening to a central radio hookup through earphones. Except for listening to a ballgame each afternoon, I spend my time reading, with a bit of physical exercise a few times a day to break up the monotony and to keep in shape.
>
> There are two things for which I am indeed grateful—a good library and an outside window. While I was in the library only once, I was able to pick up a number of books which have kept me so absorbed that often the time has passed quite rapidly. . .
>
> As for the window, how can I explain it? It's like this: It gives me perspective. While all I can see ahead of me are other windows, I can get a direct glimpse at the sky and the sun's light comes into my cell. At West Street there are no windows. There, all air comes in by blowers. To have a window with fresh air coming in, to be able to look at the sky anytime I want, to see the clouds come and go and take on so many different shapes and shades, is like being out in the open instead of in prison.

The following day we were on our way again, to the prison at Chillicothe, Ohio, but spent only one night there, leaving the next morning for Terre Haute, Indiana. There Winnie and I had a solemn farewell; we had been through a great deal together.

I spent the night at Terre Haute and left in the morning for my final stop, the Big House at Leavenworth, Kansas. The trip from New York to Leavenworth took nine days.

3

Did They Really Know?

Not long after I turned myself in, a strange rumor began making the rounds: the FBI had known where I had been all along, but it served their purpose to let me remain at large. The inference was that Winston and I had served as patsies for the FBI, enabling them to keep tab on what we were doing as well as on those working with us.

Lil told me about this rumor on an early visit, while I was still at the West Street jail in New York awaiting trial on the bail-jumping charge. "Can it be," she asked, "that the FBI did know?"

"No honey," I replied. "They knew nothing. If they knew where I was, why did they hound the family so mercilessly? Why didn't they nab me before I turned myself in? They had ample advance notice. Wouldn't it have been a feather in J. Edgar Hoover's cap?"

"But can we be sure?" she countered. "Their harassment could have been a ruse to lull you into a false sense of security."

"I don't believe it," I replied. "It's Hoover's ploy to try and make the FBI look good—that they always get their man, and that the Party is so infiltrated that they know everything."

A bizarre incident soon after my arrival at West Street confirmed my view. I had been put through the customary degrading admittance procedure. Everything I had on me and all my clothes were taken from me. My mouth, rectum, armpits and groin were searched for contraband. All hairy parts of my body were dusted with DDT. I was fingerprinted. Mug shots were taken. Finally I was put in a cell. I heard the steel door clang shut.

I was emotionally exhausted by the events of the day and relieved to be alone at last. I lay down on the bunk, shut my eyes and tried to put the kaleidoscopic images whirling before me into some kind of order: the faces of the loved ones I had at last seen again; the crowding and tumult at Foley Square when I turned myself in; the newspaper men and their questions; the cameras grinding away, and the blessed ten minutes alone with the family in a bullpen while waiting for a judge to officially remand me to the West Street pen. Suddenly my reverie was broken by the grating sound of the cell door being racked open again.

It was the guard. I was to go back for another photo. This time I was told to remove my shirt to be photographed bare-chested. I was surprised at this request, for I recalled no such procedure when I had been here during the Foley Square trial in 1949. However, I complied with the order, and then was taken back to my cell.

About an hour later I was racked-out again, for still another photo. This time I was told to remove all my clothes. Startled at this order, I asked what it was all about. The guard merely mumbled that it was the warden's order, while the inmate operating the camera shrugged his shoulders and indicated by the look on his face that he was as perplexed as I.

Unable to make any other sense of the request, I thought this was an attempt to humiliate me in the eyes of the other men. I decided to give the authorities no satisfaction.

"Hell, no," I told the guard. "I'm taking off no clothes. I'll provide no such photograph. I know no prison regulations that call for that."

At a loss as to how to proceed, and apparently somewhat embarrassed by the business, the guard led me back to my cell. An explanation came the next morning, from the warden himself.

Frank Kenton had been the assistant warden during my nearly five-month imprisonment in 1949. That he was now the warden I knew only because a guard had referred to him the day before.

Kenton appeared in front of my cell without warning and stood there glaring at me through the bars. "So you've decided to make trouble," he said. "I warn you, Green, if you're looking for trouble, you've come to the right place. Remember, what you do here will influence where you're sent and how soon you get out. Better watch out!"

"I don't know what you're talking about, Mr. Kenton. If it's about the order to be photographed in the nude . . ."

"It's not for you to say how you should be photographed. You're a prisoner now, Green. Can't you get that into your thick skull?"

"You don't have to remind me of that," I replied, "and I'm not asking for any special treatment. But I'll accept no humiliations meant especially for me. I was sentenced once, unjustly so. I don't hold anyone here responsible for that. But I'm damned if you're going to sentence me again. I'll obey rules meant for all prisoners, but no others, and I'll not provide photos for someone's pornographic collection."

His face flared up as if he'd been slapped. "How dare you talk like that to me! I see you want to spend your time in the hole. My authority comes from the Bureau. They want that photo. They want to see how deep your tan is. From the looks of you, you spent time in the sun; it may have been in the South."

So that's it, I said to myself. To him all I could say was, "Since when, Mr. Kenton, is J. Edgar Hoover running this prison and giving you orders? As for going to the hole, I'm sure people on the outside will want to know why I was sent there."

Without another word, Warden Kenton walked away. I saw him a number of times during the weeks I stayed at West Street, but never again did he address me. (Many years later my FBI files confirmed that Kenton had indeed reported to Hoover about my suntan. What the files did not indicate, however, was whether the FBI had requested a nude photograph, or whether it had been Kenton's own bright idea.)

Yet the rumor that the FBI had known my whereabouts persisted.

It even came up again eight years later, after I was out of prison and making my first trip as a free man. I stopped in the nation's capital to visit with some friends. I also had lunch with newspaperman Ed Lahey, with whom I had maintained contact over the years. On this occasion we met at his Washington office in the National Press Building. He introduced his associates, and then we took the elevator to the Press Club dining room. After exchanging pleasantries about how well we each looked, and inquiries about our families, we began to talk about events in our country and the world. Ed was curious about what my plans were and whether I was writing a book on my prison experiences. "You should know, Gil," Ed said, "that the FBI claims it knew where you were all along. A bigwig told me so."

Astonished that this tall tale was still alive, I could only repeat my reasons for believing otherwise. But could it be that I was wrong, that they had in fact known? Years later I got the answer—incontrovertible and from the FBI's own files.

On March 7, 1955—a full year before I surrendered—the Chicago and New York offices of the FBI were told by the Washington headquarters that "several of the CP leaders have recently been released from jail, [and] there is a possibility that one or more of the Communist fugitives may decide to surrender." They were ordered to keep even closer surveillance of our families and attorneys, the directive stressing "the importance of having Bureau agents arrest the fugitives rather than allowing them to voluntarily surrender."

Obviously the FBI did *not* know then where we were and clearly could not nab Fred Fine, James Jackson or William Marron before they surrendered on their own eight months later. Nor did they know where Winston and I were before we surfaced.

And there is additional evidence: Three days before I surrendered, an FBI document (February 24, 1956) carried the full text of my press release that stated exactly when and where I would appear. Across the bottom of the page someone in the FBI, presumably Hoover, had written, *"This makes us look silly."* (See reproduction on back cover.)

On the day I turned myself in, the New York FBI received a telephone call from the International News Service. INS wanted to know whether there had been prior arrangement that "Green should not be arrested before 12 noon today when he was scheduled to give himself up at Foley Square." They also inquired why I had been permitted to speak for about ten minutes to the assembled crowd.

The reply was "No comment." But at the bottom of the page on which this incident was reported, there appears the handwritten comment: *"The fact is that we just didn't know where he was as has been the case of the other 'missing' Communists."*

Even after Winston and I were in custody, J. Edgar Hoover was determined to salvage something of the FBI's reputation. A new hunt began for clues that would lead back to where we had been, so the authorities could prosecute under the Federal harboring law those who had worked with and befriended us. How resolutely this hunt was pursued is also a matter of record.

Immediately after my arrest Hoover sent a teletype to the New York FBI ordering them to "conduct all feasible investigation to determine Green's whereabouts while in fugitive status and consider all harboring aspects of this situation. All logical leads, such as examination of clothing, etc., must be handled in an expeditious fashion and the Bureau should be kept fully informed of all developments."

First, they located the New York cabbie who had driven me to Foley Square. He told them that he had picked me up at the corner of Seventh Avenue and Barrow Streets at about 11:30 A.M. He said I had had no luggage. FBI agents were immediately dispatched to that Greenwich Village area with my photograph, and shopkeepers and building superintendents were quizzed as to whether they had seen me in the neighborhood.

The driver was also asked to turn over the $5 bill I had given him for fare. But he now had three $5 bills. They were all taken from him. Their serial numbers were checked with Washington to learn to which banks they had originally been issued and whether the serial numbers corresponded with U.S. Treasury bills issued "to Soviet establishments." This hunt brought "negative results," according to the report.

Needless to say, everything I had on me when I surrendered was sent to the FBI laboratory for tests: shirt, trousers, tie, jacket, shoes, topcoat, socks, a small looseleaf notebook and a two-inch toothpick wrapper. Page after page of FBI records over many weeks detail the results of this sorry investigation. For illustration, here is the story of my shirt.

It was, the sleuths reported, of cotton and dacron, bought in a Bond Store and manufactured in a Bond shirt factory in Meridian, Mississippi. Light blue in color, it had a 15½-inch collar and 34-inch sleeves; its style was 9802-D, its cutting order, 5811. This style, color and shirt size had evidently been distributed in specifically named quantities to Bond stores located in fifteen cities across the U.S. The FBI in each area was ordered "to conduct appropriate investigation at stores indicated." FBI agents, armed with my photograph, scurried around asking store salesmen whether they recalled selling a shirt of that kind to someone like the man in the photo.

A typical response came from Cleveland: A salesman had identified me from the photo. He told the agent that he remembered me because I was a "unique customer." I had, he said, asked for this particular type of shirt and knew exactly what I wanted before making the purchase. With this vital clue, the Cleveland FBI wired Hoover:

"(Cleveland) will contact hotels and motels in the CV area and exhibit photo of subject in an effort to ascertain if subject in CV during above period."

There was also something unique about my necktie. The tie came from Carson Pirie Scott, a Chicago department store. When an FBI agent asked the store management whether they recalled who had bought a red silk tie with blue and red dots, such as the one I wore, they thought he was nuts. The agent was reminded that the store sold approximately 110,000 neckties a year. Moreover, this particular tie "from its pattern and width, was one which has not been handled by Carson Pirie Scott for at least two years, and from its appearance, could be five or six years old."

The management was right. The necktie had been given to me by my sister-in-law Florence, who never forgets a family birthday. I had worn it on the day I disappeared.

My shoes gave the FBI even greater trouble. They were mahogany color, low-cut, and manufactured (according to the inside marking) by the Burbank Shoe Company. But try as it might, the FBI was unable to track down such a company, whether shoe manufacturer or retailer, not even in the six American cities named Burbank. This fact did indeed appear suspicious. Why was the name of a nonexistent firm on the inside of the shoes?

The explanation seems to stem from the fact that they were shoes bought on sale in an Army-Navy surplus store. Perhaps they were rejects, and the manufacturer had stipulated that its trade name could not appear on the shoes, or maybe they had been manufactured in a federal prison industry for Army use, their sale on the open market forbidden. Whatever the reason, the fact remains that the shoes needed a name, and obviously Burbank had been invented to conceal the real manufacturer's identity.

The paper on which I had typed the notices to the press announcing when I would surrender was also subject to laboratory analysis. It was Permanized Plover Onionskin, produced by the Plover Paper Company. When the FBI sought to learn how much of this paper had been produced and where it was sold, they were told that approximately 20,000 pounds were manufactured every week to ten days, and it was sold throughout the United States.

So it went with one mysterious item after another: a wild-goose chase that cost the taxpayers tens of thousands of dollars and led exactly nowhere.

4
Quarantine

Leavenworth. First, the fort in 1827, to protect traffic on the old Santa Fe trail. Then came the city of Leavenworth, settled nearby in 1854 and considered the oldest in Kansas. The first prison was a military one, built on the grounds of Fort Leavenworth in 1873. Later it was transferred to the Department of Justice. Since it was considered unsuitable for maximum-security confinement, in 1896 Congress authorized a new penitentiary, which was built mainly by convict labor.

At this "new" prison, four cellhouses radiated from a central rotunda in which were situated the administrative offices, mess hall, kitchen and chapel-auditorium. An immense dome hung over the rotunda. Most of the cells measured 5½ by 9 feet and were for single occupancy. One cellblock, Cellhouse A, was divided into larger four-man cells. Initially the prison had been built to hold a maximum of 1,640 men, but during my stay the population fluctuated around 2,500. This was made possible by the use of double-decker bunks, converting many single cells into double-occupancy and four-man cells into eight-man cells.

The entire complex, including adjacent buildings, was enclosed by a high, thick brick wall. Some said it was 40 feet high; others, 30 feet. Only minimum-security men, those with little time left to do or others who had been completely tamed by institutionalization, were permitted outside the big wall to work on the prison farm.

At a cursory glance from the outside, the penitentiary resembled a medieval walled city. Even the towers and parapets were in place; only a moat was missing, but the walls at Leavenworth were to keep those inside from breaking out, not those outside from breaking in.

I spent my first month in quarantine (officially called "OA") for orientation and adjustment. Quarantine did not mean isolation, for sixty of us were herded into a dormitory pen. We were all recent transfers from other prison installations and all of us were white. The Black prisoners who had traveled with us from Terre Haute had been segregated immediately after arrival.

The dormitory was large and served as both sleeping and living quarters. Double-decker bunks jutted from the walls the length and width of the room, with barely enough space between to keep men from bumping into one another. A few small tables and chairs were placed around the room, but most of the "activity" took place at the bunks. Small knots of men would gather just to gab, or to play cards, checkers, chess or dominoes, or to kibitz others who played. Inmates would sit crosslegged on the floor or perch on a lower bunk used as a table. Because a lower bunk was also easier to climb in and out of, it was preferred to an upper. But neon light fixtures were on the ceiling, making the upper bunk more desirable for reading, so that was my choice.

We had little to do but kill time while doing time. The orientation sessions were boringly meaningless and blessedly few. Most of the men, the majority of whom were repeaters, took the talks on rehabilitation as a huge joke. I learned far more from them than from the fatuous lectures intoned to us. All of the formal preliminary rigamarole, including the so-called medical exam and IQ tests, could have been completed in a few days. Yet we remained in OA a full month.

One day I was seated before a young man in his mid-thirties who had brown hair, gray eyes and a lean muscular appearance. He wore a white hospital smock over white trousers, and a white shirt open at the collar. He had an air of authority, and appeared to be a doctor. Actually, he was an inmate, the hospital clerk.

"73-335? Green?"

I nodded, and he reached for the questionnaire in my hand. "I see you're in pretty good shape—no chronic or contagious trouble, no syph, no record of mental illness. Good."

This was all part of preparing me for admission to "general population," he explained. Then he glanced at the paper in his hand, looked at me quizzically, and asked, "What did you bring with you? A nickel, a dime, a quarter or a dollar?"

Puzzled, I was sure I had misunderstood. "I'm somewhat hard of hearing," I mumbled apologetically. "I didn't get your question. Would you mind repeating it?"

"All I'm asking, man, is what did you bring with you—a nickel, a dime, a quarter or a dollar?"

This time I knew I could not blame my ears. What was this about? I thought. He knows I brought no money with me, that it was all taken away when I was arrested. He also knows that it's a highly punishable offense to be found with currency in a federal pen. What then does he mean? Is this his idea of a joke—or a trap?

"I don't know what you're talking about. You know that I brought nothing with me."

He glared at me incredulously. "Man," he burst out, "don't get funny with me. I'm asking you for the last time, what did you bring with you?"

"And I'm telling you for the last time, nothing."

Speechless, he looked at me menacingly, and then, suddenly, it seemed as if my own state of bewilderment engulfed him, too. "Tell me, man," he asked, this time in subdued voice, "what in the hell are you in for anyway?"

Relieved at a question I could readily answer, and hoping that somehow this would help me get out of the present jam, I responded, "I'm a Communist; I'm in for my political beliefs."

Bafflement faded from his face as he began to chuckle. "Well, I'll be a sonofabitch! Another square in Leavenworth! What I'm simply asking you man, is how many years did they give you? Five, ten, twenty-five—or life?"

"Oh," I replied, with a smile, "I brought eight cents with me—five for being a Communist and three more for not turning myself in on time."

In talking with the prisoners I learned something about the prison system I had not known before. Quarantine's real purpose was psychological. Being cooped up with nothing to do made us look forward to entering the prison population as though that would indeed be freedom. We envied the men who had work to do that took them outside their cells. We envied them their long Saturday and Sunday daylight hours in the yard. (We were limited to one hour a day in a small secluded area.) We also wanted the right to buy things in the commissary—cigarettes, fruit, candy.

Men more prison-wise than I helped me to see the long-range motives behind quarantine. Strange as this may seem to some, even prison requires a degree of consensus. Since all the real work is done by inmates, should they go on a prolonged strike or refuse to obey prison rules, everything would come to a halt, and violence could take over. Hence they must be made to accept their imprisonment as a fact they cannot alter, to which end the prison authorities find they have to make such small concessions as will win a modicum of cooperation.

In a quarantine, we learned that we had no rights, only privileges granted us, and that these could easily be taken away. There was always "the hole" for those who defied authority or disobeyed prison rules. There were also the refined distinctions between minimum, medium, and maximum security inside each institution and among the different prisons of the Federal system. All thirty-six U.S. installations—penitentiaries, reformatories or correctional institutions—were but separate links in a highly integrated and centralized prison chain. Men considered unruly in Leavenworth could be shipped to Alcatraz, "the Rock" in San Francisco Bay, where conditions were harshest. There the men had no commissary privileges, not even the right to daily newspapers. Inmates in lesser-security prisons were "privileged" with electrified, barbed-wire fences instead of a big wall, but could always be threatened with transfer to Atlanta or Leavenworth—both regarded as tougher places in which to do time. The Bureau of Prisons also had the power to recommend or withhold parole, to give meritorious "good time" or take it away.

Quarantine therefore prepared us psychologically to accept conditions we would certainly abhor but which we knew could be made still worse.

At first, the only reading matter I had available in OA was the paperback whodunits borrowed from other men. These had never held interest for me, even less so now. But finally we were taken to the library. It boasted some 26,000 books, gathered over more than half a century. (I later learned that the library had once had a number of shelves of Marxist and socialist books, but these were removed—actually destroyed—at the height of the McCarthy frenzy.) There were many books on history, economics, philosophy and the natural sciences. There was also a full range of classical literature and current fiction. This was one gleam in the darkness.

One of the first books I borrowed was *The Friendly Arctic* by the renowned explorer Vilhjalmur Stefansson. My brother Ben had recommended it. He thought it held a moral for me. It did, in fact. Stefansson stressed that life in the Arctic was not all barren or friendless. The same could be said of prison, but with this immense difference: Stefansson was in the Arctic by choice, and for scientific purposes. I was in prison under compulsion, for punitive purposes.

Even before reading this fascinating book I had reflected on how to make prison life somewhat less unbearable. A guard at West Street, a Black man who had been friendly to Henry Winston and me, said to us before we were transferred to Federal penitentiaries: "Don't serve time, let time serve you." It was a standard line, but he was not preaching rehabilitation; he had already told us he didn't believe we belonged in prison. So his advice was something to think about.

My visit to the library in Leavenworth helped convince me that I could make the time serve me, at least to some extent. I began outlining a general approach. First, I decided that I was not going to become a jailhouse lawyer, plowing through heavy legal tomes to find a gimmick that would miraculously spring me. I knew that some had done so, and with considerable success. But I was fortunate in having the services of excellent lawyers, in whom I had complete confidence. It didn't make sense, therefore, for me to try and quarterback them.

I was a victim of political hysteria, and I recognized that only an improvement in the political climate could help reduce my sentence. If this came about, and I fervently hoped it would, fine. But if it didn't, I had no intention of watching the clock and counting the hours and days. I could keep time by checking off only the holidays and years.

The library offered me the opportunity to become a more knowledgeable person. I would not bemoan the years as a total loss. A program of self-study would help me mentally flee the prison walls for extended periods of time.

I decided to concentrate on three subjects: Spanish, a language I always wanted to learn, world history and anthropology. I would have liked to include the writing of articles or a book, but I was warned in advance by the parole office that my writing was strictly limited to three letters a week—"and nothing else." I was cautioned against trying to keep a prison diary, even against referring to prison matters in my letters home.

My study plan was not meant to turn me into a recluse or a

bookworm. On the contrary, during working hours, yard time, and any other periods when not locked into a cell, I would make friends, participate fully in prison life, and engage in physical sports and exercise to keep my body active. Physical exercise was to be a daily ritual, in the open air when possible, in my cell when not.

I also decided on something that may seem trivial to those on the outside: to shave every morning, even when I didn't feel like doing so. I had noticed that men who did not, who were slovenly in appearance despite strict rules to the contrary, were frequently on the verge of demoralization. I knew this would not happen to me, but I wanted everyone, especially those in authority, to know that they were not going to get me down.

As the weeks passed I grew more and more impatient to get into the general population, for more than one reason. I hadn't seen Lil and the children since I left West Street and was, of course, eager to see them as soon as possible. This could not happen until I left quarantine. And, as soon as I had learned that I was being sent to Leavenworth, I had begun to look forward to seeing my friend and comrade Gus Hall again. He had been in Leavenworth for the past four years. I wanted to compare notes with him about developments outside prison walls, to learn what I could expect and what to look out for, inside the walls. I also knew that through him I could more rapidly get to meet other prisoners I should know.

I entered quarantine on April 27 and left it on May 30. On May 29, I appeared before the Classification Committee for an institutional work assignment. The committee included the prison bigwigs—the warden, two associate wardens, the chief parole officer and a few others. I was struck with the resemblance of the scene to that of a board of director's room of a large corporation as depicted in a Hollywood movie. Smug, self-important fellows seated around a large handsome mahogany table.

As I stood before them, the warden came right to the point. "Green," he said, "now that you are leaving OA, what kind of work would you like to do?"

"Well, sir," I said, (the "sir" was obligatory) "my preference is to work in one of the prison's industrial shops, where I can earn something toward my family's upkeep. But as I have been told that such an assignment is not available to me at the beginning, I thought I might work in the library. I have had some experience of this kind at West Street."

If I thought my mention of West Street would be a recommendation, I couldn't have been more mistaken. "Do you know what a tuckpointer is?" the warden asked.

"No, sir," I replied, "I do not."

"Well, Green, that needn't bother you, you'll find out fast enough. That's what you're going to be."

I had never heard of a tuckpointer. I would have guessed it was some kind of hunting dog. Tuckpointing, I learned, is the craft of repairing outside building walls, working on a scaffold, and knocking out loose mortar and cracked or broken bricks with a pneumatic hammer and replacing them with new mortar and bricks.

I became part of Labor Gang #4 and immediately earned the monicker "old man." I was fifty years old; the others averaged half my age. Needless to say, the walls we worked on did not include the *big* wall.

5

Cellhouse A

Cellhouse A was the largest of the four cellhouses, and held more than a thousand convicts. When I first entered, I was overwhelmed by the sight of iron and steel everywhere. I had seen exposed steel skeletons of buildings under construction, but here the mass of steel was internalized in the building's bowels.

It was as if a giant hand had piled immense steel cages one on top of the other five stories high and for the length of the building. The first row of cages was on the ground floor, the stone flag. The others were on tiers above, surrounded by a steel walkway reached from a circular iron stairway. The cell block occupied the center of the structure and was separated from the walls by fifteen or twenty feet of open space. Thus the windows could not be reached from the cells and could only be raised or lowered by a device operated from the stone flag. Men who wanted more air would set up a howl, "Open the windows! Open the windows!" in the hope, often a vain one, that a guard would respond. Periodically bedlam broke loose, with some shouting for the windows to be opened while others wanted them shut. And sometimes an inmate, determined to get more air, took things into his own hands, especially if he had a good pitching arm. Then the sound of crashing glass indicated that a hard object had reached its mark.

Each cell had three sides of solid steel and one with steel bars. The door also had bars and was opened or shut electrically from controls at the end of the tier near the spiral stairway.

It was a world of cold heartless steel. Even the blistering heat of a Kansas summer could not melt the icy oppressiveness.

I had been moved into an eight-man cell on the third tier. It was a white tier, as were the two below. Above me were two Black tiers. Their occupants had to do more climbing, sometimes as often as six and seven times a day, and also suffered most from the unbearable summer heat.

The cell furnishings were Spartan: four double-decker bunks with lockers below; a small square table and several chairs; a couple of shelves for books; two washbasins with space above for toilet articles, and two "stools," with only the bare bowl to sit on. Privacy was a world away.

Sunlight trickled through dimly; the windows were too far off. Even during the day, most of the light came from two 60-watt bulbs dangling from the ceiling. These were hardly adequate for comfortable reading, but that was the only size available. The inmates met this problem in a typically resourceful fashion. When a new bulb was screwed into the socket, it would be slapped firmly once or twice with a towel until the filaments suddenly flared up and threw off an illumination nearly twice as bright.

This, of course, shortened the life of the bulb—but who cared? If the authorities were on to this device, they wisely refrained from making it an issue.

Even this ingenuity didn't help me. One night, while reading, I was baffled to find the printed words playing hide and seek with me. So I got my first pair of reading glasses. Poor light and diet may have been contributing factors, but an honest glance in the mirror pointed to the main one—I was getting older and my eyesight was not what it had been.

Life in Leavenworth was completely regimented. We were up at 6:15 a.m. and were ready for the head count soon after. Breakfast, like all meals, took place in two shifts, since the dining room was not large enough to accommodate all the men at one time. A separate, smaller shift of kitchen help ate much earlier. Except for this crew, all work began at 8:30 a.m. The day was broken up by four or five counts; one or more counts took place as we slept. When awake, it was a "standup count," each man close to the bars. Sometimes the count had to be repeated a number of times before the correct total was reached and the "all-accounted-for" signal could be given. We ate in shifts, alternating both by cellhouse and tier. Each tier was "racked out" only when its turn came.

Bells and gongs signalled all moves, so it was possible to approximate the time of day. Not everyone wore one of the cheap wristwatches that could be bought in the commissary. The regimentation served a double purpose—to keep better physical control over us, and to induce a form of psychological dependence.

We were being conditioned to the bells and the oral commands so that—like Pavlov's dogs—our reflexes would become completely automatic. The men resisted this institutionalization in many ways, but the longer one was subjected to it, the harder it was to avoid. Some men had become so institutionalized that if a bell failed to ring within an established period of time, they would become irritable, as though about to miss an important date.

Stan was such a one. I had met him during my spell in quarantine. He had asked me to help him fill out his questionnaire. He was quiet, unassuming, about 35, with thinning brown hair and gray eyes. His hometown was Cincinnati, but he had not been there in years. He was a repeater, as he told me, in and out of jail many times. Yet he didn't have the swagger of some repeaters and didn't try to impress me with his prison wisdom. As we got to know each other better, it became clear that he was not too bright and that some of his scrapes with the law were for the dumbest things imaginable. His last escapade had been stealing a Ford, taking it across state lines—a Federal offense—and then trying to sell it to a dealer. His actions made no sense unless they indicated, possibly, a subconscious desire to be returned to prison, preferably a Federal one.

Stan told me that he never knew his parents. He grew up in an orphanage. When he was old enough to get a job, he was released for work in a restaurant as a dishwasher. He neither liked nor disliked the job. He simply could not cope outside an institution. Little bits of wisdom that children pick up at home automatically—such as that every marketable object has a price, which can or cannot be afforded—Stan never learned. He relished the idea of buying things himself, but was unable to relate purchases to income. He was always short of cash, especially at the end of the month when room rent was due. He took to petty thievery and soon landed in a reformatory. That was the beginning of his prison career. While locked up, he always yearned to get out, but once he was released the cycle only repeated itself.

It is true that Stan was somewhat simple-minded, but that cannot be said of another convict I met, though only once, who also suffered from psychologically disabling institutionalization. His name was similar to mine, and as a result our prison records got mixed up. When I applied for my own under the Freedom of Information Act years later, his file was sent to me. Of course I returned it.

This man was about my age. He had spent more than twenty-five years in and out of prison. He had done time for auto theft, burglary, robbery, hijacking, grand larceny, and counterfeiting. *In prison,* his record was perfect: He caused no trouble, cooperated fully with the authorities, and had an exceptionally good work record. He had great mechanical talent and took immense pride in his workmanship.

In one prison he had been asked to solve an extremely complicated problem which required inventing a completely new mechanical device. He met this challenge with confidence and determination. The F.O.I.A. report said he had worked "long hours on his own time," including Saturdays and Sundays. He needed no supervision, although his work was in a machineshop where he could have, had he so desired, fashioned steel weapons for a possible escape attempt. He succeeded in building the needed machine entirely from "parts taken from our salvage yard," the report said. In recognition of this achievement he received a "meritorious award for work, ingenuity and tenacity surpassing all expectations."

In another penal institution he rebuilt all the dental equipment, including the X-ray machine. His superiors reported that he "can do about anything he sets his mind to do in the mechanical field."

So impressed were the authorities with this man's prison record and mechanical ability that they decided to go out of their way to find him the kind of job he could really relate to. They found one that offered him an average starting wage and the promise of rapid upgradings based on performance. He was happy about this opportunity, and left prison with enough money, accumulated from prison work, to get him to St. Louis and to tide him over until his first paycheck. But he never got there. Instead, he became involved in a number of scrapes along the way and was finally sent back for violation of parole.

Here was a man who loved to work at challenging jobs, but only in prison. On the outside, he just couldn't make it, even for a few days, so thoroughly had he become institutionalized.

During my years in the underground I had developed an erratic sleep pattern. I turned off the lights only when drowsiness came, but then I would sleep for only from ten minutes to an hour. I soon learned that tossing in bed was more enervating than loss of sleep, so I would turn on the lights, get a can of beer from the kitchen refrigerator, and read until my eyelids grew heavy again. After that I would sleep soundly, usually for the rest of the night.

I wondered how I would handle this routine in prison, where the lights went out at ten p.m., there was no switch for me to turn on, and there certainly was no refrigerator containing beer. It was a needless worry. Sometimes it would take me a while to fall asleep, but once I did, I generally slept through the night. It seems that even while sleeping I knew there was no other recourse—and I slept.

I got along well with the men in my cell, although—as at West Street—they first tried to check me out to see if I was "for real." None of them had ever met a Communist in the flesh, and some of them were convinced that I must have a "pile stashed away"; no one, they felt, would risk a long prison term "for nothing."

To get to know them better and to have them accept me as a regular guy, I had to forgo much of my reading plan for cell activites. After the evening yard period I would generally become the fourth hand in a bridge game. Once I agreed to play the first time, I was hooked—I was the only fourth hand available in the cell. The card game became an almost nightly routine. When it was not on, the single chess player in the cell was after me for "just one game" with him. I had foresworn chess a few years back—while in the underground—having found that Lord Byron was right: Life is too short for chess. But I couldn't say no under these circumstances.

The bridge game was played for "money," which in prison means cigarettes, preferably Camels. Why Camels? I never learned. Was someone in the commissary getting a kickback from the company? Or had it infiltrated one of its advertising men into prison? Whatever the reason, it was for Camels that we played. The stakes were low—single cigarettes, not packs—but the men wouldn't think of just playing for the fun of it. A bit of betting lent a bit of spice to the game, brought excitement to their lives.

Not realizing this, at the very beginning I made a gaffe. It didn't matter to me whether I lost or won a few cigarettes (I had by that time given up smoking), so I should have cheated in reverse, playing to lose. Instead, my bridge partner and I won our first game. Call it luck. My partner was elated, but the two who lost insisted on getting even. Without any desire or enthusiasm on my part, I perforce became a bridge player. But I also determined to get into a one-man cell as soon as possible.

Playing cards for cigarettes was the very mildest form of prison gambling. Men wagered, sometimes heavily, on every sports event—who would win a ball game, the pennant, a championship bout. It was, of course, one way of escaping the boredom of prison life, of participating in exciting events outside the walls. Those who loved to play the horses spent long hours figuring out their own systems for beating the track. One, I recall, advocated playing the jockey instead of the horse; the more modest the jockey's reputation, the better the choice. The logic behind this was that every jockey had to win sometime, otherwise why would the stable have hired him? Thus, if a $2 ante were doubled each time the jockey lost, the winnings would be fabulous when he finally placed.

After a major sports event so many cartons of cigarettes changed hands that the big gamblers had to worry about where to stash them. The loot could not be kept in their own lockers, for often it would not fit. But even if it did, there was another problem. According to regulations, no prisoner could possess more than $15 worth of commissary items at any one time. That was the amount he was permitted to spend per month. Everything above that amount was regarded as contraband. The solution was to get non-smokers to store cartons for those who did smoke. Thus my locker usually held cartons of cigarettes that belonged to others.

Gambling frequently led to bloodshed. When a man's debt to another became too great and he had no means of repayment in prison, honor required that the debt be met through intermediaries on the outside. Inmates who found themselves in this fix, fearing for their lives, would often ask for institutional protection—being placed in cells isolated from the rest of the prison population.

Sometimes cells were entered and the lockers broken into when their occupants were at work, at mess or in the yard. At least two men generally collaborated in such heists. One would do the actual break-in—most of the time on his own tier, where he knew when the men would be back—rapidly passing the loot to the accomplice, who was either on the tier below or that above. If the loss was reported, the cells on the tier would be searched, but of course nothing suspicious would turn up.

In one episode, two men in my cell were suspected. Both came from the Deep South and lived somewhat apart from the rest of us, to the extent that was possible in our crowded circumstances. What made them suspect was that cartons of cigarettes were constantly being moved in and out of their lockers. These transfers could have been for their gambling winnings or losses, but it didn't seem so to us.

One night our cell was suddenly shaken down by the guards and a knife was found hidden behind a narrow ledge on which the door slid open and shut. From the manner in which the search was conducted, it seemed the prison authorities knew what they were looking for. But from the way we were shoved down the stairs and out of the cellhouse to the central offices it appeared that they did *not* know, or at least were not sure, to whom the weapon belonged, or how many of us were involved.

We were interviewed one at a time. I was the first to be questioned. Robert J. Kaiser, an associate warden, conducted the probe. "You're new here, Green, and I hate to see you involved in something as serious as this. But you can help us and yourself. Whose knife was it? You better tell us."

"What knife, sir?" I asked, "I never saw or heard of one until a few minutes ago"—which was the truth.

"Don't tell me that, Green. You had to know, living in the cell. Why do you want to cover up for others? You have nothing in common with them. You're not a criminal."

"I'm not, sir? Then what am I doing here? So long as I'm here, I have a great deal in common with the other men. But as I've told you, I know nothing about a knife. Had I known, I certainly would have been disturbed—it could have been meant for me. As you know, sir, one of my co-defendants had his skull crushed at West Street."

"But if you don't know, you must suspect someone. Who?"

"I suspect no one. This whole thing may be a frameup."

The interview ended with a warning that unless they got to the bottom of this, all of us would be thrown in the hole until they did. That did not happen. One of the two we suspected squealed on the other. We never saw either of them again.

This episode further strengthened my determination to get into a single cell as soon as possible. I sent a copout to the warden, mentioning the matter of the knife and asking for a single cell.

There were some men who could, even had to, live in a fish tank all the time, but I needed time to myself. Being with others was fine—but not *all* the time.

6

The Yard

My first visit to the main yard was on May 30, 1956, the day I was released from quarantine. I had looked forward to this event with genuine anticipation. It would mean more time in the open air and sunshine. Then, too, I would meet Gus Hall again. He had sent me greetings via the prison grapevine and knew the day I would be released to the general population. I found him walking along the big wall at the far end of the ballfield.

The markings of the baseball diamond were evident as I first entered the yard. Behind home plate were solid concrete bleachers, built like the stepped rows of a typewriter keyboard. The bleachers could hold from four to five hundred men. No baseball was being played, but men were sunbathing with their shirts off; some were chatting, while others concentrated on chess or card games. In left field, in a straight line from third base, fellows were lifting weights. Some were holding their breath as they raised heavy iron bars over their heads, then the air was forcefully ejected as the bars dropped to the ground with a bang. To the extreme far left, the big wall had been marked off into courts, where perspiring men were swatting small, hard, black handballs.

On the opposite side of the yard, in a direct line from first base, some twenty men were seated on the ground or on stools, strumming or plucking string instruments. Near them a smaller group of Mexican mariachis were plaintively crooning their ranchero songs to the accompaniment of their guitars.

Except for the human animation, the yard would have been a dismal place indeed. Its soil was barren and parched, with only a few tufts of grass and several scrawny trees. But I was immensely grateful for the open space, the scanty green leaves, the broiling sun, the sight of men relaxing, and the chance this offered to escape from time to time the oppressive steel trap of a cellhouse. Even the big wall lost some of its ugly symbolism when men could play handball against it.

Gus and I exchanged hearty embraces, inquired about each other's health and family and swapped news. He looked well, although he had lost considerable weight, some of it because of stomach ulcers. The greasy prison food had not agreed with him, he reported. Yet he was in good humor. He had friends among the men, and was liked and respected. Gus told me he worked in the shoe factory office as a piecework checker. This, I learned, was an important job that helped assure the men an honest count in calculating their meager piecework earnings.

Soon I met two of Gus's friends: Jim Leather, who worked in the butcher shop, and Tom Kilbane, who was in the shoe factory office. Both were extremely intelligent men, and I got to know them well. I also met Oscar Collazo, Ervin Flores Rodriguez and Julio Pinto Gandia, three Puerto Rican pro-independence political prisoners. Soon my association with them, as well as with one of their comrades, Rafael Cancel Miranda, (after he was transferred from Alcatraz to Leavenworth) became close. They patiently corrected my mutilation of their beautiful Spanish language as we paced the yard. From them I also learned a great deal more of the history of Puerto Rico and the struggles of its people.

That first afternoon I sat with Gus in the bleachers and watched my first Leavenworth softball game. A few days later I played a game of handball doubles with Gus as my partner. I do not recall who won, which may well indicate that we two did not. In any event, I was getting to meet people and rapidly becoming part of Leavenworth yard society.

It was fortunate for me that Gus was there when I arrived. He made it easier for me to learn whom to trust and whom to avoid. Gus was by now a "short timer"; had less than a year to do. We spent many hours in the yard (the only place we could meet, since he bunked in Cellhouse D) discussing the events outside prison walls—national and world developments, and problems facing the Party.

Gus was not the only Communist to serve time in Leavenworth; some others had left by the time I arrived. Irving Potash and Carl Winter, two of my co-defendants in the Foley Square trial, had been there, as had Sid Steinberg and Sam Coleman, sentenced for harboring Bob Thompson in California. Sid, I learned, had built his own guitar in prison and was remembered as the guy who could play chess blindfolded against a number of men simultaneously—and beat them all.

On Saturday afternoon, if the weather was bad and the yard forbidding, I would sometimes go to see the regular weekly movie, although generally it left me with mingled feelings. One could be carried away by love scenes (even of the spurious Hollywood variety), or by portrayals of families with children living normal lives, but the letdown when the lights turned on again was hard to bear. I did watch some of the films, and thus learned something about the psychology of inmates at Leavenworth that I would not have fathomed otherwise.

My first surprise came at a typical cops-and-robbers film—the men were cheering the defenders of the law instead of the culprits. This was true except when the "bad guy" was portrayed as a sort of Robin Hood—or when he was a person of great courage and good looks, clever at outwitting the louts portrayed as representatives of the law. Generally it was the detectives, sheriffs and police in the films who possessed human qualities, and the hunted were the inhuman ones, so the men identified with the former. Regardless of the crimes they may have committed, the convicts saw themselves not as depraved but as human beings, victims not only of circumstances but above all of society. Often they would refer to those fellow prisoners they despised as animals, regarding themselves as different.

Surprising, too, was their reaction to sentimental scenes or those depicting deep physical or emotional suffering. In the darkened movie theater I would spot men drying their eyes, sniffling, or blowing their noses. Often, as we left at the end of the film, one could see reddened eyes. Some were men who boasted of their toughness—they were going to "get" someone when they got out—but in the theater, swept along by the human drama they were watching, their own buried humanity emerged. While they identified with the pain suffered by others, their eyes also welled with tears for themselves.

7

Pinpricks

Lil and the children came to visit me on May 31, the day after I entered the general population. Regulations limited visits to two hours a month, so we could get in another visit in June.

Seeing them again was both joyful and painful. We were not permitted to embrace, hold hands, or even touch. Our conversation took place over a glass divider. We talked about many things: what they were doing, their plans for the summer, my mother's health and her recent marriage, my first impressions of Leavenworth, how Gus was getting on, and news of friends outside. We agreed that the time had come for my mother to visit me, if possible in June. We also discussed a new problem.

Only those men who worked in prison industry could have weekend visits. Those, like myself, who were on maintenance jobs, were to have visits only on weekdays. But Lil's office job required that she be on hand every day; there was no one to replace her. I had sent copouts to the warden and the associate wardens explaining this situation and asking either that she be permitted to come on weekends or better still, that I be transferred to an industry job. I had applied for industry work before, and knew that of the men in quarantine with me who had asked for such assignment, I was the only one put off.

Having learned from Gus that his request for industry work had been favorably acted upon soon after it was made, Lil and I decided to be patient while continuing to press for that solution.

When our family visit was over I was given no chance to bask in its afterglow. Immediately I was ordered to strip, thoroughly searched, and subjected to the humiliating act described by the inmates as "asshole inspection." When I reached my cell I threw myself on the bunk; angry, frustrated, bitter. It was to be like this after every visit.

Other problems soon surfaced. I was informed that Edwin Lahey had been turned down as a non-family correspondent, because, they said, he was a newspaperman. And days would pass without letters from home. This worried me, for I knew that Lil typed a letter to me every morning upon getting to her office. Was she sick? Was there something wrong with the children? Was bad news being kept from me?

I soon got the answer. Letters that Lil and Ben had sent me had been confiscated and placed in my "institutional jacket." My own letters to them had suffered a similar fate, allegedly because they referred to political events in the United States and abroad. All of us received a curt warning from Warden Looney that correspondence was not a right but a privilege, which would be withdrawn if we persisted in writing on political matters. (I was only recently able to read the letters sent to me that had been confiscated—in my FOIA files.)

My brother Ben wrote to my attorney, John Abt, asking for advice. Abt urged that we "cool it" for a while. This we did. However, the same kind of petty badgering was to continue over the years. To cite only one example, my prison files contain a copout I sent to Associate Warden Kaiser on June 22, 1960, four years after the first incidents:

> Dear Sir:
>
> I am at a loss to understand your action and your explanation for it. I am not writing for publication! If any letter of mine has been published I'd certainly like to know about it. My letters are letters and nothing else. Certainly I refer to and discuss world events. What else am I to write about?—my life here? Or am I to be limited to meaningless "I am well; how are you?" type of letters? It seems to me that I owe something to my correspondents; namely, to write them intelligent letters on matters of common interest. To do less would be to insult them. What harm is there in expressing my views? Or am I to be muzzled even in respect to members of my own family?

Mr. Kaiser never deigned to reply.

My prison files confirm that even the privileged confidential relationship of lawyer and client was violated. My conversations with John Abt were systematically monitored. John visited me about twice a year. We discussed possible or pending court appeals; whether to apply for and the chances of getting parole or clemency; the status of the amnesty movement, and the many problems I faced with prison authorities. When these subjects had been covered, if time permitted, naturally I would utilize the opportunity to learn what I could about events outside. I had known John and his wife, Jessica Smith, for many years; they were my close friends. Certainly I could not confine a visit from him strictly to legal matters.

The authorities had neither a moral nor legal right to monitor our conversations. It was clearly unlawful for them to tune in on discussions relating to possible legal moves. Nevertheless, they did. On October 22, 1958, the warden informed officials in Washington that "Mr. Abt is quite likely deeply involved in the Communist movement in addition to serving as their legal counsel. At least it would appear so *from the conversations audited.*" (Emphasis added.) In the margin of this letter appear the words, "well known."

Sometime later there was talk of forbidding visits from Abt. But this scheme was abandoned for it "would not change the situation much, since the wife and brothers are heartily in accord with Green's feelings and could likewise serve as couriers [sic] if he so desired."

The local FBI chief, who was in on all this, refused to recommend either approval or disapproval of Abt's visits. What this gent was interested in was "cooperation from institutional officers in providing information that might be gleaned from the interviews that would be of importance to the welfare of the nation." Citing this high-minded motive of the FBI, the new warden, J. C. Taylor, wrote to the director of prisons: "Although we hesitate to infringe upon the confidential relationship of Attorney Abt and his client, the activities of these people are certainly not in the best interests of the country."

Only one report of an alleged conversation between Abt and myself appears in my prison files; that is, in the truncated portion I was able to get under the FOIA. This purported record of what we are supposed to have said is a complete and total fabrication. A sample should prove this: "Conversation then drifted to Harrisburg where Irving is a leader. Jerry and Edna are organizers. Organizing cells is progressing in leaps. Everything is okay. Some money is to be split between Edna and the Chicago cell."

This "conversation" is pure invention. I never knew anything of "organizing efforts" in Harrisburg; did not know who Jerry, Irving and the other names referred to were (if they existed at all); nor were Party branches called "cells." This stuff was straight from James Bond.

The reason for such planted gibberish was made clear a bit further on. "Abt," the alleged report continues, "was talking about a trip to Russia, where he was given rubles (he was sent there as a delegate of a union). Abt told Green that while he was in Russia, he conversed with Khrushchev. 'When they come to the United States, we will take care of them'."

So linkage is established—from Abt, to the USSR, to rubles, to Khrushchev, and to the promise to take care of "them"—whoever "they" may be—when "they" come to the United States.

What a clumsy attempt at a frameup! Abt *did* visit the Soviet Union, as part of an official CIO delegation, but in 1945, *fourteen years earlier!* He hadn't been there since. Even more preposterous was the reference to Khrushchev. In 1945 Khrushchev was a Party leader in the Ukraine, and remained there until 1949. His rise to prominence began only after Stalin's death in 1953; until then he was completely unknown to Americans.

What was the purpose of this crudely whipped up scenario? Was it the overzealous invention of an FBI agent bucking for a promotion? Was it to provide evidence to convince prison authorities to legalize the monitoring of our conversations as "in the best interests of the country?" Or was this a scheme to create evidence for possible disbarment proceedings against Abt? It should be recalled that my attorney in the Foley Square trial, Abraham Isserman, was disbarred from legal practice for eleven years.

Ma came to see me in June. With her were Dave Sennett, whom she had recently married,* my brother Ben, and my son Ralph. I had looked forward eagerly to this visit, yet was apprehensive about how my mother would stand up to this first trip to the high-walled penitentiary to visit a son she hadn't seen in five years. Life had always been difficult for Ma, and her response to it often made it worse. She had never learned to laugh so as not to weep. When she did laugh she was apologetic, as though it were a sign of weakness. "How can one laugh with life so cruel!"

When I was permitted into the visiting room, they were already seated, awaiting me. I approached jauntily with a big smile, as though everything was going my way. "Gee, Ma," I said, "you look simply wonderful! How do you keep so young and beautiful?" Her lips, drawn to a thin fine line when I entered, now relaxed, and with a slow smile she said, "You look good, Gil, you really look good."

*Her second husband, Mr. Williams, had died in the early 1930s.

The fact is that each of us had feared the worst. During my years in the underground, she must have pictured me—if not dead—on the run like a hunted beast, without a pillow for my head. After I turned myself in, she visualized me in prison stripes, at the mercy of murderers and desperados. So she was relieved to see me . . . looking somewhat older but well and in good spirits.

On my part, I had imagined her all gray, her face wrinkled, her body badly stooped. But here she was, as straight as ever, her hair not much grayer, neatly dressed—and a bride again. Above all, her smile, wan though it was, reassured me that my fears had been unfounded. Only much later did I learn from Ben what toll those years had taken.

When she first saw the high prison walls and started to climb the steep stairs leading to the rotunda, she paled, and then, midway, fell in a faint. Ben and Dave revived her and carried her the rest of the way. After she rested for a time and regained her composure, she was urged not to break down when she saw me; then they proceeded to the visiting room. I wrote to Lil about the visit that evening:

> I was happily surprised by my mother. She kept her promise and met me with a smile. Secondly, she looked extremely well. . . .
>
> In addition to telling me about her romance she spent considerable time singing paeans of praise to you and the children. She tried to tell me how wonderful you and the children are. But don't let it go to your heads; I haven't said I believed or agreed with her. She not only praised you to the skies but also her other daughter-in-law, Florence. And I really think she meant it. At last, after all these years, I guess she has become convinced that her daughters-in-law are worthy of her sons!

Ben brought with him the published copy of *The Enemy Forgotten,* the book I had written in the underground. He asked the warden for permission to show it to me, but was denied. International Publishers had mailed me a copy when the book came off the press, but it was returned. I was not allowed to see my own book.

The fact that I had written a book had been mentioned in the news at the time I surrendered, and its publication date was later announced in the Book Review section of the *New York Times.* One day an inmate who worked in one of the prison factories (there were five of them) spoke of me to one of the civilian overseers, and mentioned the book. This civilian happened to be an adherent of the Henry George single-tax school and a critic of capitalist society. He became interested in me and my book and ordered it from the publisher. He read it, liked it, and decided to sneak it into prison to me.

I was, of course, delighted to set eyes on it and to see it in print. I let others read it, choosing them carefully, so the book was read by a score of inmates, Jim and my Puerto Rican friends being among the first. Had the book been found in a shakedown, I would have been sent to the hole.

After making the rounds, the book was returned to its owner. Strangely enough, I never met the man who brought it into the prison.

8

McCarthyism Again

I liked my job as tuckpointer. It was hard physical labor, but it had some redeeming features. First, it made me feel good to be able to keep up with men half my age. I even enjoyed their joshing and being called "Pop," or "Old Man." The work was in the open, which also was a plus, and though every pore in my body felt as though it was being pierced with particles of brick dust, we had the right—glory of glories—to take a shower every day. This definitely put us in a privileged class; only the men in white—kitchen, bakery, butcher shop, hospital and barbershop workers—had a similar privilege. The rest of the sweltering population could shower and change clothes only twice a week.

The foreman of our gang was on the whole a decent fellow who, so long as the job was being done, had sense enough to turn the other way when some shenanigan was taking place. At various times I would notice him eyeing me, but not in a mean sort of way. So I would return his look in the same spirit. I've since seen his monthly report on me: "Inmate does good work. He's been getting along well with the other inmates."

One problem wouldn't go away. The constant *rat-a-tat* of the air hammer was gradually turning me deaf. Already hard of hearing, this constant battering threatened to complete the process. The foreman noticed—he would shout something and I wouldn't hear him—and offered to shift me to ground work, which involved mixing the mortar, shoveling it into pails, and hoisting them by pulley to the men on the scaffold. But I turned the offer down. We all needed periodic spells away from the incessantly jarring noise of the hammers, so we took turns working with the mortar. It would not be fair—nor to their liking—for me to have that chore all the time.

I could have applied for another maintenance job, but I hoped that my request for industry work would be acted on soon, and I didn't want to jeopardize that chance by being marked a misfit who couldn't hold down a job. I did, however, ask to see the Kansas City ear doctor on his next visit to Leavenworth.

His examination confirmed my worst fears. He found a nerve-hearing loss, probably triggered by a siege of scarlet fever as a child, and bone-conduction loss of more recent origin. He warned me against working under conditions of excessive metallic noise and particularly near an air hammer. He recommended to the prison authorities that I be transfered to an industry job where I could earn enough money to purchase a hearing aid.

His recommendation was accepted, except for the industry job. I was given a new maintenance assignment. I became a box man in the clothing issue room. On the way to the showers, the men picked up their clean clothes in a room about fifty feet long, with a counter running its full length. On the left side, as one entered, were men handling the clothes; on the right, others clamoring for them. The clothing was stacked in ten cubicles of equal size, each about the area of a single-man cell. Over each cubicle was a number, from zero through nine. The walls of the cubicles were completely covered with shelves, subdivided into box-like apertures just large enough for one man's issue; blue work shirt, blue denim trousers, and underwear. Each item, except socks, was stenciled with the inmate's registry number.

The last digit of the registry number was the important one. It determined in which cubicle the clothing belonged. I was the box man for cubicle six, which meant that all clothes whose numbers ended in 6 were shunted my way. I would fold them, sort them, and store them in their designated spots on the shelves.

On shower days the men would come tearing into the room like a run of bulls at Pamplona. The air would be filled with the shout of registry numbers until complete bedlam reigned. My hearing loss was no asset in this situation. But somehow I managed. With their clothes safely in hand, the men continued their mad rush to the shower room.

But nearly always something went wrong. Clothes would be misplaced; what belonged in cubicle six would be in cubicle nine; a new pair of somewhat better-fitting denims would be "borrowed" by someone in the laundry. Men who claimed that they were short of something might have torn it up and flushed it down the toilet in order to get a replacement. On such occasions the lines would pile up and the rush to the shower turned into a crawl. Life on non-shower days was quieter and a more leisurely sifting and sorting of clothes was possible.

While everyone, except those in whites, wore the same kind of duds, some men preferred to be more equal than others. A pack of Camels judiciously slipped into the hands of a laundry worker could accomplish wonders in transforming what would have been a mangled pair of pants into steam-pressed or starched ones. To keep such items from being wrinkled, they reached us by "special delivery." All this was *sub rosa*, but everyone knew it was taking place. Those with sharply creased trousers and starched collars would strut along the big wall as though on Fifth Avenue on Easter Sunday.

Paying for better service was the norm. A pack of Camels—better yet, two—would guarantee that one left the barber chair without being shorn. Tipping was a necessary vice. Men in industry earned a little for their labor, but those in maintenance, though the place couldn't function without them, received nothing. Many men were penniless, with nothing for their commissary needs.

As the months dragged on I became more and more impatient to be transferred to industry. But all I could get was a runaround and an evasive "Not yet." In September I requested a personal interview with Mr. Hyde, who was in charge of work assignments. I had seen him once before (from a distance) when he addressed our quarantine group on the great opportunities the institution offered for rehabilitation.

I explained to Mr. Hyde that I wanted to get an industry job to earn something to send home and to enable the family to visit me on weekends. I reminded him that I was the only one of my quarantine group who had asked for industry work and hadn't obtained it.

Hyde's response was prompt. "You've got a lot of f--ing nerve asking for favors after plotting to overthrow the U.S. Government. If it's up to me, you'll never get into industry."

As I listened, I grew angrier. What I had suspected had now been blurted out. "Let me tell you something, Mr. Hyde," I began, "I plotted to overthrow nothing. But if I had, a judge sentenced me. You can't do it a second time. As long as I'm here I'm going to demand the same treatment, the same rights, as the other men—whether murderers, rapists, bank robbers or con artists. I'm not asking for favors from you or anyone else, but neither will I accept discrimination."

On this note the interview ended. Much later, during my last year at Leavenworth, I asked for another interview (not with Hyde—I never spoke to him again), with the warden, regarding Hyde. Word had come to me from a number of inmates that Hyde had been needling some of his cronies over "why that s.o.b. Commie Green was getting along so well. Doesn't anyone have the guts to give him what he deserves?"

When these reports reached me, and from men I trusted, I promptly asked for an interview with the warden "on a most urgent matter." I told him what I had heard, that I believed it, "knowing Mr. Hyde," and that I wanted it stopped immediately. "I don't want to alarm my family," I said, "but if this doesn't stop I shall be compelled to inform them on their next visit and have them reach Mr. Abt as well. Moreover," I went on, "if anything should happen to me here, you will be held responsible. I'm telling some of my short-time friends that if anything happens to inform my family of this interview with you."

From his response I knew that he was convinced I was telling the truth. He neither became indignant nor accused me of insubordination. Instead, he tried to reassure me. "You're wrong, Green. Mr. Hyde is a decent man; he would never do anything like that."

"Oh no?" I replied. "Then let me suggest something: bring him here and let him deny the accusation to my face."

"No, Green, I can't do that. I'll speak to Mr. Hyde myself. Don't worry." So I had an enemy in Leavenworth by the name of Hyde.

I continued to press for an industry assignment. At first I thought that the denial was directed by J. Edgar Hoover, who never forgave Winston and me for outwitting his army of snoopers. This, no doubt, was a factor, but not the only one. My prison files indicate that a change of policy had occurred somewhere along the line.

A document dated July 23, 1956, reports that the Classification Committee had once again turned me down. "The Committee noted," the report stated, "that Green is a Communist and that policy does not permit the awarding of extra good time."

This referred to a statute that entitled Federal prisoners working in industry extra time off their sentences: two days per month off for the first two years in industry, four days a month for the third and fourth years, and five days for subsequent years. It is this extra time off that the authorities objected to. They wanted to keep me in prison as long as they legally could.

The policy emanated from Washington. In a letter sent to Warden Looney, James V. Bennett, Director of the Bureau of Prisons, wrote: "We have changed our previous policy about cases of this kind." Each individual should be judged on "the extent to which we believe he is attempting honestly to rehabilitate himself and intends no longer to engage in unlawful activities."

To which Looney replied, referring to me: "He has shown no indication of leading a life any different from that which he followed prior to commitment, nor of taking up different employment," adding: "When he was informed of this decision by the Board he of course expressed deep disappointment, and it will be noted, from the attached copy of a letter to his wife, that he is going to try every means of forcing us to place him in industries. He indicates also that he will campaign to force us to permit his wife to visit him on weekends so that it will brook less interference with her work. . . . I will keep you informed as to developments in this case."

Recently, to refresh my memory of the prison years, I read Bennett's autobiography, *I Chose Prison.* In it I learned something that may have had something to do with the change of policy.

Writing of the 1950s, Bennett describes a "nerve-wracking episode [which] began for me, as it must for many public servants, where a disgruntled ex-employee publicly charged me with softness on Communism and offered no evidence to support the preposterous accusation."

He relates how he was called before Senator Pat McCarran's subcommittee on appropriations without any prior notice as to the subject of inquiry. "I was not allowed to bring any of my associates, even though it was presumably an open session." He says that he was prevented from making any general statement or to correct the record. "This," he declares, "was a 'star chamber' proceeding if ever there was one." A legion of FBI agents then, according to Bennett, swooped down on the Bureau of Prisons to investigate, "without the request or approval of the Attorney General."

It was indeed a traumatic experience for Bennett, but he was not a man to ignore the lesson. He promptly joined the Inquisition. He even forgave Hoover for letting the FBI loose on his province, and notes, "I developed a considerable respect for Hoover . . . we were in day-to-day contact."

So Bennett's ordeal may have had something to do with the determination not be "soft" on me.

9

Holiday Cheer

The holiday season was the most difficult time of the year for me. It had been so in the underground as well. A special taunt was the artificially induced festivity. Christmas trees were brought in and decorated with gaily colored lights and bright tinsel trimmings. As I wrote home, "Everything is being set for a happy holiday season! It'll be just like home—even better, for there will be none of the rowdy tumult of the young, no last-minute hustling to buy gifts, no worry about what to do with unwanted ones, and no gorging or drinking to excess. A safe and sane Christmas and New Year—that's our goal!"

A package of cheap hard candy wrapped in Santa Claus paper was tossed to us in our cells with a cheery wish from one of the custodians for a Merry Christmas and a Happy New Year—cruel mockery for men locked in cages.

On holidays I was even grateful for the high wall that separated us from a view of the outside world—of cars speeding by with laughing children, of well-lit homes where men and women could be seen through windows toasting one another and the New Year. I wished them well, but I preferred not to see them.

I could, however, celebrate one important gain compared with the year before. I was now in regular contact with my family, both by visits and by mail. I even joined vicariously in their birthday and holiday dinners.

An important family event was about to occur. Dan, at nineteen, was in love, and the couple had decided on an early marriage. This was cause for rejoicing.

The one time of year when gifts from the outside were permitted was Christmas. I could receive a package of goodies and a book. The book had to come directly from the publisher and pass prison censorship. The last time Lil had visited me, I had asked her to send me Frederick Engels' *Dialectics of Nature.* Even though Marxist books were banned, I figured that the censor had never heard of Engels, and did not know he was a close co-worker of Karl Marx, that the title would throw him, and that all he would do was thumb through the pages to make sure they didn't contain smutty pictures. And that is how I got my first Marxist book in Leavenworth. Lil told me that two close friends had bought it. They continued to send me a book each Christmas I was in Leavenworth.

The box of bonbons came from Florence. It was of the very finest quality, even though each piece had been sadistically crushed in a pretext of looking for contraband. The chocolates came in time to offset an unwanted gift—another official denial of my request for an industry assignment. The reason? I had not shown "evidence of rehabilitation."

The approach of the New Year was nonetheless an important milestone. I had become a well-established resident of this walled city, knew my way around, had made friends and felt confident that I could face whatever lay ahead. I had not yet won my battle for industry work, but by this time I had gained a single cell in Cellhouse B, which made it much easier for me to find time for reading, study and reflection. Hence I felt that I had weathered the worst. In this mood I wrote home my predictions for 1957:

> 1. There is bound to be a great world-wide discontent with the weather. 2. There will be many important changes—some good and some bad. 3. People will continue to spend today what they *hope* to earn tomorrow.

4. Crops will be generally very good—especially of new children. 5. Dan will discover, all over again, the ancient truth that two can't live cheaper than one. 6. Josie will lose her great fear of geometry in direct ratio to her separation from that subject. 7. Ralph will take another great stride toward becoming a scholar. 8. You, my dear, will continue to ask time to pass swiftly but without making you any older. 9. I shall continue to live a model life of regularity and discipline, without even a teeny bit of dissipation. 10. Good, bad, or indifferent, the year 1957 will be succeeded by 1958.

These are my daring predictions!

10

Crime and Punishment

The men at Leavenworth were reputed to be hardened criminals and among the most incorrigible. They had long sentences; some were lifers, and a large percentage were repeaters. About a third were Black, a considerable number Chicanos, other Latinos, and Native American Indians—largely from the reservations of the Southwest.

Some of the inmates were anti-social in the sense that they blamed *all* of society for their plight. I met men in Leavenworth who never had a kind word about another human being, yet went out of their way to befriend a bird with an injured wing. One of them had caught a mouse in the cellhouse and turned it into a pet, bringing it crumbs of food and protecting it as his dearest possession. This man had been convicted of murder.

All were victims of a society where a person's worth is measured by material possessions, not by human qualities. Above all, many of the inmates were victims of poverty. To my knowledge, there was no son of a banker or corporation president in Leavenworth.

Eugene V. Debs, the popular labor and Socialist leader who spent years in Atlanta Penitentiary for his opposition to World War I, described his experiences in these words:

"The inmates of prisons are not the irretrievable, vicious and depraved element they are commonly believed to be, but upon the average they are like ourselves, and it is more often their misfortune than their crime that is responsible for their plight . . . a prison is a cross section of society in which every human strain is clearly revealed. An average prison, and its inmates, compare favorably with any similar number of persons outside of prison walls."

This was my own experience as well. Treated decently, humanely and as equals, the men reciprocated in every way. There were exceptions, but no more than on the outside.

The deep resentment that men in prison feel arises from being regarded as social pariahs and from strongly held convictions that the punishment imposed on them did not fit the crime. Many times I heard words like, "Had I gone out for bigger stakes, I wouldn't be here. It's only the small fry that end up in prison—the big thieves become big shots in business and government."

They were particularly resentful of the shocking disparity in punishment for similar offenses. Black prisoners, for example, are painfully aware that their real crime is the color of their skins. The death penalty is used mainly against racial minorities. Since the installation of the electric chair in the state of Virginia in 1908, for example, 56 executions have taken place. All of the victims were Black. It is also an accepted fact that Blacks charged with crimes against whites generally receive the severest sentences; those against Blacks, the mildest.

It has been recognized by many that the length of prison terms in this country is a scandal. In a single year, 15,000 offenders received sentences of five years or more; in England, for the same year, there were only 150. If it could be shown that such inhuman sentences deterred crime, that would be one matter. But facts bear out the opposite. Philadelphia, with a population of two million, for example, has approximately the same number of murders yearly as England, Scotland and Wales combined, with their total population of forty-five million!

A large number of men were at Leavenworth on narcotics raps. Some were users, others pushers; and, of course, some were both users and pushers. I had great compassion for those, mostly younger men, caught in a habit that held them like a vise. But I had no sympathy at all for those who pushed drugs as a business. As was to be expected, some rationalized this kind of free enterprise by insisting that if they didn't engage in it someone else would.

I recalled the news headlines at the time of the arrests of some of the narcotics dealers. The authorities always claimed that another big dope ring had been busted. But I learned that the so-called big shots were only small fry. The men who really owned, ran and profited from the multi-billion-dollar narcotics traffic were nowhere near Leavenworth or any other prison. They were living in palatial homes, riding in the highest priced Cadillacs and keeping company with other successful big-business men.

One fellow I had met in quarantine, with whom I later worked on one of my prison jobs, was serving a ten-year sentence for bringing less than an ounce of marijuana across the Mexican border. He insisted it was for his own use.

Another, Juan, was a favorite among the men: decent, lithe of body and gentle of spirit, and one of the best handball players in the joint. He had become a victim of the habit while very young. Desperately needing a fix one day, he robbed a drugstore. On his way out, he opened the cash register and grabbed some bills. He was not aware that the drugstore also served as a U.S. postal sub-station and that the till held postage-stamp money as well. As a result, he was found guilty of robbing the U.S. mails, a Federal offense carrying a mandatory twenty-five year sentence. Juan's sentence dated from the days of the great train robberies of yesteryear, and he was in Leavenworth long before I got there. Near the end of his sentence he was transferred to a lower-custody prison in Minnesota, from which I assume he was finally released.

Another fellow inmate was a Black musician from Detroit. We met at a music appreciation class held one night a week at the prison school. This man, too, had been busted on a narcotics charge. He had been caught getting his shot before a performance. He was convicted of using and possessing, and had been sentenced to five years.

We talked of our families; he had some familiarity with the labor movement and told me that his wife, whom he missed terribly, held an executive post in Solidarity House, the headquarters of the United Auto Workers Union. He was bitter about his conviction, for, as he observed, the use of narcotics was widespread in the musical and theatrical professions. And, he could have added, in the medical one as well.

Another large group of men in prison were those convicted under the Dyer Act, which outlaws the transport of stolen autos across state lines. Most of these men were also young. Some had "borrowed" cars because they had none of their own in a culture where anyone without a car is considered to be a nobody. Others, however, were involved in stealing cars as the legmen in a larger racket.

The great disparity in sentences among these violators arose because anyone who took a stolen car across a state line was liable to double jeopardy: could be tried and sent to jail by both the state *and* the Federal government. If he crossed more than one state line, *each* state could prosecute him. Often a man wouldn't know until the end of one sentence whether a "hold" was waiting for him in some other jurisdiction.

In this respect, as in others, the word "rehabilitation" was the most abused in the English language. To the men it was a hideous joke—punishment was the name of the game.

11

Bank-robber Friend

I had a disproportionately large number of friends who had been sentenced for bank robbing. I am not not sure why this was so, but I know Gus Hall had the same experience. One explanation may be that the bank robbers were less clannish, not as tied to cultural enclaves based on race and nationality. Another reason may be that the philosophy some of them espoused was quite uncomplicated, even though obviously self-serving. One put it this way: "When I need food I go to a supermarket; when I need money I go to a bank. And when I take money from a bank I'm harming nobody. I'm not hitting some bloke over the head on a dark street, pushing drugs on high-school kids, or conning an old widow out of her life's savings. I'm just taking money from an outfit that's lousy with it, and it hurts nobody."

One bank robber I got to know well was Jacobs, who was assigned to the prison school. He said he had robbed a bank only "to grab a sizeable chunk of dough to continue my education." The government accommodated him with more time than he bargained for—at Leavenworth "U."

Jim Leather, to whom Gus introduced me that first morning in the yard, became a very good friend of mine, although he was twenty years younger and came from a totally different background. Jim had become acquainted with the Communist prisoners who preceded me, and he saw in me a possible continuation of a relationship he evidently found stimulating.

Jim's closest friendship was with Irving Potash, a long-time Communist, a trade union leader, and one of my co-defendants. Both wore whites—Jim in the butcher shop and Irving in the bakery. Jim felt indebted to Potash for broadening his outlook on life and helping him decide to "straighten out."

"With Irving celling next to me," Jim related, "I was curious to find out what kind of a man he was. I knew very little about Communism and was affected by anti-Communist propaganda. So I used to badger Irving with the most idiotic questions imaginable, but he never responded in a way that made me feel like an idiot. In his quiet way he would just say, "Let's talk about it, Jim.' And we did, at every opportunity. I still marvel at his patience and thoughtfulness."

One night, talking through the bars, each from his own cell, Irving suggested to Jim that he read a book he'd picked up in the library. It was on comparative economic systems. Jim told me that while reading this book he first began to understand the distinction between different social systems—past and present. Jim's curiosity was stirred. "I had never really read a book to the end before," he told me, "but now I wanted to know more and more, and on many subjects." He began to take classes in the school and surprised himself by excelling even in what to him were abstruse subjects—algebra and geometry.

If Jim's interest in me arose out of previous contacts with Communist prisoners, my interest in him stemmed from having followed in the press the escapade that landed him at Leavenworth.

Jim (whose home town, like mine, was Chicago) and three companions, one of them a young woman friend, had jointly planned the robbery of a Milwaukee bank. The men were to do the actual stickup, while the woman was to help in the getaway. Two cars were used: the one in which they drove to Milwaukee, and another stolen from a parking lot. The men went to the bank in the second car. Once inside the bank, things went as planned. Then, with their loot of $94,000, they drove to the other side of the Milwaukee line and, on a deserted road, switched to their own car. Jim sat in front with the young woman, and the two men squeezed into the car's trunk with the money. They were stopped at a first roadblock but were permitted to continue. The police were on the lookout for three men, not for a young couple in a car that answered to an entirely different description.

Jim and his companions, however, did not know that a retired postman looking out his kitchen window had seen them switch cars. His suspicion aroused, he had informed the FBI. The four were picked up at the next roadblock. After a brisk trial, Jim got fifteen years.

The robbery and arrest had made sensational headlines. Jim was depicted as the leader of a group of desperados who had terrorized the bank employees and patrons with sawed-off shotguns. What I did not know at the time, nor did the reading public, was that the guns were not loaded. "We decided to take safeguards against becoming trigger nervous," Jim explained.

"But how would you have responded if an armed guard shot at you?" I asked.

"That would have ended it," he answered. "But it wasn't likely. Most people don't realize that bank personnel are usually told not to resist. Remember," he added, "insurance covers such bank losses. Of course, had the police been alerted and gotten there in time, it would have been a different story."

It was this prior "safeguard"—as Jim called it—that surprised me. But Jim told me that he had an aversion to killing living things. "That's why I never went hunting; I consider it barbaric. I remember shooting a sparrow with a BB-gun when I was about ten. I picked it up, saw its torn wing and watched it die in my hands. I felt such shame and remorse that I broke the gun in half and never used one again."

Jim worked in the butcher shop and had a reputation for being hot-tempered. He had mauled a few inmates badly in fist fights. On such occasions the blood would rush to his face and it would become as red as the hair on top of his head. "That's true," Jim admitted. "When I become mad at what I consider an injustice, I not only look red, I also see red. Then I lose control of myself, and later regret it. But it's never because of malice or a desire to hurt anyone. I just become blinded with rage."

Jim was the best all-round athlete in Leavenworth and exceptionally good with his fists. As a result, few tried to tangle with him. He never picked a fight, at least as far as I knew, and was scrupulously fair in any sport competition. Yet he was firm in his opinions if he thought he was in the right, and that, combined with a hot temper, would often get him into a jam.

When I last saw Jim—some 20 years later and with the writing of this book in mind—I asked him to tell me again something about his childhood, and when he had first gotten into trouble.

"I was in the eighth grade and a few of us kids went around to back porches to steal empty milk bottles and pop bottles for deposits. One day we saw a back door open. When we were sure no one was home, we moved up from stealing bottles to burglary.

"One burglary led to another, until we had pulled off about fifteen. Then we got arrested. The Juvenile Court Judge, a colonel in the Reserve named Hill, took one look and said, 'You're a big fellow, why don't you join the National Guard?' But I was only fourteen; the judge said all I needed was a note from my mother saying I was eighteen. She wrote it. This was October 1940. In March, 1941 the National Guard was nationalized into the U.S. Army. Then my mother got me out because I was under age, and I got out in January 1942."

After Jim left the army, women began to play an important role in his life. To impress them he developed his skill as a boxer and as a guy with money. Now there were robberies of small department stores, haberdasheries, etc. At sixteen he was sent to a reformatory in Pontiac, Illinois on an indeterminate sentence of one to ten years. After serving seven years and eight months, he came out in 1950. Four bank robberies had intervened before the one in Milwaukee.

During his stay in Leavenworth, Jim began to look back at the Milwaukee bust as a lucky break. "I don't know what would have happened to me had I continued in the same way. Now I know I won't be back."

Our daily contact was interrupted for about a year when Jim and about fifty other inmates were suddenly shipped to Alcatraz for participating in a food strike in Leavenworth. Our friendship continued upon his return. After leaving prison we continued to see one another from time to time, more often when we both lived in Chicago and only occasionally since then. The many years Jim spent in prisons and the army did not institutionalize him. He kept his word about changing his mode of life. Those years did, however, turn him into something of a loner.

12

Strike!

There are various versions of what triggered the food strike. Jim believes it started because a popular supervisor in the culinary department had been replaced. James Bennett says in *I Chose Prison* that the trouble began when some Italian-Americans were removed from their assignments in the bakeshop. According to him, these men threatened "a hunger strike . . . so we quickly picked up one after another and bundled them off to Alcatraz. . . . But the tension lasted for weeks."

More than just some Italian-Americans from the bakeshop were bundled off to Alcatraz. And this action was hardly taken to prevent a strike. It took place after the strike was well under way.

Meals in Federal prisons are generally better than in state penal institutions and infinitely better than in county or city jails. Yet food cannot be judged for its calories, vitamins or taste alone. Other factors enter, often intangible. Where life is so devoid of human amenities, meals can become the volatile focal point of general tension and frustration.

Conditions in prisons where sentences are relatively short cannot be compared with those where incarceration is for many years—even life—where the caged humans do not know if or when they will ever get out. Surprisingly, the Federal prison with the reputation for the best food was Alcatraz.

Even less appropriate is a comparison of penal conditions in poor, underdeveloped countries with those in wealthy lands such as ours.

Prisons are like small islands, microcosms of the larger society, and inevitably the larger society seeps in.

During my years at Leavenworth, for example, only a few of us were regarded as political prisoners. A decade later, a majority of the inmates were referring to themselves as such. Mounting struggles for freedom and equality outside prison walls had influenced consciousness within them.

The food strike while I was at Leavenworth was a relatively minor incident compared with the prison upheavals that followed, yet clearly it was related to them.

The food at Leavenworth was generally palatable but on the greasy and starchy side. Men suffering from ulcers and gall-bladder trouble had a great deal of difficulty digesting the food. The meat was mainly pork, which came from the prison farm. This choice was understandable: Cows bear one calf a year whereas sows carry several litters. And a unique recycling system was in effect. We ate the hogs and our leftovers went to the farm to feed more hogs. No waste!

Holiday meals were the best and usually consisted of chicken. These birds did not come from the prison farm but were bought on the market. The farm chickens were mainly for egg production. Only when the hens were too old to lay their quota were they eaten. The Sunday noon meal was the best of the week.

Ironically enough, our diet benefited from the Federal farm-surplus program. A shipment of surplus eggs, butter and cheese would arrive at Leavenworth quarterly. While these items lasted, the quality of the food improved. Vegetables, when fresh, came from the farm; otherwise we ate canned ones. Not much fruit was served, but during the year we would have watermelon and cantaloupe for a few days. Sometimes there might be an orange or an apple, but generally these had to be bought from the commissary.

When I arrived at Leavenworth, the meals didn't seem bad. I found it difficult to understand why so many inmates complained so bitterly. But the longer I was there the more insipidly tasteless, colorless and maddeningly monotonous the food became. Yet the great majority of people in Africa, Asia and Latin America and many millions of poor people in the United States do not eat as well.

The cycle of menus was repeated with hardly a variation. A bulletin issued to kitchen personnel that listed every item to be served—meal by meal for a ten-day period—made its way into the general population. Therefore we knew in advance what to expect, and some men would miss a meal periodically—particularly an evening meal of leftovers—preferring fruit, candy and peanuts bought from the commissary.

I first learned that trouble was brewing when a story that was making the rounds reached my ears: Ten or twelve inmates had become ill, supposedly from eating spoiled frankfurters the evening before. The story grew with the telling until it was being said that perishable foods like frankfurters were customarily put back into the refrigerator and then served again; sometimes more than once.

Whether true or false, this story set off the spark. But no strike could have occurred had there not been a long-time accumulation of combustible material. When someone proposed, under the heightened tension, that everyone stay away from the evening meal in protest, the idea met immediate support.

When the gong rang for evening mess and the cell doors were racked open, we looked out to see what the response would be. There was no sound of feet rushing down the stairway. An immense feeling of elation swept the cellhouse. Later we learned that the same thing had occurred in the other cell blocks. No more than a handful had gone to mess.

The same thing happened when the gong sounded for breakfast. We were then ordered off the tiers and racked back into our cells. When the time came for work we remained in our cells. The food strike had become a work strike as well.

If there were any leaders of the strike, they did not make themselves known, nor did I know who they were. No demands had been drawn up, no committees elected, no meetings asked for with authorities. It was a spontaneous protest demonstration, nothing more. My role was as a participant, not a leader. When the action first started, I noticed that a guard had been posted where he could watch any activity around my cell, especially whether I was sending or receiving "kites" (messages) from the men on either side. He had nothing to report.

As the day wore on we learned—how, I do not recall—that a large number of inmates, the so-called ringleaders, had been shipped by bus to Alcatraz. We were warned that more would follow if the strike continued. This had an intimidating effect, and the number of men who went to evening mess, while still small, was larger than for the earlier meals.

It was clear that the strike was coming to an end. Under these circumstances I felt that it would be wiser to end the strike in a united manner, rather than permit it to peter out, leaving the inmates divided and demoralized. The next morning, everyone went to breakfast.

Once the strike was over I learned that Jim had been one of those shipped to Alcatraz. They really had nothing on him. This became clear a year later when they sent him back to Leavenworth with all his lost good-time restored.

13

A Brahmin and an Untouchable

About six months after my request to correspond with the newspaperman Ed Lahey was denied, John Abt met him while on legal business in Washington. "Why hasn't Gil written?" Ed asked, "I had expected to hear from him."

"Don't you know?" Abt said, "Gil's request was turned down because you're a newspaperman."

"That's ridiculous!" exclaimed Lahey, "Are you sure? I'm going to look into this."

My FOIA prison files show that Lahey wrote Prison Director Bennett on January 3, 1957, stressing that the initiative for correspondence with him had come from me. "But if a Federal prisoner is denied the dubious privilege of writing to me because I am a newspaperman, it would be most interesting to know."

Bennett replied: "You can be sure that Gil Green or any other Federal prisoner could write to a newspaperman if he were on the inmate's list of correspondents. . . . There is nothing in his file to indicate that he has applied for the privilege of writing to you."

Warden Looney received a copy of Bennett's letter and wrote to him to set the record straight. He acknowledged that I had submitted Lahey's name as correspondent immediately upon entering Leavenworth and that a "routine inquiry" had indicated that the request met with Lahey's approval. However, the warden added, "After due consideration of the matter and in view of the nature of the case it was decided that Mr. Lahey's name would not be placed on Green's correspondence list."

The letter went on to inform Bennett that a Mr. B. Cortez Tipton of the Bureau of Rehabilitation in Washington had informed him that Lahey was well-known in the capitol, yet "Since he reported Mr. Lahey to be both an attorney and a newspaperman . . . it was still considered appropriate to deny Green's request." The warden's letter concluded, "if you feel that correspondence should be permitted between Mr. Lahey and the prisoner I shall make arrangements at once."

The Bureau of Prisons, however, hedged on such permission. Acting Director Frank Loveland replied to Looney's letter: "For the present we see nothing to be accomplished by permitting Green to correspond with Mr. Lahey, unless he expresses a particular desire to do so. If he does, I would not object to your granting him permission, but for the present let us let sleeping dogs lie."

But Lahey had shown Bennett's letter to Abt, who wrote the Director on February 3, 1957:

> You state that there is nothing in the file to indicate that Mr. Green ever sought permission to write Mr. Lahey. This is difficult to understand since Mr. Green informed me that he had applied for such permission and later asked me to supply him Mr. Lahey's home address and to secure the latter's agreement not to make use of the correspondence, both of which were required by the parole officer as a condition to processing the request.
>
> Since your letter indicates that Mr. Lahey will be approved as a correspondent if Mr. Green makes application, I shall advise him to reapply.

After a brief delay, my request was finally granted. Ed and I began corresponding almost immediately and continued intermittently for the entire period of my imprisonment.

In my first letter I informed Ed that I was restricted to writing three letters a week and that the members of my family would naturally get preference. But I promised to write occasionally. Knowing how busy he was, I was sure that he, too, had more compelling commitments. As it turned out, we both enjoyed this opportunity to learn more about one another. Ed's letters to me confirmed Henry Adams's astute observation that newspapermen tend to have double personalities—they write in one vein and think in another. The letters disclosed to me a side of Ed's personality not revealed in his newspaper work.

Several of his letters apparently shocked the prison censor and became matters of communication between Leavenworth and Washington. One of them affected me directly, bringing about repeated shakedowns of my cell (not in search of contraband), but in a meticulous examination of my personal notebooks and papers.

Lahey had written: "I got news for you, pal. You can write the language. I do hope you're keeping a journal during your stay at Jim Bennett's hostel. It would make good reading." Then he told me of his friend Ammon Hennessy, who had spent time in Atlanta Penitentiary for his opposition to World War I. Hennessy had recently written *Autobiography of a Christian Anarchist,* in which he related his prison experiences. "It is to my mind a classic," Lahey wrote, urging me to tell my story, too.

A photostat of this letter was sent to Washington with a "Personal and Confidential" message from Looney. He wrote: "As you will observe, columnist Lahey is encouraging Green to keep a day-to-day journal of his experiences here, looking toward possible publication at a later date. Mr. Lahey seems to be something less than conservative in his expressed viewpoints."

Ed's letters provided an interesting paradox: I, a prisoner, was evidently at greater peace with myself and had a far more optimistic view of life and the future than he. Yet Lahey was not only outside, a free man, but a highly respected and prestigious journalist on first-name relations with many of the men running the government.

In an early letter he wrote of being in a rut, but "I'm too far along in life now to expect to do anything about it." To which I replied, "Your letter had an undertone of weariness and resignation that surprised me. At 55, you say, 'nothing much can happen to me, good or bad.' I beg to differ. It's only the seventh-inning stretch, not the last of the ninth. Fifty-five is by no means old nowadays. Even if it were, even if you were 65 or 75, it's the wrong approach to life." Then I told him of my favorite cartoon. It showed two tough-looking guys sitting in a prison cell, one saying to the other, "Don't worry, pal, in twenty years we'll be laughing at this."

Ed was completely irreverent toward those in power and was appalled by the Washington scene. He wrote:

> I can't recall in my many years here when the sense of mental torpidity so enveloped our lords of creation. I've stopped reading the papers,

> because I can never figure out how it's going to come out even in evaluating all these charges and counter-charges of what's happening to the missile program.

Ed was a devout Catholic and was outraged by the manner in which the Christmas Spirit had been commercialized and debased. One Yuletide season, when his wife, Grace, was in Italy with their daughter, Jayne (who had been badly hurt in an auto accident), he gave himself the assignment of investigating an underworld gambling ring that operated in Miami.

> This means that I can almost completely escape the vicious spirit of Christmas and all its good will. The only concession I'll make will be to attend midnight mass in Miami, then call my family in Italy about 3 a.m., to exchange greetings. I'll take my Christmas dinner in a Jewish delicatessen and spend the afternoon at Tropical race track, after which I shall be ready for the underworld investigation. That's why Miami at Christmas will look especially good to me. It's peopled with folks who cope with basic problems, like how they are going to get their shirts out of the laundry that night and if so, how are they going to eat afterward.

I read some of Ed's articles in the Chicago *Daily News* which I received via the hand-me-down route from another prisoner, and joshed Ed about some of them being "shallow." His reply was good-natured but with a barb:

> What you should bear in mind is that superficiality is the essence of journalism, necessarily. It may sound cynical to you, but I have observed that rule for a long time. I recognize that I have the depth of a one-pound box of candy, and I can't think of a better place to use that faculty than in daily journalism, where we must wrap up human tragedy, national disaster, or a Senate debate in 300 to 400 words. It helps at times to recognize that under certain conditions, shallowness is a necessary attribute.

I read and reread this letter and it made me feel guilty that I had ever used the word "shallow." It had come out mean and deprecating. There *are* limitations inherent in trying to wrap up a disaster in less than two triple-spaced pages of typewriter copy. So I hastened to write him: "You must forgive me for stomping on your most sensitive bunion. The truth is I like your writing. You have a gift for imagery and the art of boiling down a complex equation into a fresh, simple, earthy, and often humorous, word picture. Quite a feat. And in my school, simplicity is not the opposite of profundity. Often the measure of a person's understanding is reflected in his ability to state a proposition simply and clearly. My criticism of your writing over the years is mainly political, which under the circumstances is quite understandable."

I also knew, as did he, that part of the problem was the unseen censor constantly looking over his shoulder. As chief of the Washington Bureau of the Knight newspaper chain, Ed could not very well disregard the views of its owner and publisher.

Every time I thought of Ed's boss, John S. Knight, I wondered whether he had been informed of our correspondence. It so happens that I had a brief contact with Knight at the very outset of the Cold War, but only by long-distance telephone.

I had tried to get the editor of the Chicago *Daily News* to publish a fifteen-hundred-word reply to a series of five scurrilous articles the paper had published on Communism and the Communist Party. He turned me down. I then placed a long-distance call to Knight at his office in the building of the Miami *Herald*. But I got no further than his secretary, who wanted to know who I was. Expecting to be told, "Sorry, Mr. Knight is in conference," I merely said, "Tell Mr. Knight this is Green of Illinois."

"Pardon me, Governor," she replied apologetically, "I'll get him at once." Seconds later he was on the phone. I explained that I was Green of Illinois, but not the governor of the state, as his secretary mistakenly thought; only the Illinois state chairman of the Communist Party.

"Well, what is it you want?" he asked briskly. I explained that I had turned to him as a last resort, certain that he would see the fairness of my request. He heard me through and said, "OK, Green of Illinois, you've got it—a fifteen-hundred-word article on the editorial page.

"Thank you very much," I said, "but there's one more thing. I want no changes in the article without my prior agreement.

"What if there's something libelous?" he asked.

"There isn't," I assured him.

"OK, bring the article in; it'll be published. (It was, March 29, 1948, in three columns on the editorial page, with the head, "Communist State Chairman Replies to Sweinhart Series.")

So this single contact with Knight—some years before Joe McCarthy became a national figure—had been a cordial one. And from that experience I knew that Knight had the last word on all his papers.

The letters between Ed and me touched on many subjects, personal as well as political. In writing to me as frankly as he did he showed considerable courage, for he knew that his letters were being sharply scrutinized.

After prison, when I finally was again permitted to travel, I saw Ed from time to time. Not many years later, he died. He had suffered from emphysema for many years. I grieved his loss—for his wife, his daughters, and for myself. Despite philosophical and political differences, we had become friends.

14

Battle of Broken Knee

When the Leavenworth authorities again turned down my request for industry work during the 1956-57 holiday season, I protested. I asked how much longer this privilege, open to everyone else, was to be denied me. The warden responded with a promise to give consideration to the request on May 1, 1957. As if in preparation for industry work, I was transferred from the clothing issue to the carpentry shop.

This shop is not to be confused with the furniture factory, which produced desks, chairs, tables and cabinets for sale to other government institutions. Strictly limited to serving Leavenworth's needs, the carpentry shop belonged to the category of maintenance.

I made this change in work assignment at the beginning of 1957. The shop was large and airy, with sunlight streaming in from windows on both sides. About twenty inmates worked there, two men to a bench. The place was well-equipped with a variety of mechanical tools: huge ripsaw, planer, jointer, etc., and all the hand tools required for the craft.

Several of the inmates were skilled carpenters. I was assigned to work with John, whose specialty was the restoration of old furniture. In his mid-thirties, from a small town in the Middle West, John was easy to get along with. He was especially proud of one job assigned him, the restoration and finishing of the furniture in the warden's home. Brought to the shop one at a time each piece was taken apart joint by joint, new parts made where old ones needed replacement, and then each sofa, chair, table or bookcase was carefully reassembled, sandpapered and finished to look like new.

The civilian foreman of the shop was Ralph E. Pearsley, a man five to ten years older than I. He was a decent person, liked by the inmates working under him. We got along well. His quarterly report referred to me as a "good worker" who caused no trouble.

Civilian work foremen were as a rule far superior in their relations to the inmates than were the guards. Most of the foremen had been workers on the outside, applying for prison work only when steady jobs were unavailable in private industry. Also, their specific responsibilities were different: they wanted certain jobs done, and for that they had to treat the men in a more humane way. Many of the guards also had entered prison employment for lack of anything as good on the outside, but the sordid occupation of holding other men down, and the consequent fear of them, had a decidedly debasing influence on character. Some of them actually enjoyed their power; it made them feel superior. But in fairness it should be said that there were some guards who treated the prisoners decently.

All things considered, I liked work in the carpentry shop. Were it not for my desire to earn something to send home, to ease Lil's problem of visiting me, and to earn the extra good time that industry work made mandatory, I would have liked to continue there.

May 1st came and went with no word from the warden. Once again I had been given the runaround, so once again I sent a copout to the warden, protesting.

On the morning of May 20, I was returning to my workbench from the bandsaw, my arms laden with strips of lumber, when I tripped over a one-inch air hose stretched across the floor where it should not have been. It had been used the previous afternoon to blow out shavings and sawdust that clogged the planer. Had my arms been free, I could have regained my balance or at least checked the fall. Instead, I fell awkwardly, my left knee striking the concrete floor under the full force of my body weight. The break rang out like a pistol shot. Unable to rise, I was carried by stretcher to the prison hospital. An X-ray showed that the patella (kneecap) had been broken into four pieces.

After viewing the X-ray, the chief surgeon, Dr. R. C. Lam, came to my bedside. He checked my medical record, felt my leg muscles and told me to prepare for surgery that afternoon.

"How bad is it?"I asked, "Will I be crippled?"

"That's too early to say," he answered, "We must first decide whether to remove the patella or try to suture it." If the patella is removed, he explained, the knee loses its protective shield. "But suturing at your age could lead to a calcification of the patella to the knee bone, freezing the knee permanently stiff. However, he added, "I'm going to recommend trying to save the patella. Your muscle tone is good, and if you agree to work hard at an exercise I'll show you, I think we can save it."

"By all means, try," I urged. "If exercise is needed, doctor, it's as good as done."

Dr. Lam operated that afternoon. The break proved to be clean, without jagged ends, making suturing easier. The leg was then placed in a plaster-of-Paris cast, from ankle to upper thigh. The exercise which Dr. Lam prescribed was simple yet difficult, and at first excruciatingly painful. It required alternately contracting and relaxing the thigh muscle attached to the patella so as to move it forward and backward as frequently as possible. This would help prevent calcification of the knee. What made it difficult was that the leg was in a cast and I had to learn how to mentally isolate the thigh muscle in order to exercise it.

I did so by first placing a finger on the opposite thigh. Once the sense of touch registered the muscle mentally, it was easier to locate its opposite mate. I was told to contract and relax the muscle consecutively until I could no longer endure the pain, and then to repeat the ordeal a little later.

Dr. Lam was a first-rate surgeon, far above the average prison doctor. He was born and educated in China and left there when the Revolution brought the Communists to power. From a well-to-do family, he feared the new regime and fled, first to Hong Kong and from there to the United States. He entered the U.S. Public Health Service as a way of rapidly acquiring the experience needed to qualify as a Board-certified surgeon. His presence at Leavenworth was a stroke of luck for me.

In the weeks that followed I got to know Dr. Lam well. At first I feared he would be prejudiced toward me because of my political views. As it turned out, he was not. Although he had fled the Chinese Revolution, he had an abiding love for China and was intensely proud of its growing strength and independence. He followed events in his homeland closely, subscribing to a monthly pictorial magazine about the new China, which he lent me regularly.

Second only to the worry about how serious my accident would prove to be was my concern with how the family would react to the news. Ben was bringing my mother to visit me in a few days and I feared the effect on her of seeing me on crutches or in a wheelchair without prior warning. So when the operation was over, I sent a copout to Mr. Huber, the parole officer, asking that he send the following wire to my brother: "Please postpone your visit. An explanatory letter follows. Much love, Gil." I added a footnote to the copout that the cost of the wire could be deducted from my commissary account.

Huber visited me at the hospital the next morning. He told me that he had not sent the telegram because he feared it would produce the very anguish I sought to avoid. He urged that the scheduled Friday visit be kept, but that I immediately send an airmail letter to my wife and a special delivery letter to my brother informing them to prepare my mother to expect to see me in a wheelchair. He promised to get the letters out at once and was certain they would reach Chicago before Friday.

I immediately recognized the wisdom of his proposal and was relieved to know that the wire I had suggested had been held up. I wrote the notes to Lil and Ben and the next morning sent thanks to Huber for his prudent advice.

However, my mother's visit was postponed after all, but for other reasons. When I learned this I sent a follow-up letter to Lil explaining in greater detail what had happened and that I would remain in the hospital in a cast for a number of weeks, since my condition made climbing the tiers in the cellhouse impossible. "Of course," I added, "if you know where a new kneecap can be found for an old 1906-model chassis, let me know."

My injury caused considerable concern to my family and among my friends. Some of them feared I was concealing something: that the injury might have been due to an act of violence. Others were dubious about the quality of the medical care I was getting. "Why should a good surgeon be working in a prison hospital?" they thought. Even two months later they were still proposing that an outside medical consultant be brought in. I tried to convince them that I would have been the first to raise hell if there had been poor medical treatment; I certainly did not want to end up stiff-legged. I was, of course, grateful for their concern and knew that the constant inquiries of family members and John Abt had helped assure proper care. But I wanted it known that I had confidence in Dr. Lam.

There was still another problem. Should I hold the prison administration responsible for the accident? The air hose had no business being where it could be tripped over during working hours—a clear violation of safety regulations. But I had to ask myself: Who would be the ones hurt if I raised this question publicly?—the prisoner who had carelessly left the hose and the foreman who had not seen to its removal. I had nothing against either man. I did not want Pearsley, the foreman, to be made the goat for an unfortunate accident. But the episode did effect a change: it was decided to string the air hose overhead instead of on the floor.

The cast remained for eight weeks, and nearly all members of my family, including my mother, Florence, and even my brother Harry from Los Angeles, had an opportunity to look it over. Wearing it in the summer heat was torture. There were times I wanted to rip it off to get at an itch that was driving me mad. Finally the day of liberation arrived. The operation had been a success, but a great deal of active exercise would be necessary for the knee to regain its full range of motion.

As soon as I was released from the hospital and could go out to the yard again, I began to fasten heavy weights to my left foot, and with the knee bent used my arms to pull the lower leg closer to the back of the thigh. This was painful, but each bit of adhesion broken increased the knee's range of movement.

When the family heard of these exercises, they asked the opinion of a friend who was an orthopedic surgeon. He urged a more conservative treatment, warning of possible lasting injury. I thought he might be right, but I still had confidence in Dr. Lam who encouraged me to continue, and in my own instincts.

One incident I recall: Dan and his wife Norma came to visit me. It was Norma's second visit and I was completely charmed by her. In the course of our conversation, Dan told me about the orthopedist's warning. Dan urged: "Why take the chance, Dad, you're walking okay now; what difference does it make if you don't regain full knee range?"

"It makes a difference to me, Dan," I replied. "I also want to be able to run again."

The two young people said nothing in reply, but the look they gave each other told me what they were thinking. It was: "My God, the old codger wants to run again, and at his age!"

Within six months, at Jim Leather's urging, I was back on the handball court.

Perhaps my broken kneecap helped break the impasse in the warden's office. While I was on the operating table, the classification committee met and granted my request for industry work. It was a consolation prize I gladly accepted.

15
Convict Labor

In August, 1957, with my leg relatively in shape again, I was transferred from the carpentry shop to the shoe factory. Before starting work I signed a contract. It provided that 75 percent of my earnings would be sent home and the balance placed in my commissary account. The starting wage would be 12 cents an hour.

The shoe factory was the largest of the five industry units inside the walls. The others were the clothing, brush, furniture, and print shops. Production was for sale exclusively to federal institutions. The print shop published government documents. The shoe factory manufactured cheap footwear for federal prisons and a better quality shoe for army personnel.

Knowing nothing about shoe production, I was immediately struck by the hundreds of detailed operations involved. Cutting machines stamped out soles, vamps, quarters, tongues, linings and insoles. Other machines sliced thick hides into thin wafers, still others compressed leather and plastics into predetermined shapes.

Each component had to be prepared separately and in its proper size and shape. Then two more were joined by sewing, stitching or cementing, or by a combination of these methods. Then came the loosely fitted assembly of the upper parts on a wooden last and the application of pincers and fasteners to draw this tightly together into a snug fit.

Each worker was assigned a specific operation. There were three different gradations of pay, depending on the complexity of the work. The piecework system prevailed. Hence, some workers never reached their theoretical hourly wage, while others went somewhat above it.

I worked at various jobs assembling, sewing, cementing, and later as a piecework payroll clerk. My job on the sewing machine was a nightmare. The machine was like an ornery bronco that refused to be tamed. When I wanted it to trot, it galloped. Whenever the foreman was watching, it decided to show him who was boss. This didn't make for the even stitching that made the foreman happy. The only positive gain from this experience was a renewed respect for my father the tailor, and my mother the dressmaker. If only their skill had been passed on to me! Because of this lack of cooperation from the sewing machine, my first month's earnings were a munificent six dollars. By mutual consent, the machine and I separated. I was assigned to work at a glue pot.

I sat at one side of a long table, another prisoner facing me. Between us was a large pot of white liquid glue and a rotating porcelain cylinder that reached the cement but was never submerged in it. At the other end of the table, two inmates were similarly seated. Our task was to glue white flannel linings to the backs of leather tongues.

I had no special fondness for this job, but had no difficulty maintaining the required speed and proficiency. It was even possible to do this while the mind wandered. The four of us broke the monotony by ceaseless talk.

One of the men sitting at the far side of the table came from a small town in western Pennsylvania and constantly bemoaned the absence of the Dexedrine and Benzedrine pills on which he got high when he was on the outside. "All I need," Joe would lament, "is a pill and a bottle of Coke."

After listening to this time and again, Lem, who sat across from him, said, "You can't get the Coke here, but if you really want a pill I can get it for you."

"What do you mean you can get it? How, where?"

"As you know, Joe, before coming to this glue pot I was an orderly in the hospital. It has Dexedrine. I can get it, but it'll cost you two packs a pill."

"But is it the real stuff?" Joe asked.

"You'll have to take my word for it, if you really want it," Lem replied. The deal was agreed to, and Lem promised to have the pill on Friday afternoon.

After the noon break on Friday, Lem gave Joe a capsule, which he gulped down immediately with water. Ten minutes later he was, as he put it, "higher than a kite," laughing, singing, gay as could be. Fearing that others would notice this, we urged him to quiet down. The same thing was repeated, one Friday after another.

What Joe did not know was that the capsules contained nothing more than powdered aspirin. When Lem let me in on the secret, I could hardly believe it. After all, I had seen Joe's spirits soar only minutes after he took a capsule. So Lem let me monitor his operation. During the lunch break he placed two aspirin tablets in an envelope, stomped on it with his foot, filled a capsule with its granules, and after returning to work, gave the capsule to Joe.

I did nothing to stop this deception. Joe was delighted with his weekly fix; it would have been cruel to disenchant him.

This was not the only example of how the power of suggestion did its strange work. Later, when I was a piecework payroll clerk in the office of the shoe factory, I sat next to Kenneth, a prisoner about my age who was a U.S. citizen but had lived in Mexico for a number of years. He was married to a Mexican woman and they had two children. Kenneth told me that he would tell his wife periodically that he had to return to the States on business matters and would stay away anywhere from a few weeks to many months. Once his feet touched U.S. soil his character changed and he became a modern Bluebeard. He did not murder women; he only swindled them. He bragged about the wealthy widows he had swept off their feet, made love to, and then, in a variety of ways, conned out of thousands of dollars.

Ken suffered from a bad case of ulcers, but they weren't due to a bad conscience. His prison time was growing shorter and as it did his worry grew, because the state of New Mexico still had a "hold" on him. His worst pain came at night, making sleep difficult. Finally, the prison doctor told him that without enough sleep there would be no improvement in his condition.

He prescribed a "strong drug," to be taken every evening after dinner for two weeks. This would put him into a deep sleep that would last until morning. "But I cannot give you these pills. You'll have to take one in the lieutenant's office on your way from the mess hall, and then go immediately to your cell. Remember, the pill is strong. It'll knock you out rapidly. So as soon as you get to your cell, undress, wait for the count, then go to sleep."

Ken followed instructions, but by the time he reached his cell he was so drowsy that he fell asleep and had to be awakened and reprimanded for not standing up for the count. Then he slept the rest of the night. The same thing happened the next night, but this time he forced himself to stay awake until the count was over. In two weeks he felt like a "new man."

The "strong drug" he was given was a placebo. In Joe's case the power of suggestion had "turned him on"; in Ken's case it had "turned him off."

The most important job and the one I held longest was that of piecework payroll clerk. It was similar to the work Gus Hall had done while he was in Leavenworth. I had not applied for the job; it was offered to me. Apparently they were looking for someone who would not finagle figures by giving credit to cronies for work done by others. With so many different operations and piecework rates, and with inmates often shifted from one job to another during the month, it was difficult for many to know exactly what their earnings would be. It was important therefore that there be confidence in the final tabulation.

I earned the maximum hourly rate of pay, which averaged, in my last year, 1961, about $48 a month. Thus, working in prison industry was beneficial to me. It also made it possible for the family to visit on weekends instead of workdays, and earned me mandatory industrial good time, which reduced my sentence by several months.

Yet work in prison industry was a form of servitude in which convict labor was miserably exploited. Those inmates who could cover their own commissary needs, and who were relatively sure of making parole or earning meritorious good time in other ways, shunned work in industry like the plague. They preferred jobs in maintenance where the pace was more leisurely and the pressure to make a buck absent. Some inmates even looked upon industry work as slave labor, and they were not far from wrong.

In a report to a U.S. Senate subcommittee, Director of Prisons Bennett praised federal prison industries highly. He reported that the men working there in 1961 had earned an average of $40 a month. This at a time when workers in manufacturing industries were averaging $92 a week. Thus, workers in federal prison industry were receiving every *month* only 43 percent of what workers outside prison walls earned every *week*.

It is this abominably low wage scale that explained why federal prison industry earned a much higher profits-to-sales ratio than private industry. In U.S. manufacturing industry for 1961 this profit ratio was 6 percent, but in federal prison industry it was 18 percent.

If prison labor brought the same rate of pay as workers outside receive, it would add immeasurably to inmates' feelings of self-respect and pride. It would also enable them to leave prison with enough money to help them cope with the problem of finding employment. Under the existing conditions, it was no wonder that so many turned to their old ways and before long ended up back in prison.

16

Puerto Rico Libre

As the years passed, I spent more and more time with the Puerto Rican political prisoners. We did not cell or work near each other, so our meeting place was the prison yard. Weather permitting, I would play handball, exercise, exchange pleasantries with inmates, and then stroll in the shadow of the high wall with my Puerto Rican friends.

We generally talked in Spanish. They preferred it and thought it would help my less-than-good hearing become accustomed to the spoken language. But often I found it impossible to follow what they were saying. They spoke with machine-gun rapidity, telescoping words and chopping off syllables along the way. I knew Spanish was a phonetic language, but it didn't sound that way to me. I had begun reading Spanish newspapers, and later novels, but the spoken idiom was something else again. I would implore, *"No tan rapido, por favor!"* They would slow down until the warmth of the subject set its own rhythm again. And when I tried to speak Spanish I was so concerned with proper grammar that I soon was making a bollixed-up jumble of both languages.

We would fill each other in on the latest news, and when I read something I wanted to relate, I mentally rehearsed it in Spanish so as not to fumble in telling it. They invariably found a verb conjugated incorrectly or some other unpardonable grammatical sin. But I was learning, not only their language but about them as human beings and how deeply they felt about their beloved Puerto Rico.

Oscar Collazo was doing a life sentence. On November 1, 1950, he and another Nationalist Party member, Griselio Torreselo, tried to force their way into Blair House in Washington. It was being used at the time as President Truman's residence while the White House was under repair. In the encounter, Torreselo and a security guard, Leslie Coffelt, were killed. Collazo was gravely wounded.

At his trial, Collazo was found guilty of murder and sentenced to death. Worldwide protest influenced Truman to commute the sentence to life imprisonment. At the time of the Washington events he was 36 years old, married, and the father of a young daughter.

Ervin Flores and Rafael Cancel were serving 25-to-75 year sentences. They, too, had been convicted of a violent act. On March 1, 1954, they and two companions—Lolita Lebron and Andres Figueroa Cordero—had gone to the House of Representatives in Washington, taken seats in the gallery, and then at a signal unfurled the Puerto Rican flag, shouted *"Libertad para Puerto Rico!,"* and opened fire into the ceiling and the well of the House. Five congressmen were wounded by ricocheting bullets.

Lolita had given the signal to fire. A note in her purse took full responsibility for the action. She said at the trial that their intent had not been to kill anyone. Lolita was 33 at the time of their action, Ervin and Andres 29, and Rafael 23.

The violent actions in Washington, I was told, were a desperate response to massive repression taking place in Puerto Rico. In the face of a worldwide movement of third-world countries to end colonialism and gain independence, the U.S. Government was under pressure to do something about its colony, Puerto Rico. But instead of granting independence, it devised a plan to camouflage the island's colonial status by turning it into an "associated free state" in a U.S. "commonwealth." Thus, at a time when the British Commonwealth, the French Community, and other similar pseudonyms for empire were tottering from colonial revolts, the United States was setting up a so-called commonwealth of its own, with Puerto Rico as hostage.

Incensed at this fraud, the island's independence forces sought to halt it. The struggle soon took on a now-or-never quality. As government repression increased, the Nationalist Party on the island attempted to organize a popular insurrection. The decision of Collazo and Terreselo to go to Blair House was made when they received word that U.S. armed forces were being used to put down a pro-independence takeover of the town of Jayuya.

At the time of the Washington episodes I questioned these violent acts, as did many friends of Puerto Rican independence. I feared they would be used to justify even greater repression. However, I never discussed this with my Puerto Rican friends in Leavenworth. It was no longer an issue.

In prison, Oscar, Ervin and Rafael decided that under no circumstances would they apply for parole or ask for a commutation of sentence. To do so, they felt, would be to recognize the authority of the U.S. Government over them, and, by inference, over their country. If freedom came, it would have to be unconditional, without their asking for it or agreeing to anything. Lolita—in the women's prison in Alderson, West Virginia—and Andres, in Atlanta, also shared this view.

They were quite different personalities. Oscar, who had worked as a metal polisher, came from humble surroundings in the farming community of Florida, Puerto Rico. Yet he could well have been a college professor. In prison he became something of a linguist, mastering Italian, French and Portuguese. He was also a passionate student of history and a walking encyclopedia on many subjects.

Oscar was soft-spoken, reserved, considerate, and had the patience of Job. He was well-liked, but not too well known. He stayed much to himself. His physical activity consisted of walking the prison yard, which he could do for hours at a stretch. His other yard activity was strumming a mandolin. He learned to play like a virtuoso.

Oscar suffered terribly from hay fever. One year, during the weeks when the hot Kansas winds swept up more pollen than usual, he was so ill I feared he would die. Yet he refused to ask for medication or to be checked into the hospital. He would say, "I'll ask these people for nothing. They represent the power that oppresses my people and I'll have nothing to do with them."

I would argue, "But Oscar, will you help your cause if you die here? Your job is to live, to survive all this, so that you can continue your struggle. As a prisoner you should *demand* proper medical care, not reject it."

He took the same position at first toward using the school facilities or working in industry. Yet he needed the money to buy the books and publications he wanted and the commissary items he needed. His family was not in a position to help him.

I never won the argument. But during one particularly bad hay fever season he became so desperately ill that he had to be taken to the hospital. In time, he also made use of the school, helping other inmates study Spanish. And still later, after I left Leavenworth, I learned he was working in industry. (Ervin and Rafael had gone into industry much earlier.)

It took me a bit longer to get to know Ervin. He spoke a halting English at first and I had great difficulty in understanding his Spanish. Ervin had been employed at a number of trades, particularly tailoring and cabinet making. He had also had trade union organizing experience. He was the shortest of the three, about 5 feet, 3 inches. This gave him the appearance of a youngster not yet fully grown. As if to make up for his short stature, Ervin would always walk tall, head high, back straight, chest out. Yet he was modest and shy. As he began to feel more at home in the English language, he became something of a counselor for inmates with personal problems. With a laugh he told me that sometimes he felt like a social worker. His specialties in the yard were handball and weightlifting.

Ervin was single, and for the years I was at Leavenworth he received neither mail nor visitors. Apparently his family had abandoned him, whether because of political disagreement, fear of persecution, or lack of means to travel. However Ervin was a stoic and never talked about his personal problems, but I knew how much it meant for a prisoner to have people on the outside who cared.

Rafael, the tallest of the three, was neither shy nor diffident. It didn't take him long after arriving from Alcatraz to become well-known and quite popular. He had a habit of punctuating his sentences with the phrase "By golly," and so he became known as "By Golly."

When he was not yet seven years old, something happened that Rafael never forgot. On Palm Sunday, 1937, his parents, ardent supporters of the independence cause, had gone to Ponce to participate in a peaceful pro-independence march. The mayor of the city had issued a permit, but an hour before the march was to start, the U.S.-appointed governor of the island, Blanton Winship, rescinded permission and ordered the mobilization of the police. When the march proceeded nonetheless, the police opened fire. Twenty-one persons were killed and approximately 200 wounded. "My mother left home dressed in white," Rafael recalled, "she returned dressed in red—in blood. To save herself she had crawled over fallen bodies."

The child was stunned and horrified. A week later, he committed his first act of rebellion. He refused to stand up in his classroom to salute and pledge allegiance to the U.S. flag.

In his youth Rafael had been very devout and had considered studying for the priesthood. "Two things prevented this," he explained. "First, I became too involved in the independence movement, and then I fell deeply in love."

Rafael was living in a fifth-floor Brooklyn tenement with his wife, two children, a brother-in-law and sister-in-law when he left for Washington in March 1954. After the FBI and New York police searched his apartment they reported that one wall bore a large colored picture of Pedro Albizu Campos, legendary leader of the Puerto Rican Nationalist Party.

Rafael and his wife had been married only three years when he was arrested. He spoke of her with pride and sadness. I was surprised when he told me that she was not involved in the independence movement and had known little about it when they fell in love. "She must be a wonderful person," I told him, "to stand by you so bravely."

Rafael loved baseball. He was a good pitcher and fun to watch because of his good-natured banter. The last game I saw him pitch, shortly before I was released, was a one-hit shutout.

As much as I longed for the day of my release, I dreaded the moment I would have to say farewell to my Puerto Rican friends. Yet there was reason for hope. The Cuban

Revolution, which we had watched develop and then celebrated while in prison, had a special significance for Puerto Rico. For four hundred years, the two islands had shared a common cultural and political history. Together they had fought against Spanish colonial rule and U.S. occupation. Lola Rodriguez, a Puerto Rican poet, had compared them to the two wings of a single bird receiving flowers and bullets in the same heart.

It took eighteen more years before Oscar, Lolita, Ervin and Rafael were released. Andres had been freed two years earlier, suffering from terminal cancer. (I had never met him.) For two years his cancer in the lower colon had been treated by prison doctors as bleeding hemorrhoids. Counting the time in jail awaiting trial, Oscar had spent 30 years in prison; Rafael, Lolita and Ervin—26 years each.

Shortly after their release on September 12, 1980, I greeted them again on their native soil, under clear blue skies, amid the exotic flora of the lush, beautiful island. The three had obviously aged since I last saw them, but they were full of life and eager to help unite all the island's forces favoring independence. From them I learned something of the changes that had occurred in Leavenworth since I was there. Each of the three had spent time in the hole. Rafael had been kept there for six months, then shipped to Marion, Illinois—the maximum security prison that had taken the place of Alcatraz—and had stayed in Marion's hole for sixteen additional months.

Most prisoners now were from racial minorities; they saw themselves as victims of racism and poverty, not as criminals. This had greatly increased their militancy and their determination to be treated as human beings. A number of concessions had been won by this militancy: mail privileges had been enlarged—inmates could write to anyone; each cellhouse now had a telephone from which prisoners could make collect calls; recreational and athletic facilities had been expanded, and the Leavenworth prison population had been reduced from the former 2,500 to about 1,800.

At the same time, however, the screws of repression had been greatly tightened. The reduction in size of the prison population, for example, was part of a general trend to assure better control—establishing more Federal prisons with fewer inmates in each. There was also less talk of rehabilitation and a more candid acknowledgement that the prime purpose of imprisonment is punitive.

I learned that a number of food strikes, riots and work stoppages had taken place at Leavenworth. Rafael had been thrown into the hole for speaking up for a Chicano prisoner who had been treated unfairly in the brush factory.

The horror of horrors was Marion—the prototype of the prisons-to-be. Rafael referred to it as "a model of the most sadistic prison system imaginable." Everything there, he reported, is controlled electronically, yet there is a guard for every two or three inmates. The object is to turn inmates into robots, without independent wills, trained to respond automatically and without question to every command. Prisoners are permitted to move in or out of a corridor only during "move time"—a ten-minute interval every hour, five minutes before to five minutes after the hour. No movement is permitted in between. Should a man fail to complete his move before the ten minutes are up, he is frozen where he is until the next move time arrives.

Closed-circuit TV screens monitor the corridors; electric eyes monitor the cells. Loudspeakers in the corridors become receivers at the push of a button. Even worse is the wholesale use of valium and other powerful drugs for behavior modification purposes. Rafael said that some prisoners are so doped up all the time that they walk around like zombies. "During my seven years in Marion," he told me, "I refused to touch a pill—not even an aspirin, vitamin or sleeping pill. I was convinced that they were all doctored to turn us into vegetables."

In addition to these refined techniques of human torture, Marion had become notorious for the use of old-fashioned physical force. Rafael told me of seeing men beaten into unconsciousness. To get a man in his cell and to make sure he could not resist, a machine called a Big Bertha was employed. This was brought directly in front of the cell, its gun nozzle pointed between the bars, and a stream of tear gas shot into the cell. When the victim had been overcome, guards wearing gas masks would enter the cell, stand the inmate up against the wall, and then beat him into a pulp.

Rafael referred me to a Federal court ruling in 1978, which called the "sensory-deprivation boxcar cell," used in Marion for punishment purposes, "an updated version of medieval torture methods." Yet the Marion model is being copied in both federal and state prisons, including the Alderson Federal Prison for women, according to Rafael.

17
Segregation

Racial segregation was deeply ingrained in the Federal prison system. In Leavenworth, Cellhouses B and D were for whites only; Cellhouse C, for Blacks only. Cellhouse A was the exception—whites occupied the lower tiers and Blacks the upper ones. The dining room was also segregated: whites on one side, Blacks on the other. They sat in opposite wings of the movie auditorium. It was prison apartheid.

The major impetus for changing this pattern came from events outside prison walls. The U.S. Supreme Court's decision in 1954 in *Brown v. Board of Education* rejected the "separate but equal" concept. It ruled that segregation in education was a violation of the 14th Amendment to the U.S. Constitution. This was a signal victory for the Black people in their struggle to end the Jim Crow system.

Even more important, in some ways, was the simple and courageous act of Rosa Parks in the old Confederate capital of Montgomery, Alabama, in December 1955. By refusing to move to the rear of the bus she set in motion a wave of civil rights struggles that continued for more than a decade and influenced all aspects of American life, including life behind prison bars.

Prisons are a mirror of society, especially of the conditions of the most exploited and oppressed. At the turn of the century, the majority of prison inmates were European immigrants or their children. But the more recent migrations of Black people from the South, and of Puerto Ricans and Mexicans from their native lands, have brought new kinds of ghettos, different from those of the past because escape from them is nearly impossible. Present-day ghetto-slum poverty is grinding, degrading and overwhelming. This is what fills our prisons today. (When I was in Leavenworth, about one-third of the inmates were Black.)

At the time of the high court's decision on school segregation, Ben

Davis, Jr., former Communist New York City councilman, was serving a five-year sentence under the Smith Act in the Federal prison in Terre Haute. Davis, a Harvard Law School graduate, made application to the U.S. District Court in Washington, D.C., on December 17, 1954, for a writ of mandamus on behalf of himself and "all other Negro inmates similarly situated in prisons and penitentiaries." He asked the court to direct U.S. Attorney General Herbert Brownell, Jr., and U.S. prison director James V. Bennett, "to discontinue the unlawful and unconstitutional practice of segregating petitioner and other Negro inmates of prisons and penitentiaries."

On the day Davis's lawsuit was filed, he was placed in solitary confinement to "facilitate his protection." According to Davis, however, there had been no inmate threat of violence against him. The real motive for his isolation soon became clear. The Government responded to Davis's allegations by claiming that he was no longer being segregated racially, for he was no longer eating in the mess hall or using the other facilities that he had listed as being segregated; furthermore, that his solitary confinement was not a form of racial discrimination, for there were four other inmates in isolation—two white and one Black.

When, four months later, in April 1955, Davis's suit came before the district court, it was dismissed as moot. He had been released from Terre Haute a few weeks earlier for transfer to the Allegheny County jail in Pittsburgh, Pennsylvania, to serve a 60-day sentence for contempt of court. In testifying for the defendants in a state sedition trial, Davis had refused to name names of other Party members.

In Pennsylvania, too, Davis took legal action to challenge the segregation of and discrimination against Black prisoners, acting as his own attorney.

Word of Davis's bold legal assault on the system of prison segregation soon spread throughout the prison chain. It became an issue that could no longer be ignored.

Under increasing criticism for failing to halt the growing racist terror in the South, the Government was doubly sensitive to the charge that it was sanctioning segregation in an area under its direct supervision—the federal prisons. As a result, the Bureau of Prisons began to move toward desegregation, but in the minimum-and medium-security institutions first.

Rumors regarding these efforts had reached us at Leavenworth. These rumors included wild tales of racial tension and violence. How much truth there was to these allegations we did not know. It was apparent, however, that measures to desegregate Leavenworth would not be long in coming. Some of the most racially-bigoted white inmates talked of "burning the joint down" should such steps be taken. Most whites said nothing, but there was increasing fear of racial disturbances.

By the time Leavenworth's turn came, the authorities had acquired enough experience to avoid violence. They pursued a policy designed to make clear that they would tolerate no opposition to changes, and that *all* prisoners would benefit by what they had in mind. But they proceeded piecemeal—the dining hall first, the movie auditorium next, and finally the cellhouses.

The seating arrangement in the dining hall had remained unchanged since the prison was first built. The hall was divided lengthwise into four sections, with long rows of seats closely jammed together. White prisoners sat on the left side of the hall and Blacks on the right. Guards stood along the walls.

Counters barely wide enough for a food tray ran the length of the rows. These were the tables we ate from. They were attached to the backrests of the men seated in the row ahead. Inmates filed into the hall, picked up their trays and food at serving tables, then continued up an aisle, one at a time, until they reached the row with the first vacant seat. As each row was occupied, the man next in turn would take the seat at the far end of the next row. This procedure continued until all inmates were seated.

We sat facing forward and were permitted to talk only to the man on either side of us; even this conversation was sometimes frowned upon. When we finished eating we waited our turn to leave. The signal given, we filed out in the precise order in which we had come in. On the way out we disposed of our trays and utensils, which were checked to see that everything was accounted for.

This seating plan was, of course, an abomination. The hemmed-in overcrowding, which made it difficult to bend an elbow while eating, plus the total regimentation, seemed designed to upset even cast-iron stomachs.

The changes in the dining room were radical: seats and counters were torn up and discarded section by section. As each section was cleared and the floor redone, tables for four were installed. We were now permitted to sit where and with whom we pleased, as long as a seat was vacant. This held for everyone, Black and white alike.

At first only a few of the white inmates invited Black friends or acquaintances to eat with them or, if the Blacks were already seated, asked whether they could join them. There were angry looks from some prisoners, but the practice was soon accepted as normal. Integration, however, never became complete. Most of the inmates ate with members of their own race or nationality and with their close friends. But no one could be denied the right to an empty seat, no matter where it was or who else was sitting at that table.

Nor did we wait our turn to leave the dining hall. We left when we finished eating. This innovation was welcomed enthusiastically. It helped neutralize whatever opposition there was to dining hall desegregation.

Changes, too, were made in the auditorium seating for movies. Up to then, as in the dining hall, whites sat on the left side of the theater and Blacks on the right. We filed in, one at a time, to occupy seat after seat, starting with the front row, irrespective of hearing or seeing needs, or friends we would have liked to sit with.

All this was changed, by a simple announcement: Henceforth we could sit where we desired, on a first-come first-choice basis, and this applied to *everyone*. As each cellhouse proceeded to the movie in rotating order, the inmates of each would get their turn for first choice of seats. This reform, too, was welcomed, even though some of the bigoted whites were aware that its purpose was to bring about desegregation.

The final changes were the most difficult and sensitive, for they related to the desegregation of living quarters. On this issue some of the racists were rabid in their opposition. I was living at the time in Cellhouse D, occupied exclusively by white inmates working in industry. (Black industry workers occupied Cellhouse C). My cell was D-407, and next to it, on my left, the occupant was Ed Smith, a Texan. "Smitty" was among those who had threatened "dire consequences" if Blacks were moved in to "our" cellhouse. I tried to reason with him, to explain why segregation was wrong and had to go, but to no avail.

The authorities, meanwhile, were biding their time. The first signs that something was afoot came when we noticed that cells were being vacated and remained vacant. This was unusual, for as a rule the daily "snitch-sheet"—which carried all in-and-out movements of prisoners—listed the name and registry number of a new inmate on the same day that an old one was reported going out. But now days went by and more and more cells stayed empty, until there were about twenty unoccupied in our cellhouse. Then one day around noon, without prior notice, all the empty cells were filled with Black inmates, who were now located on each tier.

Smitty and some of his like-minded friends were, of course, furious. During the next two days a number of mattresses of new occupants were set on fire. Then everything returned to normal. Even the worst racist bigots were sobered into the realization that they had a great deal to lose and nothing to gain by continuing their frantic opposition. Their concern was not only with the chance of landing in the hole, losing accumulated good time, or being shipped to Alcatraz, but with another more pressing, concern. Television had just come to Leavenworth.

A large TV set had been installed on the stone flag of each cellhouse. After dinner, inmates were permitted to come down from their cells to watch the programs. This was an innovation they had fervently wanted. Most of the prisoners were long-timers, some of them lifers, and television was a new, exciting experience, an escape from the boredom of confinement, a window to the outside world. The prison authorities stipulated, however, that in the event of cellhouse "trouble," the TV would be yanked. Everyone suspected that the introduction of television was somehow linked to the desegregation move. However, faced with the risk of losing the prized TV offerings, even the most blatant racists hesitated.

Not long after these changes were put into operation, Smitty made friends with a fellow Texan, a Black prisoner on the tier.

18

Bad News from Terre Haute

Each time John Abt visited me—about twice a year—he brought news of Henry Winston's health and how he was doing at Terre Haute. As Winnie's attorney, he corresponded regularly with him and visited him usually on the same trip that brought him my way. Thus Winnie and I kept in touch with one another through Abt.

I learned that Winnie, in his usually high spirits, had adjusted to prison life but was being given a hard time by prison authorities. Having had experience with Ben Davis, who had waged his legal battle against prison segregation from the same prison, officials were doubly concerned about Winston developing any influence among the Black inmates. He was warned against "proselytizing," kept under close watch, and given an especially menial job calculated to isolate him from other inmates during working hours.

Winston's job was to keep the "rec" building clean. On the main floor was an auditorium, which also served as the movie house, and there was a gym upstairs. Winnie worked with a broom, mop, brush and rags. He swept, mopped and polished the floors, dusted the seats and cleaned the toilet. When he was finally admitted to an industry job, it was to polish brass fixtures.

All this time I learned from Abt. What neither he nor I knew at the time was that about the end of 1957 or the beginning of 1958 Winston had begun to suffer from severe headaches. The aspirins prescribed when he appeared in sick line brought no relief. Instead, his condition became progressively worse and he started to get dizzy spells. When Winnie reported this to the hospital clinic staff, he was told that his headaches were caused by "nervous tension." He was urged to relax and was given sedatives. However, his headaches and dizziness became worse and he was now having trouble walking. When he described these symptoms to members of the medical staff he was accused of malingering. Yet work—as he told them—even menial work, was far preferable to being locked up in a cell all day.

Winston finally wrote to the warden, complaining of the treatment he was getting, and demanded a thorough physical. He was examined on April 22, 1959, more than a year after his first symptoms appeared. The chief medical officer of the prison reported the results of this examination to Mayden, the associate warden. (These were the "findings" as set down in the medical records later obtained under the FOIA.) They read:

> As requested by you, the above named inmate was seen by Dr. Flood this date, for physical examination. Dr. Flood's report reflects that this 44-year-old colored man is complaining of vertigo, trouble with his teeth, shortness of breath, and weakness of arms and legs . . . .
> Dr. Flood diagnosed (1) gross obesity and 2) vertigo, etiology undetermined.
> Treatment recommended was weight reduction as well as treatment with an anti-vertigo namely dramamine.

Thus, the physician prescribed nothing more than a pill for seasickness.

Eight months after this examination, in early January, 1960, Winston's wife, Edna, and their children — Larry, 13, and Judy, 10, came to see him. During the visit, Winston got up to fetch the boxed lunch (in Terre Haute prisoners were permitted to have lunch with family visitors). It was then that Edna noticed her husband had difficulty getting up and that in reaching for the food his eye focus and hand coordination were off. She asked him what was wrong and for the first time he told her, for he had not wanted to worry either his family or his friends.

Alarmed, Edna reached John Abt as soon as she returned to New York. He put everything aside and caught an early flight to Terre Haute. When he saw Winnie he knew something was seriousy wrong. He spoke to the warden and insisted that an outside neurological specialist be permitted to examine Winston. The warden refused, but promised that a consulting neurologist would be brought in. An examination took place on January 20. The diagnosis indicated a brain tumor and the recommendation was for immediate surgery.

The next day Winston was taken by prison bus to the U.S. prison medical center in Springfield, Missouri. Travel by bus was chosen despite his condition. Their indifference was spelled out in the instructions to the bus personnel. In "the event of convulsions," Winston was to be given sodium phenobarbital to induce sleep. If the convulsions were "unusually severe," he was to be administered sodium pentothal—an anesthetic and hypnotic! (From the medical records obtained under the FOIA.)

As soon as Abt learned that Winston had been transferred to Springfield for brain surgery, he reached Director of Prisons James Bennett. Abt insisted that the operation be performed by a qualified neurosurgeon chosen by the family and in a non-prison hospital. After the sorry record of prison-medical bungling, he would not permit his client to undergo so dangerous and delicate an operation in Springfield and by a prison-assigned surgeon. This position was supported by a large number of highly reputable surgeons and doctors who added their voices to Abt's.

Ten days later, on January 31, 1960, Winston was released to the custody of Abt and taken by him to the Montefiore Hospital in the Bronx. Winston's words to Abt as he was being wheeled out of the Springfield hospital were: "Am I that bad off, John, that they're letting me out?"

"Don't worry, Winnie," Abt assured him, "it's only for the operation. They want you back as soon as it's over."

"That's better, John," Winnie said.

The operation took place on February 2, and was a success. The tumor was found to be benign. Its removal had come in time to save his life—but too late to save his sight. Winston was blind. There had been two years of misdiagnosis and criminal negligence, as there had been for the Puerto Rican prisoner, Andres Figueroa Cordero.

"I was terribly shocked by the news of Winston's operation, "I wrote Lil on February 5. "I hadn't suspected anything quite as serious. I had written to John Abt some weeks back asking how Henry was as John had visited him in Terre Haute immediately following his visit here. Today I received a reply, delayed until after the operation. According to this the operation was successful and Winnie is on the road to recovery. I hope this proves to be the case. I have a great fondness for Winnie—who does not? . . . It breaks my heart to think of what he must have gone through before the real malady was discovered. I'm sure it must have been diagnosed as just psychosomatic, a bad case of nerves. Please keep me abreast of everything you hear about him. John writes that he was 'released' under custody to go to New York for the operation. I don't exactly know what that means. I hope this doesn't mean he will be sent back. It would be a double crime to do so."

But this was exactly what the government had in mind! It sought to send him back to the Springfield prison hospital, and from there to Terre Haute. To stop this, John Abt took the matter to the courts.

On March 25, 1960, I wrote home:

> Your letter about Winnie's case going to the Circuit Court arrived this evening. I'm heartened by the news. I hope, however, that the Administration's offer to send him to a New York prison hospital instead of to the one in Missouri doesn't produce a relaxation in the efforts to win his complete freedom. At the first signs of such relaxation Winnie will be hustled off to Springfield, Terre Haute or some other such place. That's how things are done.
>
> The charge of inhuman treatment may have stung some people a bit, but not enough to make them relent. Hasn't Winnie paid enough for a crime that never was? . . . . In my opinion what is decisive in giving him an even break is that of removing him from the dark, damp, dreary, depressive and cruel status of prisoner and placing him in the life-giving, all-curing sunshine of freedom.

At that point I had not yet been informed that Winston had lost his sight. When I learned the tragic fact, I wrote, on April 20, 1960, "I am dismayed at the state of Henry's health. I hadn't realized he was just about totally blind and thus far incapable of using his lower limbs. To live in eternal darkness and to wear shackles on top of it?"

Twice the Parole Board refused to grant him medical parole. The policy was set by the Administration, which was determined to keep this now-blind Communist leader under lock and key. From Montefiore Hospital he was transferred to the U.S. Marine Hospital on Staten Island, and from there to the U.S. prison in Danbury, Connecticut.

But the disgrace and inhumanity of Winston's treatment caused worldwide anger. Winston was finally released on June 21, 1961, in an order of clemency issued by President John F. Kennedy, nearly a year and a half after the operation had left him blind.

19

To Shorten My Time

When I entered prison I was prepared to serve my full sentence of eight years minus whatever good time I could get. Yet I hoped that unfolding events would bring my time to an end much sooner. Each sign of abating cold war tensions, the growing feeling of shame over the McCarthy years, raised these hopes. I soon learned, however, that it takes a great deal more to halt or reverse the wheels of repression than to get them started.

When I began serving time in February 1956, a national movement to halt Smith Act arrests and jailings already existed. The National Committee to Win Amnesty for Smith Act Victims had been formed at the end of 1951, with Dr. Edward K. Barsky chairman, Carl Marzani treasurer, and Marion Bachrach secretary. A national conference on amnesty had taken place on June 14, 1952, in New York City. Muriel Draper, Dr. W. E. B Du Bois, Dashiell Hammett, Albert Maltz, Vito Marcantonio, William L. Patterson, Paul Robeson and Dr. Harry F. Ward were among its sponsors.

A number of important national organizations had also spoken out against the Smith Act prosecutions. The Congress of Industrial Organizations, the Americans for Democratic Action, the National Association for the Advancement of Colored People, and the American Civil Liberties Union had called for repeal of the Smith Act. The 1951 national convention of the CIO termed the Supreme Court's upholding of our convictions *(Dennis v. U.S.)* "a grave blow to America's precious heritage of freedom of speech."

This movement continued to grow in the next few years, but so also did the list of Smith Act victims. In January 1955, for the first time a leading Communist was convicted under the "membership" provision of the Smith Act; Claude Lightfoot, Black Illinois C.P. leader, was sentenced to five years. Three months later, Junius Scales of North Carolina was likewise convicted. Although war tensions had visibly declined and McCarthyism was in retreat, the government's repressive machinery kept on operating as though nothing had changed.

At that point, A. J. Muste, prominent leader of the Fellowship of Reconciliation, decided to initiate an independent appeal to President Eisenhower for a 1955 Christmas political amnesty. He was joined by Eleanor Roosevelt, Norman Thomas, Elmer Rice, Prof. Henry Steele Commager and Lewis Mumford, among others. Their appeal, too, went unheeded.

Even though these efforts failed to win amnesty for anyone, they constituted an important moral-political force influencing the national political climate. The turning point came in 1957 with the U.S. Supreme Court's decision in the California Smith Act *(Yates)* case.

When the high court had upheld our convictions in the Dennis case in June 1951, it specifically excluded from its review the sufficiency of the evidence presented against us. This was admitted by Chief Justice Fred Vinson: "*Whether on this record petitioners did in fact advocate the overthrow of the Government by force and violence is not before us*" (Emphasis added-GG).

In the *Yates* case, six years later, with Earl Warren as Chief Justice, the tribunal *did* review sufficiency of evidence. It found that, "When it comes to forcible action at some future time, we cannot but regard this record as deficient." As the records in all the Smith Act cases were basically similar, the Yates decision laid the basis for the subsequent reversal of nine Smith Act cases then pending for review in the U.S. appeals courts, involving approximately seventy defendants. But it did not open up for review those cases already adjudicated, such as our convictions in *Dennis v. U.S.* Since court decisions are not retroactive, such a reversal could come only after a rehearing. But when our attorneys asked that our case be reheard, the U.S. Supreme Court turned us down.

Hence, even though the Warren court decision had in effect reversed that of the Vinson court, Henry Winston and I were left exactly where we were—behind bars.

The *Yates* decision had, of course, made it far easier to convince people of the injustice of our imprisonment. But with only two of us left in prison, and no new Smith Act cases arising in the foreseeable future, much of the former urgency to win broad amnesty had been removed. In fact, for all practical purposes there was a danger that the amnesty campaign might phase out. Although I could understand this, I could not agree with it. Of course I had a personal stake, wanting to get out of prison as soon as possible.

But there was another consideration. What real assurance was there that the repression was now over? More than a dozen Communist Party leaders still had Smith Act membership indictments hanging over their heads, and the Department of Justice showed no signs of dropping them. The House Committee on Un-American Activities was still in business, holding its shameful hearings around the country. Then there was the McCarran Act, with its repressive registration provisions. To have the fight for amnesty relax now, I felt, would encourage illusions that all was well. Continuation of the amnesty campaign, even if it failed to reduce our sentences by a single day, was important to alert people to the still continuing existence of political repression.

I did not have to convince members of my family or friends in Chicago that the fight for amnesty must continue; they were as determined about it as I. Although there had been a letdown in the campaign nationally, the Party's national center took measures to reverse it. William L. Patterson headed a Party committee for this purpose and Simon W. Gerson, also designated the personal representative of the Winston-Green families, assumed coordination of the national effort. His was an extremely difficult task, for considerable inertia had set in by that time.

Much had been done in the Chicago area. A Smith Act Families Committee had been active in Chicago for a number of years. It provided information, exposed the FBI harassment of Smith Act victim's families, sent speakers to church, labor and community groups, arranged public meetings and affairs, published a Families Committee news bulletin, held Christmas, Chanukah and birthday parties for the children, and raised funds for its work and to defray the cost of family prison visits.

Lil, Ben and Florence were all deeply involved in the committee's activities (as were, of course, many others). The children helped to lick postage stamps, seal envelopes and run errands. Lil's role was, of course, crucial. Her courage and tireless activity inspired everyone. Florence was also indispensable. She was the treasurer of the Families Committee and within the Green family circle made it possible for Ben and Lil to devote much of their time to public activities.

Ben was concerned with all aspects of the committee's work but had the specific responsibility of helping extend the movement for amnesty. He was an excellent organizer, with immense vitality and determination, and a range of vision linked to good common sense.

The Chicago Committee to Defeat the Smith Act, led by Richard Criley, concentrated on showing how the Smith Act prosecutions endangered the hard-won provisions of the Bill of Rights. A first amnesty appeal emanating from Chicagoans appeared in 1953 and was authored by Rev. William T. Baird and Prof. Robert Morse Lovett.

The most important national appeal following the Supreme Court's Yates decision appeared in September 1958. It was cosponsored by Dr. Reinhold Niebuhr and Norman Thomas, joined by thirty-four other prominent Americans. Among them were Clarence E. Pickett, Kermit Eby, Prof. Alexander Meiklejohn, Rev. John Hayes Holmes, Rev. A. J. Muste, Bishop Edward L. Parsons, Joseph L. Rauh, and four well-known Chicagoans—Dr. John A. Lapp, Dr. John B. Thompson, Prof. Maynard Krueger, and Prof. Curtiss MacDougall of Northwestern University. When the appeal appeared in the Chicago press it included the names of additional prominent Chicagoans.*

Despite advancing age and failing health, Norman Thomas spent a great deal of time and energy on the amnesty effort. When the *New Republic* turned down an advertisement of the amnesty appeal, Thomas addressed a personal letter to the magazine's publisher, Gilbert Harrison. "I felt under some moral obligation," he wrote, "to raise the case of the only two Communists now in prison for a Smith Act offense which I do not believe would have resulted in conviction had the Supreme Court reached the position it took in the Yates case."

The thousands of letters addressed to Eisenhower urging amnesty brought a standard reply: Presidential clemency was a last resort after all other means had failed. As we had not yet appeared before the Parole Board, and were now eligible to do so, it was suggested that we try that avenue first.

I had misgivings about taking this course. I wrote Lil on April 16,

*Among them were Frank R. Anglin, Rev. William T. Baird, Rev. Frederick E. Ball, Harry Barnard, Earl E. Dickerson, Jessie C. Binford, Annette Dieckman, Prof. Murray Edelman, Pearl M. Hart, Lillian Herstein, Sidney Lens, Prof. Stephen Love, Prof. Victor Obenhaus, Prof. William T. Starr, Rev. Alva Tompkins, and Rabbi S. Burr Yampol.

1958, "It is hard to believe that a parole board will have the gumption to grant parole when there is still another indictment pending against us [that of membership in the CP]. And while the likelihood is that the other indictment will never stand up in the courts, the fact is that it has not been withdrawn and therefore cannot be discounted as a factor in the total picture."

But family and friends argued that my failure to apply for parole could become the Administration's pretext for not acting. I therefore filed an application.

About a month before the parole hearing in Washington (it took place on November 13, 1958), a member of the board came to Leavenworth to interview me. She was Mrs. Eva Bowring, the widow of a Nebraska congressman.

When I entered the prison office, I saw Mrs. Bowring—a tall, mannish-looking, middle-aged woman—and a younger woman with a stenographic notebook in hand. Mrs. Bowring went straight to the point. First she made sure that I was the right person (she was to interview others as well) and then asked, "Mr. Green, are you still a Communist?"

I was surprised at the question, for my application for parole had made clear that my political views had not changed. But recognizing that to her the word "Communist" apparently had a special sinister connotation, I said, "That depends on what you mean by that word, Mrs. Bowring. If you define a Communist as one who loves his country and because of that believes the present outmoded social system, capitalism, should be and someday will be replaced by the American people with a more equitable system, socialism, then I certainly am a Communist."

"So, Mr. Green, you are and you aren't. Which is it?"

"No, Mrs. Bowring, I am only what I am, not what someone else may think or say I am."

A great deal of work had been done in Chicago to prepare for the parole hearing. It climaxed with a Parole Dinner in a hotel on October 5, 1958. About 500 participated.

At the parole hearing in Washington, nine witnesses testified in our behalf. Their remarks were necessarily brief, as the total time allotted was only an hour. Among those who spoke were Rev. Shelby Rooks of Harlem, Rev. William T. Baird of Chicago, Charlotta Bass of Los Angeles, and Si Gerson, as a close personal friend. Edna Winston, Lil and Ben spoke for the two families, and John Abt as our attorney. Abt referred to the changed political climate since our trial and said that if the board treated our case on its merits, "then no doubt there will be parole. But here, frankly," he added, "the real problem is that these men are political prisoners—they are Communists."

The board members sat mum. Not a single question was asked. Describing the scene later, the Families Committee news bulletin still chose to stress the positive. "The parole hearing," it said, "has at least cleared away any procedural obstacles which, according to the Justice Department, blocked consideration in the past [of executive clemency]."

No sooner had this "procedural" obstacle erected by the Department of Justice been removed than another replaced it. Now those who wrote the President were informed that before clemency would be considered, Winston and I had to formally petition for it. It seemed clear to me that this was just more runaround. Eisenhower did not need a formal petition from us to act, and this was the Administration's way of dodging the issue.

I wrote Lil on May 18, 1959, "After you left here I sat down and formulated my petition for commutation of sentence and put it on ice for a few days just to see whether it holds its flavor when cold. As you know I have no taste for this venture. I do it only because I do not like the idea of people getting letters from Washington that nothing can be done to grant my release because I had not made formal application." My petition read in part:

> Petitioner is a political prisoner serving a cruel and unjust prison sentence solely for holding and advocating what may be to some unpopular political views. As a member and leader of the Communist Party of the United States, petitioner never concealed or tried to conceal his political philosophy and party affiliation. His beliefs have always been an open book from which any and all could read, be it to agree or disagree. The petitioner believes that the public avowal of his views, from speakers' rostrum and printed page, represent the very opposite of conspiracy and deceit. But in the frenzied hysteria of the McCarthy era a mere belief in socialism and/or communism, let alone active leadership in an organization advocating these goals was considered tantamount to treason. It was in this stifling anti-intellectual, "Know-Nothing," fear-laden atmosphere that the petitioner and his co-defendants were indicted and convicted.

Referring to my bail-jumping I wrote:

> Petitioner was also convicted of contempt arising from his failure to begin serving his sentence in July 1951. He began serving it in February 1956 when he surrendered voluntarily. This delay in surrender cannot be understood without reference to the atmosphere of repression at the time, in which it seemed that the nation was on the brink of a complete black-out of civil liberties. It is also necessary to point out that at the time this occurred there was no Federal law against bail-jumping. Therefore, petitioner's act of becoming a fugitive did not constitute a crime.

The amnesty campaign for Winston and myself did not miss the vigilant eye of J. Edgar Hoover. Nor did he and the FBI permit such "dangerous" activities to continue without FBI snoopers reporting them regularly. Special warnings were forwarded to the President and to the Parole Board, as though these perfectly legal activities constituted another "Communist threat" to the ramparts of the Republic.

On December 18, 1957, a letter from Hoover was delivered "By Courier Service" to the "Honorable Sherman Adams, the Special Assistant to the President, The White House." Hoover's letter refers to a report submitted on November 10, 1957, about the campaign "to obtain the release from prison of Communist Party leaders Gilbert Green and Henry Winston." (A copy of this report is *not* in the FBI files given me—G.G.)

The purpose of this letter to the President via his special assistant is to inform him "that Ben Green has indicated that his immediate goal is to try and see as many important people as possible, and particularly people who influence the administration." Hoover promised to send Adams "additional pertinent data" on this matter.

My FBI files reveal that on October 27, 1958, Hoover received a report of a national campaign to influence public opinion for parole. "The method used," the report states, "is direction of a continuous flow of mail to the Federal Parole Board." Twelve days later, on November 8, 1958, Hoover wrote to George J. Reed, Chairman of the Parole Board, about a delegation being organized to attend its hearings on November 13. This letter is marked "Classified Confidential." It states that "the information came from a highly confidential source [and that] . . . unauthorized disclosure of the information could result in disclosure of the source which would have an adverse effect on national security." No less!

How crazy this is can be seen in light of the fact that the matter of a delegation to the parole hearing had been publicly discussed at the

Chicago Parole Dinner on October 7, a full month earlier! There was more of this Hoover to White House and Parole Board nonsense.

But the most bizarre incident involved an exchange of letters between Richard M. Nixon, then Vice-President, and J. Edgar Hoover. On July 2, 1959, Nixon wrote to Hoover asking how to respond to a letter on amnesty that he had received from Earl Browder, who had been removed from his post as General Secretary of the Communist Party in 1945 and expelled from the organization the following year.

According to an FBI memo of July 8, 1959, Browder "purely on my own" had suggested to Nixon that the commutation of our sentences "would add strength to Nixon's future international role" and that "wiping this particular slate clean at this particular moment will strengthen America's moral position in a world where great populations hunger for a rebirth of morality."

The FBI memo discounts Browder's concern with morality. It suggests a more self-serving motive. It claims that Browder was trying to form a new organization and thought that delivering Nixon's support for amnesty would enhance his own standing. The FBI memo also questions Browder's reliability. "He admitted he is no longer a Communist but has consistently refused to furnish information in his possession which would have been of great value to this country's intelligence coverage."

On the same day, July 8, a "Dear Dick" letter was delivered by courier service. In it Hoover stressed that Winston and I had been convicted of a "heinous" crime. He said that we were not "political dissidents" but long-time, hard-core" Communists. He advised Nixon that should he decide to reply to Browder's letter, it be in that vein. Furthermore, that should Winston or I make applications for executive clemency "they will be afforded the same treatment, through established channels, as an application filed by any other convicted criminal."

How much influence Hoover had on the actions of the Parole Board and the President is a matter of conjecture. That he actively intervened against amnesty is a matter of record.

20

Jailhouse Intellectuals

With the passage of time I became more and more determined to salvage as much as I could from these wasted years. In my letters home I frequently referred to the books I was reading and classes I was taking. On April 3, 1959, I wrote: "In addition to my continuing study of Spanish, I am also spending considerable time on economics, anthropology and history." I then enumerated some of the original sources I was turning to in my study of economics: "Aristotle, Adam Smith, Ricardo, Malthus, Say, Marx, the Millses [James and John Stuart], and such contemporary writers as Veblen and Keynes. Anyway, as you can see I'm quite busy. Everyone here, if he's to keep from going insane, must find some avenues of escape and I guess mine is as good as any."

Later that year I wrote, "I'm up to my ears in study. I'm in the midst of a heavy philosophy program, concentrating nearly exclusively on the contemporary philosophers. I've just finished a book by Whitehead, *Science and the Modern World*, and am in the midst of reading Ortega y Gassett's *The Revolt of the Masses*, as well as Henri Bergson's *Creative Evolution*, and John Dewey's *Reconstruction of Philosophy*. This is part of a University of Chicago correspondence course in Contemporary Philosophy." Then, as an aside, "I'm also doing some study of German."

"Where I get the drive," I wrote, "I don't know. I guess it's just an inner compulsion not to mark these years on my life's score card as all lost."

Most of my studies were without benefit of classroom direction. However, when the opportunity arose to enroll in a correspondence course, or better still, an organized class, I jumped at the chance.

During my last year at Leavenworth I was taking five classes a week, a correspondence course in general science, and a Great Books discussion course on Saturday nights.* Through inmate friends assigned to the school it was possible to schedule classes not originally planned. One of these was the correspondence course of the University of Chicago in contemporary philosophy, which also met as a class once a week. From twenty to thirty inmates attended. Some of them had college degrees, but most were, in prison lingo, jailhouse intellectuals. Our weekly discussions were genuinely interesting, often exciting, and for me, always stimulating.

One paper I wrote for the class was on the relationship of the philosophies of Whitehead, a mathematician, and Bergson, a biologist, to the central division in philosophy between idealism and materialism. As a result I was asked to give a talk on the Marxist philosophy of dialectical materialism. As it happened, my nemesis, Mr. Hyde, (the assistant warden to whom I have previously referred), was in charge of the school on this particular night. He prowled the aisles and peered through the glass partitions into the classrooms to make sure that nothing unauthorized was taking place. As my lecture definitely fell into that category, and his bias against me was well known, we feared he could jeopardize our class's existence. So I spoke seated, while another inmate stood at the front table as though addressing the group.

A class in world history was also organized in the same freewheeling manner. We used college outlines on ancient, medieval and modern history. These contained many names of famous men and the dates of important historic events but said little or nothing about the underlying social pressures that produced the great historic changes. This reminded me of Brecht's words:

Who built seven-towered Thebes?
In the books stand the names of kings.
Did the kings drag the blocks of stone? . . . .
Young Alexander conquered India. He alone? . . . .
Every page a victory.
Who cooked the victory feast?

Thus I focused my efforts on showing the specific conditions and social-class relations underlying historic changes. In this class, too, I was asked to give a talk, and I readily agreed. I spoke of the pattern of development that led to changes from one social system to another.

*Based on the Great Books program originated at the University of Chicago by Mortimer J. Adler.

The Great Books discussion class proved the most interesting. We met every Saturday evening, shortly after the post-dinner count. Since school facilities were not available to us on Saturday nights, we were permitted to meet in a board room in the front offices. The course was led by two men assigned by the Kansas City Great Books Foundation. One was a lawyer, the other a doctor. They had evidently received training in guiding discussion groups at the Foundation's school and were quite familiar with the books discussed.

This course was not open to general enrollment. The list of invitees had been drawn up by inmate intellectuals in cooperation with the school administration. The list had then been submitted to the prison authorities for approval. My name was stricken. Those who had prepared the list protested, charging political discrimination in violation of the principles upon which the Great Books courses were organized. Two days before the course started I was informed that my name had been restored to the list.

We sat around a long table with the Kansas City discussion leaders at one end. (A member of the prison administration was always present, but not as a participant.) Before we began discussion of the first document, *The Declaration of Independence,* one of the discussion leaders explained that the 100 world classics had been selected as the best representatives of Western culture and that the role of the guides would be to see that the discussion did not wander in all directions. They would provide additional information at times, but they were not there to impose their own views.

The first session set the tone for those that followed. It was stimulating as well as challenging. There was a general appreciation of the Declaration as one of the great documents of history—spelling out the rights of people to dissolve old bonds and declare their independence, as well as their right to "alter or abolish" forms of government which no longer "effect their Safety and Happiness."

Then came the questions. One inmate wanted to know how it was possible for signers of the Declaration to proclaim the right to life, liberty and the pursuit of happiness and yet themselves to be slaveowners. Another criticized the document for its portrayal of the native Indians as encouraging genocide. Then came the charge that we as a nation now treat the Declaration as a museum piece, not as a living document applicable to present-day realities. The United States, he said, is now opposed to revolution anywhere in the world; it even opposes oppressed nations who are seeking their own 1776. The same atmosphere prevailed each Saturday—whether a work was by Plato, Shakespeare, Thoreau, Machiavelli, or de Tocqueville, whether it was James Madison's Federalist Papers or the Gospel of St. Matthew.

High point of the series for me was our discussion of *The Communist Manifesto* by Karl Marx and Frederick Engels, published in 1848. One of the group leaders opened the discussion to help "place the Manifesto in perspective." He reminded us that it was more than a hundred years old and that the capitalism it described was not that of today. Millions of people who now own corporate stock have turned it into a "people's capitalism," he assured us.

Of course, I challenged this view. Capitalism had indeed undergone changes, but in the direction of an ever greater concentration of wealth in the hands of a few. The general standard of living is higher because advances in science and technology have greatly expanded the productive forces of society. But, I argued, the gap between immense wealth on one side and abject poverty on the other is greater than ever. The basic analysis of the Manifesto, I contended, is still valid.

The discussion that followed revolved largely around this issue. When the class ended, not everyone had had a chance to speak, so one of the inmates (I think it was my friend Jim) proposed that we indicate by a show of hands where we stood: Was, or was not, the Manifesto still relevant today? A sizeable majority voted in the affirmative.

On occasion, when a guest lecturer was appearing at the nearby University of Kansas in Lawrence, arrangements were made for the speaker to make a stop at Leavenworth. That is how Prof. S. I. Hayakawa happened to address about 300 inmates on semantics. (At that time he was best known as an authority in that field and was not yet the politician who would be elected U.S. Senator from California in 1976.)

Hayakawa first explained the nature of semantics. It was, he said, the scientific study of the relationship of words to things and of language to thought and behavior. Words, he pointed out, are not identical with the things they are meant to symbolize. If a great disparity develops between the two—if words begin to mean different things to different people—misunderstanding, conflict and psychological disorder are a consequence.

He gave examples: The Soviet Union uses the word democracy differently than we do. Unless there is agreement on what that word means, conflict is inevitable. Similarly with labor-capital disputes. Both parties, he said, still use the "emotive" words that come out of a long past, arousing passions and enmity, which block understanding and cooperation. Strikes are one consequence. Hence, Hayakawa continued, the study of semantics is a social imperative, for on it depends the ability to overcome the tensions of our time.

When the time came for questions and comments, I spoke up. I agreed that a precise use of words and language is important, for otherwise people cannot intelligently communicate. But I vigorously disagreed with Hayakawa that the imprecise use of words is a main cause of discord. Differences over words, I stated, are most often an expression of differences over more fundamental questions, arising from varying conditions of life and social outlook. What an employer considers to be a fair wage, I pointed out, is most frequently regarded as a grossly unfair one by his workers. In the same way, what a judge believes to be justice is most frequently considered injustice by a defendant being sentenced. "It boils down to what old Abe Lincoln said: 'The wolf and the lamb can never agree on the definition of the word liberty.'"

Enthusiastic applause greeted my remarks, and from the rear of the hall came the call, soon picked up by others, "Use the mike!" When I looked at Hayakawa, he nodded agreement and said, "Yes, come forward."

Thus urged on, I continued to outline my views. I pointed to a current tendency to change the name of something rather than its substance. When a product loses its appeal, its name is changed. So with capitalism, which is now being sold as "people's capitalism."

"But what people are they talking about?" I asked. "Certainly not us. And now we are told we must defend the free world. Free for whom?—U.S. corporate investments? or the bitterly oppressed peoples of Africa, Asia and Latin America? You can call an onion a rose, as the saying goes, but it'll still be an onion. The problem as I see it," I concluded, "is not to change words, but the kind of world we live in."

Hayakawa listened politely. "Yes," he said, there is some truth to what you say—but who are you and what are you doing here?"

"I'm a Communist," I replied, "I'm here because of my political views and Communist Party affiliation."

"Oh, so that's it," he said, and added, "While I don't agree with you, I don't think a man like you belongs in a place like this."

"Nor do most of the men here belong in prison," I responded.

Some years later, when Hayakawa broke up a student demonstration at San Francisco State College—an act which catapulted him into national visibility and which was to lead to his successful U.S. Senate run—I was tempted to write to him. I could have reminded him of our exchange at Leavenworth and asked why he had not used his knowledge of semantics to resolve the issues at the college peaceably instead of calling in the police. But his tough-guy tactics toward the students had made him the darling of the ultra-Rightists, and my letter to him would have been an exercise in futility.

21

No. 73-335 Is Released

For me, as for all imprisoned, time passed at a slow pace. But by crowding as much as I could into each day, I made it move a bit less slowly. At first I judged time by the passing years and holidays. Later, on the downhill stretch, I counted the months, the weeks, and the days left until July 29, 1961. But now the fear of not making it, that is, not coming out of prison under one's own steam and in good shape was replaced by another concern: How would I make it when I got out?

The problem of finding a job did not greatly trouble me. I assumed that with the help of friends I would find *something*. My brother Ben was already working on the problem. Nor was I unduly concerned over the fact that for the first two years after my release I would be sharply restricted in what I could do and whom I could see, and under the strict supervision of the Parole Board (even though the Board had never given me parole). My eight-year sentence had been reduced considerably by statutory time off for maintaining a clean record and by "industrial good time." It was this portion of my sentence that I would have to do "on the street." But whatever petty harassments I might have to face, it would still be a thousand times better than prison.

What worried me most was the adjustment with my family. Ten years had passed since I had left home. So much had happened in that time. The children were no longer kids. Dan was the father of two, making me a grandfather. Josie was a young adult. Even Ralph, the baby of the family, would celebrate his sixteenth birthday a week after my return.

Could I fit into their lives again? Would I be an intruder in a life they had patterned for a full decade without me? The children knew me from visits to prison and from my letters, but not as a daily physical presence.

I noticed that Josie and Ralph were a bit concerned about what changes my coming home would bring. (Dan and his family lived in an apartment of their own.) So I began gingerly to touch on this subject in my letters. I tried to reassure them by letting them know that I was aware I would be coming onto *their* turf and had no intention of changing their way of life.

And what about myself? Of course, I too had changed. The years had transformed me into something of a loner. I liked being with people, but I also needed privacy. That was why I had pushed so hard to get a single cell. Could I adjust to the intimacy of family life again?

My chief concern, naturally, was Lil. If our feelings for each other were as strong as we believed them to be, then all other problems would vanish. Yet ten years of separation was a long time. It had wrought changes in each of us. We were now older. We had learned to live apart. How sure could we be that we were as compatible as we once were—physically and otherwise? Could fires banked so long again burn hot?

It was imperative that Lil and I resolve these doubts as rapidly as possible. But this required our being alone, *completely* alone, even if only for a short time. We had not had a moment completely to ourselves in ten years' time. Lil had come alone to visit me in prison, but we were never *really* alone: watched all the time, our conversations monitored, and in a room crowded with other families. We could not even speak our innermost thoughts in our letters, ever conscious of the ubiquitous censor.

Thinking about all this, I decided I would suggest to Lil that she come alone to meet me upon my release, that we then rent a car and take our time driving back to Chicago. However, I hesitated about proposing this for fear the children would resent our going off on our own before coming directly home. Then, as if she had read my mind, Lil wrote suggesting the very same thing. I was elated.

On July 24, 1961, five days before my scheduled release, the prison loudspeaker blared: "Attention Green, 73-335; Attention Green, 73-335! Come to the lieutenant's office at once with all your belongings."

This was completely unexpected. To be ordered to appear with all one's belongings usually meant only one thing—shipment elsewhere. But why, and where? And five days before the end of my sentence. Mystified, I insisted on an immediate interview with the warden. When I asked him what this was all about, he said he had orders from Washington to ship me to New York because of the still-pending indictment for Communist membership against me.

"But why?" I asked. "My co-defendant Gus Hall also had a membership indictment against him, but was released directly from this very prison." (A local U.S. Commissioner then promptly set him free on $5,000 bond.) "Why a different treatment for me?"

"I don't know," the warden replied, shrugging his shoulders. "All I know is that I have orders to send you to New York via prison van."

"What about my wife? It would be cruel to have her come here and find me gone. And Mr. Abt, my attorney, is also coming to arrange my bail."

"Don't worry, Green, it'll all be taken care of. They'll be informed."

I felt furious and thwarted, but there was nothing I could do. To get me out without further hassle, they didn't even bother to check over my loose-leaf notebooks filled with material from my prison studies, even letting me take out the outlines of lectures I had given. (My books had been shipped home earlier.)

Once again I was shackled to a prisoner, this time to be taken back to the West Street jail. We made the same overnight stops I had made on the trip to Leavenworth so many years before, but in reverse. All the way to New York I seethed with anger at this last act of petty vindictiveness.

Many years later I learned from my FIOA files why it occurred. Warden Taylor had lied when he said he didn't know why I was being sent to New York. In fact, he had been a prime mover of this indignity.

About two weeks before my scheduled release, on July 13, the warden wrote a letter to Washington. He informed the U.S. Prison Bureau that Federal Marshal Kemper of Topeka was planning to be on hand to take me into custody until I was released on bail. He noted that "there was no indication of plans toward prosecution of the case," and that I had asked Abt to make bail arrangements. Then he added ingratiatingly:

> If that is done, we anticipate the family and possibly others will be here to meet him at the gate. While we have no knowledge of organized publicity plans, it is possible the Communists could make the most of his departure from prison as martyr. If such were the case, by transfer on the eastbound plane about July 26th, they would not have time to get organized.
>
> Undoubtedly you would want to proceed slowly on such a plan, though, and coordinate any move with wishes of the Department [of Justice]. I'm sure we can cope with any publicity that might develop out here and handle his release in routine manner.

So, to avoid publicity about the Government's prosecution of Communist leaders, a game no longer popular, I was to be sneaked out of prison without anyone knowing it.

In my last prison letter to my journalist friend Ed Lahey, I summed up my feelings: "Well Ed, my ship is finally due to dock on Saturday, July 29th. Leaking a bit fore and aft, with sails somewhat tattered and beams slightly creaking, it should enter port with colors flying. After a period in drydock, and with a fresh coat of paint to conceal tempest scars, the brig should be seaworthy again, hoping for calmer waters but determined to sail on, come what may. For as you know, an idea is a belief you hold; a conviction, a belief that holds you. . . .

"As for me, Ed, I am now older, grayer, balder, thinner, perhaps a bit more knowledgeable, but none the wiser. I have tried to make this theft of my years into a time that would also serve me. Whether I've succeeded or not, is not for me to judge.

"I have probed more deeply into many subjects, all related to why man is as he is. I have also seen, close up, the raw, ugly side of human behavior, and while horrified at the danger of biological mutations induced by radiation, I am no less aghast at the equally crippling social mutations all around me. And yet my confidence in man's ability to become brother to man, given the opportunity, is greater than ever.

"Looking at world events, even through prison bars, I confess to a feeling of exhilaration at the profound social transformations at work, at the 'sudden' rise of old-new nations from slavery to dignity. And where others may see only the pain and the danger associated with this change, I also see the inherent beauty of new birth, of social creation.

"There is one West Side boy who greets me, as I pass him in the shadow of the big wall, with the daily salutation, 'It's a beautiful day—in Chicago!' That it will be on July 29."

APPENDIX

Letter of Gil Green to Ed Lahey (as published in the Chicago *Daily News*, February 24, 1956)

Dear Ed:

I got news for you. On Monday, February 27, at 12 noon I will be at the United States marshall's office at Foley Square.

I wasn't waiting for the "revolution"—as you so quaintly suggested in your article in the Chicago *Daily News* of January 3—only for the reasonable assurance that America is going to remain true to its own Constitution and Bill of Rights and that men and women of different political views would have the right to hold and advocate them.

It seems to me that recent developments indicate that such a reasonable assurance is now in the making.

You wrote, Ed, that my Communist views had turned me into a "criminal and fugitive." But you and I know—as do most thinking people—that I am guilty of no crime and least of all, the ridiculous charge of conspiring to advocate the overthrow of the government by force.

It is not my Communist views that have been at fault, but the conditions of war-hysteria and witch-hunt, under which communism was distorted from the political philosophy and movement which it is into the political conspiracy which it is not.

I have been a fugitive, therefore, not from justice but from injustice.

In your article you referred to my five-year separation from wife and children as defying "normal human sentiment." Gratuitously, you even drew the conclusion that "a confirmed Communist" is "immune to the impulses of universal emotion."

And you chose the holiday season to pour this salt on the raw, throbbing wounds of my family and myself.

As for human sentiment and the capacity to love one's own kin, I give ground to no man. And in rejecting your caricature of myself, I likewise reject it for all Communists.

What I did five years ago arose from the very greatest love—for those closest and dearest to me, my own flesh and blood—and the human family of which we all are members. Nor can I separate one from the other.

Intellectually and morally, I consider as reprehensible the view that the welfare of an individual or family is to be pitted against the general welfare.

If the Bill of Rights and popular liberties were to become ashes in the crematorium of McCarthyite America, what kind of a country would my children be compelled to live in?

Or, if those war-minded monopolists who have been so intent upon bringing about a third world war had succeeded in their nefarious endeavor, what would be the state of my loved ones in the terrible destructiveness of hydrogen war?

But even if it were otherwise, even if I could insulate my personal family from the ills and sufferings of mankind, and from their struggles—I would not do so.

For they would lose more than they gained. They would lose the dignity and stature that make them human.

They would become lowered to the level of jungle beasts, who by instinct also fight to protect their mates and young ones, but who neither feel nor know any sense of social responsibility.

I wish nothing more for my children than that they shall grow to manhood and womanhood with the very strongest feeling of social obligation, with a readiness to make sacrifices, if these be necessary, for the greater good of their fellow men.

During World War II, a young American soldier fighting in the Pacific theater carried through an exploit so courageous, so brave and daring, that he won the highly coveted Distinguished Service Cross.

When he volunteered for the exceedingly perilous mission, he did not ask for special immunity because he had left back home a young wife and child.

If he had, the mission would not have been fulfilled and the nation would not have seen fit to honor him for special valor.

In a sense, the problem that young man faced on the battlefield is one which all men and women face at different times, if they have a social conscience.

The issue may not be one of life or death—it may not call for physical pluck—but the readiness to sacrifice for the truth is a quality which cannot and will not perish.

It is the basic ingredient without which courage and character are dead.

Every working man, who has helped establish a union in his place of employment, or who has known the empty feeling of weeks without wages during a prolonged strike, can attest to the truth of this observation.

In fact, were there not men and women ready to forego comfort and security, both for themselves and their families, America itself could not be the great nation it is today.

The young soldier I was thinking of was Robert Thompson. Today he is a political prisoner of the "cold war" in Atlanta penitentiary.

This is how his selfless idealism and courage are being repaid by a ruling class which, having lost these qualities itself, refuses to admit that they still exist in others.

On my part, so long as the national trend was toward greater and greater repression as part of a larger trend toward a new world war, I could not in good conscience do anything else but resist—and resist actively.

This course I have pursued, as have thousands of others, each in accord with how best he thought the cause of peace and democratic liberties could be served.

One would argue that the new climate now coming into being would have occurred irrespective of what one or another individual did. There is truth in this assertion.

But if every individual had met the war hysteria and witch-hunt by bending his knees to it, there would not be the straightening of knees visible today.

Or, were there any relaxation in the fight for peace and democracy at present, war and McCarthyism could still emerge the victors.

Our own James Russell Lowell wrote in his "Commemoration Ode" that those loved truth best who to themselves are true.

I have tried to be true to myself and because of that I believe I have not been false to any man, and least of all to my fellow Americans. As for my family, I am certain that they would not have asked me to do otherwise.

I write this letter to you, Ed, because I have read your articles over the years and met you personally during the trial. (I hope this doesn't drag you before the inquisition!)

It has been my impression that you have seen more of the truth than you cared to admit, even though you concealed this and salved your conscience by applying to everything a thick coat of hard-bitten cynicism.

But cynicism—which knows the price of everything and the value of nothing—is not what is needed today.

There is too much of it all about us already. That is why juvenile delinquency is so widespread.

It seems to me that the time has come to affirm that there are values which are priceless and the very first of these is integrity.

I hope some day to be able to continue this discussion face to face, over a cup of coffee or a glass of beer, and I have confidence that day is not too far off, for sooner or later the reasonable arguing-out of questions must replace unreasoned hysteria and fear.

Toward that day, and toward the day when all families can be united, I look forward.

Sincerely yours,

Gil Green

P.S. I wonder whether the so-called "free press" for which you work is free enough to publish this letter and thereby help correct the false impression left by your article.

EDERAL BUREAU OF INVESTIGA
ED STATES DEPARTMENT OF

Mr. Dise
Mr. Doyle
URGENT

To: COMMUNICATIONS SECTION. FEBRUARY 27, 1956

Transmit the following message to: SAC, NEW YORK

GILBERT GREEN, FUGITIVE, IO NUMBER TWO FOUR THREE FIVE, INTERNAL SECURITY DASH C. REFERENCE TELEPHONE CALLS FROM ASAC MOORE, NEW YORK OFFICE, THIS DATE, REPORTING SURRENDER OF COMFUG GIL GREEN. IN LINE WITH INSTRUCTIONS ISSUED DURING ABOVE TELEPHONE CALLS BY INSPECTOR J. A. SIZOO, BUREAU DESIRES YOUR OFFICE CONDUCT ALL FEASIBLE INVESTIGATION TO DETERMINE GREEN DASH S WHEREABOUTS WHILE IN A FUGITIVE STATUS AND CONSIDER ALL HARBORING ASPECTS OF THIS SITUATION. ALL LOGICAL LEADS, SUCH AS EXAMINATION OF CLOTHING, ET CETERA, MUST BE HANDLED IN AN EXPEDITIOUS FASHION AND THE BUREAU SHOULD BE KEPT FULLY INFORMED ON ALL DEVELOPMENTS.

HOOVER

BUFILE 100-35360

Proof that the FBI didn't know Green's whereabouts.

One of the posters demanding amnesty for the Smith Act prisoners.

Letter to SAC, New York
RE: COMMUNIST PARTY, USA
COUNTERINTELLIGENCE PROGRAM
100-3-104

plans can be made, the New York Office must first obtain a great deal of information concerning [redacted] such as whether or not he uses a typewriter on a regular basis or uses longhand in his correspondence.

The Document Section of the Laboratory Division advises that in order to simulate two pages in the handwriting of an ordinary individual it would take approximately 24 hours continuous work. Therefore, the briefer the material to be simulated, the quicker it can be done. It would be much simpler if a typewriter could be used to prepare the report in question which would not have to be altered to match a known typewriter normally used with a small amount of actual handwriting added at the end or interlineated throughout the typewritten report. To alter a typewriter to match a known model would require a large amount of typewriter specimens and weeks of laboratory work. It is not felt that this technique of altering a typewriter should be considered in this connection.

Once a counterintelligence plan is worked out and approved which has an excellent chance of success, the Bureau would authorize having an Agent or employee of the New York Office bring the material directly to the Bureau Laboratory for simulating the handwriting on the proper paper and return it to New York for prompt mailing. The Laboratory should, of course, have several days' notice prior to undertaking the actual assignment and should pass on the question in advance as to whether sufficient handwriting specimens are available.

The New York Office should keep the Bureau advised of all pertinent developments in this regard. Since this technique cannot be implemented against [redacted] until April, 1960, or later, perhaps the New York Office would prefer to give further consideration to pursuing this technique against [redacted]. The Laboratory has advised that sufficient handwriting specimens of [redacted] are available.

The observations and recommendations of the New York Office should be most carefully evaluated and analyzed prior to submitting them to the Bureau for approval.

- 2 -

The FBI discussing how to frame-up victims.

INDEX